# ESL
## English as a Second Language

# Grammar
## *Intermediate & Advanced*

### Mary Ellen Muñoz Page

**Research & Education Association**
*Visit our website at*
**www.rea.com**

**Research & Education Association**
258 Prospect Plains Road
Cranbury, New Jersey 08512
Email: info@rea.com

**ESL Grammar: Intermediate and Advanced**

**Published 2020**

Printed in the United States of America

Library of Congress Control Number 2006923970

ISBN-13: 978-0-7386-0101-4
ISBN-10: 0-7386-0101-2

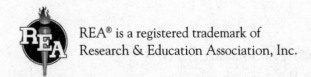

# About This Book

Open a new world of opportunity by mastering the English language. *ESL Grammar: Intermediate and Advanced* is truly for everyone, whether in school or on the job. This comprehensive and challenging guide serves as an ideal supplement to textbooks, language courses, and most other study aids and test preparation books. But with its thorough coverage of English grammar, easy-to-follow exercises, glossary, and complete answer key, this book can be used by itself with confidence.

The ability to write and speak English effectively is necessary for success in *any* study area, whether it be English, science, mathematics, or social studies. Therefore, most standardized school and vocational tests—as well as the Test of English as a Foreign Language, or TOEFL—require that students demonstrate a command of the English language, which is why we have included a helpful guide to note-taking, studying, and test-taking.

English writing and speaking skills are invaluable for getting a job and advancing in your chosen career. Employers (and their clients) often judge employees according to their ability to communicate effectively and in a productive way. This book, as well as REA's companion volume, *ESL Writing: Intermediate and Advanced*, can help you take command of English and express yourself with precision.

# How to Use This Book

This book is one of the most straightforward study guides you will find. As you can see from the table of contents, all aspects of English grammar are effectively covered. Each section contains clear explanations, simple examples, and ample exercises for you to practice and learn. The answer key at the back of the book is an ideal reference by which you can judge your progress, and the glossary stands ready to clear up any uncertainties about terms and their meanings.

REA wishes you all the best on your climb up the ladder to English-language mastery—and the success that you will enjoy in work and in life!

## About the Author

Mary Ellen Muñoz Page is a former Bilingual Training Specialist and Spanish professor at the University of Florida in Gainesville. She received a B.A. in Spanish and history and an M.A. in Spanish, both from Case Western Reserve University, in Cleveland, Ohio. As a professor, Ms. Muñoz Page received three "Voyages of Discovery" mini-grants to develop cultural modules on Costa Rica, Guatemala, and Spain. Ms. Muñoz Page is also the author of books for the TOEFL Test (Test of English as a Foreign Language) and the Florida FTCE ESOL Examination (English for Speakers of Other Languages). She was selected for *Who's Who Among American Teachers* in 1996 and 1998.

## Author Acknowledgments

This book is lovingly dedicated to my mother, Edna I. Schmidt, who always made sure that I used proper grammar. To all my ESL students whose unceasing questions prompted the writing of this manual, I give my thanks. To Maureen Jennings, for her help in the final assembly of this book, my undying gratitude.

## About REA

Founded in 1959, Research & Education Association (REA) is dedicated to publishing the finest and most effective educational materials—including study guides and test preps—for students of all ages.

Today, REA's wide-ranging catalog is a leading resource for students, teachers, and other professionals. Visit *www.rea.com* to see a complete listing of all our titles.

## REA Acknowledgments

We would like to thank Steven M. Gras for technically editing the manuscript; Pam Weston, Publisher, for setting the quality standards for production integrity and managing the publication to completion; Larry B. Kling, Editorial Director, for his supervision of revisions and overall direction; and Jennifer Calhoun for file prep.

# Contents

# PART I
# ESL

*Intermediate Grammar*

# *Intermediate Grammar*

# ESL

## CHAPTER 1

## Pronouns

# Chapter 1
# PRONOUNS

Pronouns are words that take the place of nouns and all their modifiers. They can be subjects, direct and indirect objects, interrogatives, impersonals, objects of prepositions, reflexives, demonstratives, possessives, and relatives. This chart will help you keep them in the proper order.

| Subject | Direct Object | Indirect Object | Object of Preposition | Reflexive |
|---|---|---|---|---|
| Performs action of the verb (except for linking verbs) | First receiver of the action; person, animal, or thing | Second receiver of action; usually person or animal | Prepositions followed by nouns referring to people, animals, or objects | Persons and animals perform and receive the same action |
| I | me | me | me | myself |
| you | you | you | you | yourself |
| he | him | him | him | himself |
| she | her | her | her | herself |
| it | it | it | it | itself, oneself |
| we | us | us | us | ourselves |
| you | you | you | you | yourselves |
| they | them | them | them | themselves |

| Demonstrative | Relative | Possessive | Interrogative | Impersonal |
|---|---|---|---|---|
| Refers to location | Refers back to the noun that comes before it | Shows ownership | Refers to questions | Doesn't refer to a specific person or object |
| here: | who | mine | who | it |
|   this | whom | yours | whom | there |
|   these | whoever | his | what | others |
| | whomever | hers | which | another |
| there: | | ours | | anyone |
|   that | | yours | | anybody |
|   those | | theirs | | anything |
| | | | | someone |
| | | | | somebody |
| | | | | something |
| | | | | no one |
| | | | | nobody |
| | | | | nothing |

# SUBJECT PRONOUNS

Pronouns can be **subjects** and perform action. Here are the pronouns used as subjects:

| I | he | it | they | who |
|---|-----|-----|-------|------|
| you | she | we | which | what |

Use subject pronouns for the following:

a. As the subject of the verb

> *He* writes music.          *She* sings well.

b. After *than* or *as* in comparison

> He paints better than *she*.    I am as tall as *he*.

c. After a form of the verb *be*

> It is *I*.              The winner was *she*.

In (b) if you repeat the verb, you can see that you must use the subject form.

> He paints better than *she (paints)*.   I am as tall as *he (is)*.

Pronouns can be **objects** (receivers): direct, indirect, object of a preposition:

| | |
|---|---|
| me | us |
| you | you |
| him, her, it | them |

a. Khan saw *her* last night in class. (direct object)

b. Give the money to *them* immediately. Give *them* the money immediately. (indirect object)

c. Sam bought for *us* dinner because we were working so late. (object of a preposition)

Whenever there is a compound form in a prepositional phrase, cover up the other noun and the word *and*, and then decide whether you need subject or object pronouns.

Give the books to Jane and $\left\{\begin{array}{c} she \\ her \end{array}\right\}$. Give Jane and her the books.

By covering up *Jane and*, you see that the pronoun is used as the object of the preposition *to*, and *her* would be the object form.

Pat and $\left\{\begin{array}{c} I \\ me \end{array}\right\}$ saw the movie last night.

By covering up *Pat and*, you see that the pronoun is the subject form; therefore, *I* is the correct form.

## EXERCISE 1

Circle the correct form of the pronoun. When you have finished, check your answers with the answer key in the back of the book.

**Example:** You and (he, him) will represent the class at the meeting.

**Answer:** You and (he, him) will represent the class at the meeting.

1. (She, Her) and Paul are planning on attending the concert.

2. (We, Us) girls insist on being admitted to the club.

3. Our teacher gave the extra credit to Melanie and (I, me).

4. No one saw him and (she, her) together at the game.

5. How many tickets did you buy for (we, us)?

6. I have to see (they, them) before the office closes.

7. (He, Him) travels to San Diego every spring.

8. Find the boss's file and hand it to (him, he).

9. The boys challenged (we, us) girls to a test of strength. (We, Us) won, of course.

10. When will the director present the award to (she, her)?

11. I hope that (she, her) accepts that new job in Orlando.

12. Someone told (we, us) that a new store would be opening here soon.

13. What do (they, them) plan to do about the entertainment for the party?

14. Will you please help (he, him) unload the packages?

15. How many books will he deliver to (she, her)?

16. Cal loves Myriam, and he dreamed about (she, her) all night long.

17. No one seems to know where (they, them) went after lunch.

18. My sister and (I, me) traveled through the Orient last year.

19. Can (he, him) play tennis as well as (they, them)?

20. John's father earns more than (he, him).

## EXERCISE 2

Circle the correct pronoun.

**Example:** Mother gave (us, we) the money to buy some milk.

**Answer:** Mother gave (us, we) the money to buy some milk.

1. (Him, He) and I went to see a horror movie last night.

2. The teacher encouraged (we, us) students to watch the play.

3. No one took (she, her) and (I, me) seriously when we told the story.

4. Many fans loved Babe Ruth and went to see (he, him) play ball.

5. (Who, Whom) is Dave inviting to the dance?

6. They are concerned about (we, us) because we haven't called.

7. My sister gave (they, them) the stamps for their collection.

8. Wes and (I, me) are taking a cruise to the Bahamas.

9. You and (he, him) are welcome to join us at the club.

10. The director gave Jill and (I, me) the scholarships.

11. Laura and her brother are taking a trip with (we, us) next summer.

12. Everybody wants (they, them) to win the championship.

13. How many pamphlets do (they, them) need?

14. Will there be enough food for all of (we, us)?

15. Once Kathy receives the check, (she, her) will pay the bills.

16. Sam took (I, me) to the conference in his new car.

17. Sue's husband is going with (she, her) to Toronto.

18. Rafael and (I, me) were selected as delegates to the convention.

19. (I, me) am accepting the position, and this disturbs my parents.

20. The boy (who, whom) is wearing the green shirt is my cousin.

# REFLEXIVE PRONOUNS

Pronouns can function as **reflexives** when the subject performs the action on him/herself. The forms *hisself* and *theirselves* DO NOT EXIST. Here are the reflexive pronouns:

| Singular | Plural |
|----------|--------|
| myself | ourselves |
| yourself | yourselves |
| himself | themselves |
| herself | |
| itself | |
| oneself | |

I write *myself* notes to help me remember things that I have to do.

We wash *ourselves* before going to bed.

## EXERCISE 3

Use a reflexive pronoun for each sentence.

**Example:** The child dressed *__himself__* well despite his age.

1. Nancy, you need to protect _____ from the sun.

2. Tom hurt _____ skiing last year.

3. We saw _____ in those crazy costumes and couldn't stop laughing.

4. Victor and Abbas are working two jobs to put _____through college.

5. The flying object turned _____ around and disappeared in the night.

6. I bought _____ some new clothes last week.

7. Susana calls _____ "doctor" even though she hasn't graduated yet.

8. Harry and Sam, find _____ a place to sit, and I'll be right with you.

9. Janet cut _____ while she was fixing her bicycle.

10. Each student has to teach _____ how to study well.

## EXERCISE 4

Circle the correct pronoun or possessive.

**Example:** You need to ask (you, yourself) what your goals are before you begin.

**Answer:** Give (he, (him)) the check as soon as possible.

1. (We, Us) skiers will be leaving for the mountains next week.

2. Raul is as tall as (I, me).

3. Sandy hurt (hisself, himself) while repairing the car.

4. Jason is lucky that the baseball didn't hit (he, him).

5. My daughter is older than (your, yours).

6. They are expected to do the work by (theirselves, themselves).

7. His book is interesting. (My, Mine) is boring.

8. Nancy taught (hers, herself) to play the piano.

9. We haven't seen (they, them) since they visited last year.

10. Present the awards to him and (she, her).

11. Jose paints as well as (they, them).

12. Don't get up! It's only (I, me).

13. We need to give (us, ourselves) a rest from this job.

# RELATIVE PRONOUNS

**Relative pronouns** relate to the word(s) that precedes them. They introduce a **dependent relative clause** (a clause that by itself does not convey a complete idea). This clause usually eliminates the repetition of the same word(s) and uses one of the following pronouns to connect the two clauses:

| Used only for persons | Used only for things |
|---|---|
| who | that |
| whom | which |
| whose (other living things) | |

*Who* and *whom* refer only to persons. *Who* is the subject (performer) of the action of the verb.

The girl *who is waving to us* is my cousin. (girl = who = subject)
subject + verb + indirect object

We have met the singer *who will replace Joan.* (singer = who)

*Who* functions as a subject in its clause (*who is waving to us*) (*who will replace Joan*) and refers to the girl (singer). These clauses do *not* convey a complete idea.

*Whom* is the object (receiver) of the action. (See a detailed explanation on *who* and *whom* in the Part 2: ESL Advanced Grammar.)

The guest speaker is the one *to whom you should address the letter.*

**Whom** is the second receiver of the action **should address**
(guest speaker = to whom)

The artists *about whom Jack spoke* are visiting us today.

(artists = about whom)

*Whose* shows possession and usually refers to people or other living things.

The senator *whose daughter is my friend* spoke to us last night.

(senator has a daughter = my friend)

*That* and *which* are used with things. In informal English *that* may also be used with persons. *That* clauses are vital to the sentence and are *never* set off by commas.

I have the book *that* you ordered last week. (a specific book)

The bill *that you received* last week needs to be paid tomorrow. (specific bill)

*Which* clauses are not always absolutely necessary to the sentence. When they do *not* limit the meaning of the main clause, they are set apart by commas.

Hal bought a washer, *which was delivered yesterday*.

(*Which was delivered yesterday* is not vital to the sentence.)

Monaco, *which is a very small country*, is near the South of France.

(Whether the county is large or small, it doesn't change its location. This information is not vital to the fact that Monaco is near the South of France.)

When you combine two independent sentences, you will have two clauses, each containing a subject and a verb. The **relative pronoun** will connect the two clauses and keep the speaker or writer from repeating the same words.

Glen needs a secretary. The secretary must speak Spanish.

S + V + C          S + V + C

Glen needs a secretary *who must speak Spanish*.

S + V + C       S + V + C

(main clause)      (dependent clause)

Perry is planning a vacation. The vacation will be relaxing and educational.

S + V + C        S + V + C

Perry is planning a vacation, *which will be relaxing and educational*.

S + V + C       S + V + C

(main clause)      (dependent clause)

Our company has many employees. The employees' job is to produce quality products.

Our company has many employees, *whose job is to produce quality products.*

S + V + C       S + V + C

(main clause)      (dependent clause)

Teri sent money to her son. Her son's house was damaged by the hurricane.

Teri sent money to her son **whose house was damaged by the hurricane.**

S + V +   C   +   C         S     +     V     +     C (agent)

(main clause)                       (dependent clause)

## EXERCISE 5

Combine each sentence by using a **relative pronoun** and eliminate the repeated words. Use *who*, *whom*, *whose*, *which*, and *that*.

**Example:** Omar met a teacher. The teacher spoke Arabic.

**Answer:** Omar met a teacher *__who__* spoke Arabic.

1. I met an actor. The actor's picture won an oscar.

   _____

2. We bought a house. The house cost us $150,000.

   _____

3. Sally introduced me to her boyfriend. Her boyfriend is a civil engineer.

   _____

4. Maureen bought a dress. The dress cost $45. She had to return it.

   _____

5. Jake gave Isabel a ring. The ring had diamonds and rubies.

   _____

6. Mrs. Duncan is talking to her students. The students' projects are due on Friday.

   _____

7. Norman lives with his sister. His sister is a nurse.

   _____

8. The soldiers were injured in combat. The president is awarding medals to the soldiers.

   _____

9. Mr. Franklin graded the tests. We took the tests on Friday.

_____

10. The director knows the candidate. The candidate was chosen to be the manager.

_____

**EXERCISE 6**

Using *formal* English, circle the correct pronoun in these sentences.

1. We have a package for the man (who, which) stopped by today.

2. I met the author (who, whose) book is on the best-seller list.

3. Are you sure that the book (that, which) has all the art pictures is for this class?

4. That young man (who, whom) you met seems very nice.

5. I'll be writing to the director (who, whom) you saw Monday.

6. Will you be presenting the slides (that, which) you took in Canada last summer?

7. The steaks, (that, which) my brother gave us, are delicious.

8. The fish (that, which) Lonnie caught is a big bass.

9. The income tax (that, which) he paid last year is accurate.

10. My friend (who, whose) father is a dentist wants to be an artist.

11. Henry finally found his wallet, (that, which) he lost.

12. Juan Valdez's coffee, (that, which) comes from Colombia, tastes the best of all.

# IMPERSONAL SUBJECTS
## *IT* AND *THERE*

While the word *there* is not usually viewed as a subject, it accompanies the verb *be* to show the existence of something. The real subject always follows the verb and determines whether that verb should be singular or plural.

| Affirmative: | **THERE** + **BE** + subject |
|---|---|

**There are many more empty desks** in the classroom.

**There is a message** in your mail box.

| Negative: | **THERE** + **BE** + $\begin{Bmatrix} NO \\ NOT\ ANY \end{Bmatrix}$ + subject |
|---|---|

**There** is **no time** to waste on such foolishness.

**There** aren't **any cookies** on the plate.

| Question: | **HAS** | + | **THERE** | + | **BEEN** | + | subject |
|---|---|---|---|---|---|---|---|
| | **BE** | + | **THERE** | + | subject | | |
| | **HOW MANY** | + | subject | + | verb | + | **THERE** |
| | **HOW MUCH** | + | subject | + | verb | + | **THERE** |

**Has there been** any rain here lately?

**Are there** more papers to grade?

How many stores **are there** in the mall?

How much space **is there** left in the garage?

--- NOTE ---
Be careful when you have two singular subjects joined by the conjunction *and*. This will require a plural verb.

There **are a vase and two dolls** on the dresser.

**Were** there a ticket and some money in your purse?

---
**NOTE**

In the following sentences, *there* is an adverb and refers to location. This is not the same as showing the existence of something.

---

**There** is the money for my tuition. = The money is over there.

**There** are your pen and notebook. = Your pen and notebook are over there.

*Much* and *many* are two adjectives that non-native speakers often confuse. *Much* describes things that can't be counted in certain general categories (time, money, patience, sugar, water, etc.). However, if you put these things in containers or, when it comes to time, show it in hours and minutes, and money in dollars and cents, then you have something to count. Notice the difference in the following:

There isn't **much water** in the tank.

There were **many gallons of water** when we started to sprinkle the grass.

There is **too much sugar** in this recipe.

There are **too many cubes** of sugar in the dish.

**How much money** is there in the account? (use with non-countable noun)

**How many deposit slips** are there in your book? (use with a countable noun)

When [*much* + a noun] is the subject of the sentence, the verb is singular.

There **is** too much time spent on play and not enough on study.

When [*many* + a noun] is the subject, the verb is plural.

There **are** not many days **left** to finish this project.

## EXERCISE 7

Circle the correct form of the verb.

**Example:** How much money (is, are) left in your savings account?

**Answer:** How much money (is, are) left in your savings account?

1. There (is, are) only 28 days in February.

2. There (is, are) five tickets left for the concert.

3. There (was, were) a vase of flowers on the table.

4. There (has, have) been many data published on the use of DNA in crime detection.

5. (Have, Has) there been any news about the accident?

6. There (has, have) been no new developments in that research.

7. How many people (is, are) there in the class?

8. There (wasn't, weren't) any cake left after the party.

9. (Was, Were) there any cookies in the jar?

10. How much furniture (was, were) there in the apartment before you moved in.

11. (Has, Have) there been anyone who shows an interest in buying your car?

12. There (is, are) no information available on this topic.

13. (Is, Are) there many states that have repealed that law?

14. How many tests (has, have) there been this semester?

15. (Was, Were) there a dress, a jacket, and some shoes in the box when you opened it?

16. (Has, Have) there been any inquiries into the committee's request?

17. There (is, are) no rules against dual enrollment.

18. How many pints (is, are) there in a gallon?

19. (Is, Are) there any students this year with a 4.0 GPA?

20. (Was, Were) there any toothpaste left in the tube?

The pronoun *it* is the subject in many impersonal expressions. It is not responsible for performing the action even though it functions as the subject. In these expressions, the pronoun is *not* replacing a previously mentioned singular noun. These expressions can be followed by *that* and a dependent clause or by an infinitive.

> ***IT*** + ***BE*** + adjective + [***THAT*** + subject + verb]
> (dependent clause)

Adjectives that fit into this category are the following:

| | | | |
|---|---|---|---|
| apparent | assumed | believed | evident |
| good | important | astonishing | unusual |
| improbable | probable | unlikely | unfortunate |

It is *important **that you study*** every night.

*It is good **that Sarah has completed*** the program.

It is unusual ***that so much snow has fallen***.

Another group can be followed only by the **infinitive** [*to* + base form of the verb]:

> ***IT*** + ***BE*** + adjective + infinitive

These are adjectives that fall into this category:

| | | | |
|---|---|---|---|
| dangerous | helpful | silly | wise |
| foolish | impractical | useful | worthwhile |
| frightful | practical | useless | |

It is dangerous ***to play*** with matches.

It was helpful ***to have*** my flashlight in the dark.

It will be practical ***to speak*** another language.

The impersonal *it* plus some adjectives can be followed by either an infinitive or a dependent clause.

> **IT** + **BE** + adjective + infinitive
> (dependent clause)

This category includes the following words:

| | | | |
|---|---|---|---|
| advisable | important | necessary | surprising |
| astonishing | inconceivable | possible | terrible |
| bad | incredible | preferable | unbelievable |
| exciting | inevitable | ridiculous | unfair |
| good | interesting | strange | unusual |

It is inconceivable *to put* a value on such a priceless object.

It is inconceivable *that someone has put* a value on such a priceless object.

It will be important *to translate* the poem carefully.

It will be important *that Matt translate* the poem carefully.

There are other impersonal *it* constructions that are followed by dependent clauses.

> **IT** + **LOOK** + [**AS IF** + subject + verb]
> **IT** + **SEEM**
> **APPEAR** + [**THAT** + subject + verb]
> **TURN OUT**

It looks as if *Randy has left for the day*.

It seemed that *he wanted to escape to some place quiet*.

It appears that *you have discovered a cure for the disease*.

It turned out that *we were all wrong about Melanie*.

**EXERCISE 8**

Decide whether the blank spaces require *to* for the infinitive or *that* to introduce a dependent clause. Write the appropriate word in the blanks.

**Example:** It is advisable *to* study every night.
It seems ***that*** you never seem to have any free time.

1. It has been exciting _____ visit all the places we've read about in class.

2. It's necessary _____ sign the check before cashing it.

3. It was terrible _____ the flood victims couldn't stay in their homes.

4. It won't be possible _____ see the doctor this afternoon.

5. It is apparent ___ no one has prepared the lesson for today.

6. It will be necessary _____ leave immediately after the concert.

7. It is unbelievable _____ so many people went to see the premiere of that movie.

8. It was good _____ have someone around to help with the work.

9. It is evident _____ you don't understand what I am saying.

10. It is incredible _____ the play has lasted so long.

11. It turned out _____ all the students did well in the final exam.

12. It is foolish _____ drive with no brakes.

13. It was strange _____ Janice didn't call when she was in town.

14. It will be interesting _____ see who wins the race.

15. It had been apparent _____ leaving the scene of the accident was a mistake.

16. It was advisable _____ the student change his major.

17. It would be important _____ evaluate your assets before you ask for the loan.

18. It appears _____ someone has already decorated the room for the party.

19. It seems _____ you have won the prize after all.

20. It would be silly _____ count on Randy for support.

Other expressions use the progressive tense.

***IT* + *BE* + [V + *ING*]**

It **will be snowing** in a few hours.

It **was raining** when I left the office.

It **is beginning to look** a lot like Christmas.

One of the most common uses for the impersonal *it* is used in with time expressions.

It will be **morning** soon.

It is **nine o'clock**.

It was **8:15** when the airplane arrived.

One last category refers to conditions.

> ***IT*** + ***BE*** + adjective (condition)

Here are common words used for such conditions:

| | | | |
|---|---|---|---|
| cold | hot | quiet | sunny |
| cloudy | noisy | still | windy |

It was **cold and windy** yesterday.

It will be **noisy** at the party.

It is so **still** that I can hear the wind blowing.

## EXERCISE 9

Use either *it* or *there* in each sentence.

**Example:** *It* was very windy yesterday afternoon.
I wonder if ***there*** were any new developments in the investigation.

1. _____ has been very sunny for the last three days.

2. Have _____ been any interesting programs on television lately?

3. _____ will be good to see Martha after such a long time.

4. _____ is unusual to see so many people out so early on a Sunday morning.

5. Will _____ be necessary to call Janet before the debate?

6. Will _____ be any benefit changes in the new medical plan?

7. Were _____ any messages on the answering machine?

8. Was _____ necessary to drive so far to pick up the package?

9. _____ will be important for you to attend the meeting.

10. Was _____ enough time to talk with everyone?

11. How many days are _____ before we leave for vacation?

12. I wonder if _____ is raining in Newark now.

13. Has _____ been anyone interested in buying your house?

14. Will _____ be any refreshments served after the concert?

15. How many guests will _____ be at the wedding?

16. _____ is impractical to spend foolishly and to try to save.

17. _____ was four o'clock when I left work yesterday.

18. _____ will be better days; just be patient.

19. _____ turned out that the boys had arrived on time after all.

20. _____ was quiet after the children finally went to sleep.

## EXERCISE 10

Decide which of the underlined items is INCORRECT.

1. My mother's <u>tremendous</u> fear of cats <u>makes</u> it difficult for <u>she</u> to go <u>walking</u> in our neighborhood at night.

   A. tremendous    B. makes       C. she          D. walking

2. My book differs from <u>your</u> in that <u>mine</u> has a vocabulary section <u>at the</u> bottom of each page, and yours has one in <u>the back</u>.

   A. your          B. that        C. at the       D. the back

3. Some people <u>which</u> have been working for a company <u>for years</u> suddenly find <u>themselves</u> unemployed <u>because of</u> administrative mismanagement.

   A. which         B. for years   C. themselves   D. because of

4. The professor <u>asked us</u>, Nancy and <u>I</u>, to stay after class <u>to discuss</u> the <u>make-up</u> assignment for next week.

   A. asked us      B. I           C. to discuss   D. make-up

5. If in a family the members are always looking <u>out</u> only for <u>one's self</u>, then they <u>have to be</u> aggressive <u>to get ahead</u>.

   A. out           B. one's self  C. have to be   D. to get ahead

6. People <u>whom</u> play in orchestras <u>are</u> usually adults who have studied <u>music</u> for many years and who are <u>devoted professionals</u>.

   A. whom          B. devoted     C. music        D. are
                       professionals

## EXERCISE 11

Select the correct word(s) to complete the sentence.

1. Families _____ play together usually are happy together.

    A. who         B. which         C. whomever     D. whose

2. Invite _____ you like to the party, but don't invite Mark.

    A. who         B. whoever      C. whomever     D. that

3. After giving the student a chance to prove _____, he was dismissed.

    A. him         B. hisself       C. himself      D. his

4. We wish she were here to help _____ with the decorations.

    A. us          B. we          C. ourselves     D. yourselves

5. The little boy dresses _____ every morning.

    A. him         B. hisself       C. he          D. himself

6. Do they know ___ has been chosen prom queen?

    A. who         B. whom       C. whoever     D. whomever

7. Let me divide the flowers. _____ are yours, and those are mine.

    A. This        B. That        C. These      D. This one

8. I desperately need some money. I don't have _____ to pay my bills!

    A. any         B. some       C. something    D. anything

# EXERCISE 12

Select the correct pronoun to complete each sentence.

1. (Who, Whom) do you want to serve on the board for directors?

2. Can you lend me $50 until payday? Sorry, I don't have (some, any) extra.

3. Rick is shorter than (I, me), but he's taller than his brothers.

4. (It, There) are twenty names of the candidates on the director's list.

5. Photograph (whoever, whomever) you see at the inauguration.

6. The man (whose, who's) brother is a lawyer wants to become a judge.

# Intermediate Grammar

# ESL

## CHAPTER 2

## Adjectives

# Chapter 2
# ADJECTIVES

Adjectives are words that modify (describe) a noun or a pronoun. They can also follow linking verbs (be, seem, appear, etc.). Just like nouns, they can fall into different categories: 1) **limiting—articles, demonstratives, possessives**—and 2) **descriptives**. Adjectives usually precede the words that they modify.

Limiting adjectives fall into these categories:

**Numbers:** one, five, ten, twenty, first, second, third

**Quantity:** some, any, much, many, few, little (with non-count nouns)

**Demonstratives:** this, that, these, and those (These are the same forms as the pronouns, but these must come before a noun, not replace it.) Examples: <u>**this**</u> car, <u>**that**</u> house

**Articles:** a, an, the

**Possessives:** my, your, his, her, its, our, your, their

Keep in mind that when you add '*s* to a noun, you make the noun a possessive and change it to an adjective.

The <u>**secretary's**</u> typewriter is broken.

The dog chased the little <u>**boy's**</u> ball.

All other adjectives are **descriptives**. Here are examples of common descriptive adjectives:

| | | |
|---|---|---|
| scholastic | beautiful | sorrowful |
| slow | loving | honest |
| early | hot | solid |
| future | frigid | fast |
| plain | happy | colored |
| colorful | watery | angry |

# POSSESSIVE ADJECTIVES BEFORE GERUNDS

Whenever a noun or pronoun appears before a gerund, it must be in the possessive form. This form then becomes an adjective.

> S + V + possessive form (noun/pronoun) + [verb + **ING**]

We were surprised by **his** not accepting the job.

They are sorry about **our** leaving so soon.

Nancy objects to **Jan's** calling her so late.

Referring to the first example above, we are surprised not by him but rather by his not accepting the job. In number two, they are sorry not about us but rather about our leaving so soon.

Nancy does not object to Jan but rather to Jan's calling so late.

> — **NOTE** —
> Nouns can usually become possessives by adding **'s**
> to the singular form.

boy > boy's      dog > dog's      boss > boss's

For the plural, however, the noun needs to be plural first, and then add the **'s**.

man > men's      child > children's

If the plural ends in *s*, then add only the apostrophe (').

boys'      girls'      sisters'

## EXERCISE 13

Change the noun or pronoun to the possessive form, and use it as an adjective.

**Example:** We were surprised at **_Betty's_** getting married so soon.

1. My parents do not approve of _____ dating David. (I)

2. I am so tired of _____ not accepting his responsibilities. (Peter)

3. The teacher is afraid of _____ not learning enough English this year. (her students)

4. The thieves confessed to _____ stealing the money. (they)

5. The witness testified about _____ taking pictures of the scientific experiments. (he)

6. The boss said, "I need to count on _____ taking part in all of these activities." (you)

7. We are afraid of _____ raising the rent. (the landlord)

8. Do not try to explain _____ bad driving! You taught him. (Terry)

9. You don't like it! Are you referring to _____ playing the piano? (I)

10. The children are looking forward to _____ visiting them. (you)

11. Can we rely on _____ bringing the food to the party? (Kim)

12. Kerry can't decide on _____ taking the trip or not. (we)

13. That loud music detracts from _____ doing a good job. (the workers)

14. I resent _____ giving me a ticket when I was not speeding. (the policeman)

15. We're looking into _____ being offered the job. (Tom)

16. I'm depending on _____ singing very well today. (the group)

17. George is planning on _____ driving some of the students. (I)

18. Harry objects to _____ nominating a new president. (the club)

19. The doctor is upset with _____ not taking enough vitamins. (Ann)

20. The voters are tired of _____ spending money so foolishly. (the government)

## EXERCISE 14

Change the noun or pronoun in parentheses to the possessive form, and use it as an adjective.

1. Tom's parents are dissatisfied with _____ accepting a job abroad. (he)

2. We're surprised at _____ receiving the drama award. (Helen)

3. Aimee was not jealous of her _____ winning the scholarship. (friend)

4. The children were fascinated by the _____ jumping up and down. (clowns)

5. I am depending on _____ organizing the trip for us. (you)

6. Mrs. Genovese disapproved of _____ commuting so far to work every day. (me)

7. _____ accepting the challenge depends on her commitment to doing well. (Anne)

8. The Senate approved of its _____ receiving more health benefits. (citizens)

9. I will rely on my _____ finding time to work with me. (brother)

10. The _____ thinking quickly saved his little sister from choking. (boy)

11. Mel will have to pay for his _____ breaking the window with the baseball. (son)

12. _____ exercising too much caused pains in his muscles. (Tony)

13. _____ smoking in her office caused her co-workers to complain. (Anita)

14. _____ moving to the country made a big difference in our health. (us)

15. By now we are accustomed to _____ arriving late. (they)

16. I am afraid of the _____ catching the flu this season. (children)

17. _____ fishing every day keeps him busy during his retirement. (Lonnie)

18. The _____ building their nest in our garage created some problems. (birds)

19. Maureen was interested in the _____ keeping their dog in the yard. (neighbors)

20. We are concerned about _____ driving so late at night. (they)

# SOME AND ANY

While *some* and *any* convey the same idea, they may not be used interchangeably in standard written English. *Some* is used with affirmative sentences, and *any* is used with negatives and questions. They may be used as pronouns or adjectives. For affirmative statements, use *some*. For negative statements or questions, use *any*.

**Affirmative:** Use *some*.

There are *some* papers on my desk in the office. (adj.)

I saw *some* on yours too. (pronoun)

*Some* days are hotter than others in the summer. (adj.)

*Some* are also colder in winter. (pronoun)

**Negative:** Use *any*.

Dave does *not* have *any* spare time to exercise. (adj.)

We don't have *any* either. (pronoun)

*No one* had *any* idea on how to solve the problem. (adj.)

I don't have *any* either. (pronoun)

**Question:** Use *any*.

Do you have *any* 29-cent stamps for this letter? (adj.)

Are there *any* in the drawer? (pronoun)

Have they ever read *any* plays by Shakespeare? (adj.)

Has he ever read *any* by Molière? (pronoun)

The following forms are all pronouns and can be used only as subjects and objects:

| **Affirmative** | | **Negative or question** | |
|---|---|---|---|
| someone | sometime | anyone | anytime |
| somebody | somewhere | anybody | anywhere |
| something | | anything | |

The following sentences are in affirmative:

> **Someone** is working in the kitchen right now.
>
> **Somebody** came here looking for you just a moment ago.
>
> Tony needs **something** to wipe up the juice he spilled.
>
> **Sometime** next week, stop by the office to see me.
>
> I left the book **somewhere** in my house.

The following are examples of sentences in negative or in question form:

> I can't see **anyone** in the pool. Can you?
>
> Has **anybody** turned in a set of car keys?
>
> The library did not have **anything** I needed for my report.
>
> The doctor does not have **any time** to see you today.
>
> I can't go **anywhere** without you.

Keep in mind that the forms *someone*, *somebody*, *anyone*, *anybody* can be adjectives if they become possessives by adding *'s* to the pronoun form.

> Bob lost his jacket. Have you seen it?
>
> I found **someone's** (**somebody's**) jacket in my car. (adj.)

> Are these **anybody's** (**anyone's**) house keys? (adj.)
>
> Helene doesn't think that they are **anybody's**. (pronoun)

## EXERCISE 15

Using the words from the list below, fill in the correct form in each space. Some sentences grouped together are part of a mini-dialogue.

**Example:** I know that **_someone_** bought the lucky lottery ticket.

Do you have **any** of the new coins just put into circulation?

| | | | |
|---|---|---|---|
| some | someone | somebody | something |
| any | anyone | anybody | anything |
| someone's | somebody's | anybody's | anyone's |

1. I will save _____ cake from the party for you.

2. Do you have _____ homework tonight?

3. He doesn't have _____ vacation time left this year.

4. "_____ has been sleeping in my bed," said the baby bear.

5. The children are bored because they don't have _____ time to play outside.

6. We haven't seen _____ we know here at the party.

7. Did Mr. Robertson have _____ in mind for the job?

8. While they were away, _____ broke into their house and stole their valuables.

9. Joel can't go to football games because he never has _____ free time on Saturdays.

10. No one saw _____ unusual that day. (object)

11. We hope that they will give us _____ information on traveling in the Northwest.

12. I am looking for _____ red hem lace.

13. Gail, do you have _____ ?

14. No, I don't, but I am sure Dolly has _____ .

15. Kelly has _____ in her hand. What is it?

16. It's just _____ candy that her friend gave her.

17. Mr. Jansen can't see you immediately because he has _____ in his office.

18. There wasn't _____ at home when I called this morning.

19. The defendant did not say _____ in his defense.

20. Did they find _____ interesting in that old trunk in the attic?

## COMPARISON OF ADJECTIVES

Descriptive adjectives or adverbs can have three different forms: **positive**, **comparative**, and **superlative**. Here are a few examples of the three forms:

| Positive | Comparative | Superlative |
| --- | --- | --- |
| fast | faster | fastest |
| clean | cleaner | cleanest |
| hot | hotter | hottest |
| important | more important | most important |

The first form, the **positive degree**, is the basic form of the adjective or adverb, which describes one or more persons, objects, or ways of doing something.

| | |
|---|---|
| the *big white* houses | (adjective) |
| a *crazy* cat | (adjective) |
| some *ornate* paintings | (adjective) |
| The deer ran *fast*. | (adverb) |

# Unequal Comparisons

The comparative is used to show a relationship between two objects, persons, or groups that are equal or unequal to the same element of another object, person, or group. Most one- and two-syllable adjectives add *-er* to express unequal comparisons.

> Adjective + *ER*
> Adverb + *ER*

| | |
|---|---|
| quiet > quieter | high > higher |
| neat > neater | fast > faster |
| quick > quicker | soon > sooner |

For adjectives ending in *e*, just add *r* to the root.

> Adjectives ending in [*E* + *R*]

| | |
|---|---|
| nice > nicer | white > whiter |
| fine > finer | tame > tamer |

## EXERCISE 16

For each word, write the comparison.

| | | |
|---|---|---|
| 1. wide | 6. noble | 11. late |
| 2. pale | 7. wise | 12. large |
| 3. brave | 8. polite | 13. ripe |
| 4. cute | 9. close | 14. rare |
| 5. humble | 10. stale | 15. safe |

For adjectives ending in [consonant + *y*] change *y* to *i* before adding *er*

happy > happier      dainty > daintier

pretty > prettier      lovely > lovelier

## EXERCISE 17

Change the following from the positive degree to the comparative.

| | | |
|---|---|---|
| 1. cozy | 6. heavy | 11. noisy |
| 2. shy | 7. pretty | 12. friendly |
| 3. dizzy | 8. ugly | 13. lonely |
| 4. angry | 9. merry | 14. healthy |
| 5. easy | 10. early | 15. lovely |

For adjectives ending in a [vowel + *y*], just add *er*.

coy > coyer      gay > gayer (happy)      gray > grayer

To express unequal comparison in a sentence, use the following pattern:

> subject + verb + [adjective + *ER*] + *THAN* + other element

Ben's brother is **taller than** he.

Mrs. Andrews is **older than** her son.

This blouse seems **nicer than** that one.

Beth looks **happier** today **than** she did yesterday.

--- **NOTE** ---
After comparisons, use subject, not object, pronouns.

Sylvia plays the guitar **better than I**.

He needs **more money than she**.

## EXERCISE 18

Write the correct form of the comparative.

**Example:** John's room is **neater** than mine.

History is **easier** than calculus.

1. My neighborhood is _____ than yours. (quiet)

2. Your new furniture looks _____ than the old. (lovely)

3. Our team ran _____ than your team. (fast)

4. Wanda lives _____ to the university than Harry. (close)

5. After a long diet, Jessica is _____ than her friends. (slim)

6. Los Angeles is _____ than Orlando. (hazy)

7. The children seem _____ than their parents after the long airplane ride. (sleepy)

8. The streets in the old section of town seem _____ than any place else. (narrow)

9. Buffalo feels _____ than Pittsburgh in the winter. (cold)

10. Women seem to be _____ than men in the game of love. (coy)

Some two-syllable and all three-syllable or more adjectives and adverbs use *more* or *less* plus the adjective or adverb for the comparison.

> **LESS**
> **MORE** } + three-syllable adjectives

**MORE** } + beautiful, intelligent, quietly, quickly

**LESS** } + difficult, important, interesting, economical

— **NOTE** —
Never combine *more* and the [adjective + *er*] form.

**INCORRECT:**   more happier, more friendlier, more wiser

**CORRECT:**     happier, friendlier, wiser

Two-syllable adjectives ending in the following suffixes usually use *more* or *less* plus the adjective to express the comparative:

| | | | |
|---|---|---|---|
| -ish | -ant | -like | -act |
| -ous | -ive | -ward | -er |
| -ful | -less | -ose | |
| -ic | -ing | -al | |

*MORE* + foolish, careful, helpless, cautious, active

*LESS* + blatant, verbose, regal, caring, hyper, boring

## EXERCISE 19

Write the comparative forms.

| | | | |
|---|---|---|---|
| 1. famous | 9. fiendish | 17. childlike | 25. selfish |
| 2. helpful | 10. morose | 18. alive | |
| 3. pensive | 11. cutting | 19. flagrant | |
| 4. captive | 12. clever | 20. fragrant | |
| 5. exact | 13. normal | 21. callous | |
| 6. loving | 14. sheepish | 22. forward | |
| 7. daring | 15. festive | 23. grateful | |
| 8. basic | 16. glorious | 24. useless | |

Sometimes it is better to use an antonym than to try to use the [less + adjective] pattern.

> Paul is **shorter than** Danny.
>
> Jane is **younger than** her cousins.

Use the same pattern for sentences as mentioned above.

> subject + verb + $\left\{\begin{array}{c}\textbf{\textit{MORE}} \\ \textbf{\textit{LESS}}\end{array}\right\}$ + $\left\{\begin{array}{c}\text{adjective} \\ \text{adverb}\end{array}\right\}$ + **THAN** + $\left\{\begin{array}{c}\text{noun} \\ \text{pronoun}\end{array}\right\}$

> This problem seems **more difficult than** that one.
>
> Larry finished his work **more quickly than** Tom.
>
> Since his accident, Lou is **less able** to play golf **than** before.
>
> I don't believe Leslie acts **less capably than** Brian.

To indicate a greater degree of comparison, use **much** or **far** plus the comparison form. **Much** and **far** can be used interchangeably in the comparison.

> subject + verb + $\left\{\begin{array}{c}\textbf{\textit{MUCH}} \\ \textbf{\textit{FAR}}\end{array}\right\}$ + comparative + **THAN** + $\left\{\begin{array}{c}\text{noun} \\ \text{pronoun}\end{array}\right\}$

Isa is ***much more independent than*** her sister ever was.

This jacket is ***far less expensive than*** the leather one.

A Porsche accelerates ***far more quickly than*** a Ford Escort.

Beginning students speak ***much less fluently than*** advanced ones.

It is also possible to compare nouns.

subject + verb + { ***LESS*** (non-count) / ***FEWER*** (countable) / ***MORE*** (both) } + noun + ***THAN*** + { noun / pronoun }

There are ***fewer*** people here today ***than*** yesterday.

I have ***less*** free time ***than*** anyone else I know.

We can visit ***more*** relatives on this trip ***than*** on the last.

Our professor has ***many more books than*** we have.

subject + verb + ***FAR*** + { ***MORE*** / ***LESS*** } + noun + ***THAN*** + noun

Gene spends ***far less time*** on his work ***than*** his friends.

Jack has ***far more friends*** than Bob.

## EXERCISE 20

Fill in the comparison using + (***more/ much***) and – (***less/ fewer***), and ++ (***far more***) and – – (***far less***) as your guides to the correct forms.

**Example:** Lucy is ***far less athletic*** than Jill. (– – athletic)

Michelle drinks ***more*** water in the summer than in the winter. (+)

1. Sue grades _____ exams than Lucy. (++)

2. This lace table cloth looks _____ the plastic one. (+ pretty)

3. In the summer grapes are _____ in the winter. (+ abundant)

4. As a child, Albert Einstein seemed _____ his playmates. (– intelligent)

5. The seats in first class have become _____ those in second class. (– – cramped)

6. In this class there are _____ students than there used to be. (++)

7. This morning Stan's talk was _____ it was yesterday. (+ straightforward)

8. Today we earn _____ money than we used to earn. (– –)

9. In warm weather, cars accelerate _____ in cold weather. (+ rapidly)

10. I found this book _____ the one that Jody recommended. (– – interesting)

Some adjectives cannot be compared. These are a few that cannot:

*Dead:* It is impossible to be deader than someone or something else.

*Unique:* It means one of a kind and allows for no comparison.

*Pregnant:* It is impossible to be a little pregnant or more pregnant than another.

*Immaculate:* It means pure or sinless, absolutely clean, and does not allow for comparison.

*Magnificent:* It already indicates the highest degree of perfection, superb.

*Infinite:* It already indicates without limits or bounds.

*Ultimate:* It indicates last possible or final of a series.

*Bare:* It means totally without clothing or furniture.

*Perfect:* It indicates the highest degree possible.

In winter the flowers are **dead**, and so are the trees.

Antoni Gaudi's architecture was **unique**.

**Pregnant** women visit a gynecologist.

Judy keeps an **immaculate** house.

Versailles is a **magnificent** example of Baroque architecture.

There are **infinite** ways to arrange musical notes in an opera.

John's **ultimate** goal is to become a professional photographer.

Janet's **bare** apartment was longing for some furniture and a new tenant.

Andy received **perfect** scores on all of his tests.

## EXERCISE 21

Using the following information, write unequal comparisons. Wherever possible, write one comparison using a greater degree and one comparison using a lesser degree.

**Example:** Gardenias smell very good. Violets don't have much aroma.

Gardenias smell *much better* than violets.

Violets smell *much less* than gardenias.

1. Mexico City has 20 million inhabitants. Micanopy has about 1,500.

2. Philip earns $100,000 per year. Tony earns $35,000.

3. Nancy is 35 years old and her brother is 38.

4. The millionaire has six cars. I have one.

5. The art building is 100 feet tall. The language lab is 50 feet tall.

6. A chocolate bar has 230 calories. A banana has 100.

7. It is 95 degrees in Arizona and 25 degrees in Anchorage.

8. Rudy receives C's and D's on his tests. Ralph receives A's and B's.

9. It is raining in Cleveland and snowing in Buffalo.

10. Betty learned to speak Portuguese well in three years. It took her ten years to learn Arabic.

## EXERCISE 22

Make comparisons using the following pairs of words.

**Example:** silk . . . denim *Silk is softer (more expensive) than denim.*

1. silver . . . gold

2. elephant . . . monkey

3. cotton . . . plastic

4. Coca-Cola . . . milk

5. spinach . . . cake

6. Tom Cruise . . . Paul Newman

7. yacht . . . canoe

8. airplane . . . train

9. swimming . . . watching television

10. North Pole . . . California

---
**NOTE**

When writing comparisons with *different*, it is incorrect to say *different than*. Use, instead, *different from*.

---

subject + verb + **DIFFERENT** + **FROM** + noun

Your book is **different from** mine.        ~~Your book is different *than* mine.~~

Kurt's car looks **different from** yours.    ~~Kurt's car looks different *than* yours.~~

# Irregular Comparisons

There are some adjectives and adverbs that have irregular comparisons. Here are some examples:

| | | |
|---|---|---|
| good | better | best |
| bad | worse | worst |
| far | farther | farthest |
| well | better | best |

This dessert tastes **better** than the apple pie.

Their baseball team was **the worst** of all.

Dennis writes **well**, but Dean writes **better.**

San Diego is **farther** from New York than Chicago.

## EXERCISE 23

Write a comparison for each sentence.

**Example:** Harry's writing is **_worse_** than yours.

1. Danny receives _____ grades than his brother. (good)

2. We live _____ from the university than you do. (far)

3. Nancy's students speak _____ than most. (well)

4. The food in this restaurant is _____ than in the one on the corner. (bad)

5. Ron feels much _____ today after taking his medicine. (good)

6. Ben ran _____ than any other athlete. (far)

7. Lucy sings _____ than Anita. (well)

8. This recipe sounds _____ than yours. (good)

9. Cleveland has _____ weather than Richmond. (bad)

10. Mel plays the guitar _____ than I do. (well)

# Equal Comparisons

The other type of comparisons relates equality or sameness to the elements being compared. One element is the same as the other.

> I have three oranges. You have three oranges.
>
> I have **as many oranges as** you.
>
> There are many skyscrapers in New York. There are also many skyscrapers in Chicago.
>
> New York has **as many skyscrapers as** Chicago.

The pattern for equal comparison differs from unequal comparison.

> **AS** + adjective + **AS**
>
> **AS** + adverb + **AS**
>
> **AS** + $\left\{ \begin{array}{c} \textbf{\textit{MUCH}} \\ \textbf{\textit{LITTLE/FEW}} \end{array} \right\}$ + (non-count) noun + **AS**
>
> **AS** + **MANY** + (countable) noun + **AS**

> Paul is **as tall as** Peter.
>
> Sue types **as fast as** Jennifer.
>
> We have **as much time as** you
>
> Sandy writes **as many letters as** Virginia.
>
> The Glass Boutique has **as many vases as** the Emporium.
>
> Make **as little noise as** possible, because your father is asleep.

---
**NOTE**

Remember that subject, not object, pronouns follow comparisons.

---

> They have as many books as **we**.
>
> No one studies as hard as **she**.

## EXERCISE 24

Combine the two sentences to show equal comparisons. There may be several possibilities for some of the sentences.

1. Kevin hit two home runs in yesterday's game. Dave also hit two home runs.

2. It's 75 degrees in Oahu and 75 degrees in Dallas.

3. Maureen ate three pieces of pizza, and her sister ate three.

4. Brian sleeps eight hours every night and Rita sleeps eight.

5. Phil weights 180 pounds. Harry weighs 180 pounds.

6. Tracy works very diligently in school. Trisha also works very diligently.

7. This sweater costs $10.95. The yellow one also costs $10.95.

8. Joel runs a mile in ten minutes. His brother also runs a mile in ten minutes.

9. The long dress is very elegant. The short dress is also elegant.

10. José spends four hours a day studying English and four hours studying math.

11. Some high school students do six assignments for homework every night. Some college students also do six hours of assignments.

12. Joan Collins has a lot of jewelry. Liz Taylor has a lot of jewelry.

13. In their new apartment, the Andersons have six pieces of furniture in the dining room and six pieces in the living room.

14. There are only 18 students in the chemistry class and only 18 in the physics class.

15. I paid $45 for my textbook. Anne paid $45 for her book.

## *The Same As*

Another type of comparison showing equality uses the expression *the same as*. There are no adjectives nor adverbs expressed in these comparisons.

> Your keys look *the same as* mine.
>
> His ring shines *the same as* hers.

Comparisons can also be made by using a noun to express the common element.

> subject + verb + *THE SAME* + noun + *AS*

> This gate is *the same height as* that one.
>
> Your sweater is *the same color as* Jan's.

## Superlatives

The last type of comparison involving three or more elements is called the **superlative degree**. One entity is the focus in comparison against the remaining entities. This can also be expressed in higher and lower degrees. Adjectives of one or two syllables follow this pattern:

> *THE* + [adjective + *EST*] +   [*OF* + plural noun]
>
>                                   [*IN* + singular noun]

> Dan is *the tallest of* the boys.
>
> Sandy is *the neatest in* the family.

Adjectives of three or more syllables follow another pattern:

> *THE* + { *MOST* / *LEAST* } + adjective + (noun) + [*OF* + plural noun]
>
>                                                      [*IN* + singular noun]

Many Italians say that the Vatican is ***the most beautiful of*** all buildings.

Some French think that the *Venus de Milo* is ***the most important work in*** the Louvre.

Sam thinks that math is ***the least significant of*** his courses.

Adverbs can also be expressed as superlatives.

***THE*** + [adverb + ***EST***] + [***OF*** + plural]

***THE*** + [***MOST*** + adverb] + [***IN*** + singular]

A Porsche runs ***the fastest of all***.

Tom studied ***the most diligently in*** his class.

## EXERCISE 25: WRITING

Study the information carefully and write statements, using the superlative. Use both highest and lowest degrees of comparison wherever possible.

**Example:** Glen likes to travel and is considering the following vacations. Europe—21 days, Mexico—14 days, and Canada—20 days. ***Europe is the longest vacation. Mexico is the shortest vacation.***

1. Semi-gloss paint costs $21 a gallon, satin $18, and flat $16 a gallon.

2. There are three cans on the table: 7 ounces of peas, 4 ounces of mushrooms, and 16 ounces of corn.

3. One-half cup of some fruits has more calories and is more fattening than others: apricots 128 calories, cantaloupe 35 calories, and pears 97.

4. It's hot today: Cleveland 95 degrees, Atlanta 87 degrees, and Trenton 80 degrees.

5. Distances from Olympia, Washington: Tacoma 30 miles, Bremerton 56, Aberdeen 49.

6. Helen has four holiday candles burning: red 3 hours, green 1 hour, and white 45 minutes.

7. Dan is measuring cabinets for his house: kitchen 36 inches wide, bath 27 inches, laundry 30 inches.

8. The football team went to a restaurant after the big game. The quarterback ate three hamburgers, the coach had two, and the kicker ate one.

9. Three athletes want to be healthy. Arthur jogs four miles every day and eats no red meat. Jill loves hamburgers and french fries, but she swims 35 laps every day. Ted drives to class and snacks on junk food every day.

10. It was a hot summer day. Cindy drank three glasses of lemonade, Suzy two, and Diane four.

## EXERCISE 26

For each sentence, supply the correct form.

1. Your house is _____ (far) from the university than mine.

2. I like this soup _____ (good) of all.

3. Today is much _____ (hot) than yesterday.

4. This furniture is _____ (expensive) than that.

5. Elvis Presley is _____ (famous) than Perry Como.

6. Your book seems _____ (boring) than mine.

7. This guide is _____ (helpful) than the one that the travel agent recommended.

8. Pete was _____ (interested) in the demonstration than his younger brother was.

9. Good students attend class _____ (frequently) than poor ones.

10. Paquito is the _____ (bad) player of all.

11. Mary's child was so nervous that he sat the _____ (quietly) of all the children.

12. The first contestant answered the questions the _____ (quickly) of all.

13. The Green Bean is the _____ (good) restaurant of any I have visited.

14. The North Pole has _____ (cold) temperatures than Alaska.

15. Marrying Tim was the _____ (foolish) thing Mary had ever done.

## EXERCISE 27

Use the correct form: *than*, *as*, *from*, or *more*.

1. Your dictionary is quite different ___from___ mine.

2. His job is not the same _____ yours.

3. An unskilled laborer is less qualified _____ a skilled one.

4. The dress costs far more _____ the skirt.

5. Skiing on snow is as dangerous _____ skiing on water.

6. Enrique speaks Spanish as well _____ English.

7. Paramedics are different _____ specialists.

8. These answers are the same _____ the ones I wrote.

9. Jackie's hair is longer _____ her sister's.

10. Algebra is different _____ geometry.

11. Spring is _____ pleasant than winter.

12. The girls play _____ rough as some of the boys.

13. Sara's culture is so much different _____ mine.

14. The _____ you earn, the more you spend.

15. The plot of this play is less interesting _____ the one you are reading.

## EXERCISE 28

Circle the underlined item that is incorrect.

1. In a marriage it is necessary for <u>each</u> of the partners to know <u>as</u> much as <u>it is</u> possible <u>about each other</u>.

   A.  each         B.  as         C.  it is         D.  about each other

2. Nobody <u>asked</u> me <u>about</u> my friend's <u>winning the lottery, and I didn't volunteer</u> any information.

   A.  Nobody         B.  me         C.  my friend         D.  any

3. The football team made <u>too much</u> errors and fumbles that the players <u>literally</u> gave <u>the win</u> to <u>their</u> opponents.

   A.  too much         B.  literally         C.  the win         D.  their

4. It is interesting <u>that</u> Medieval thought was <u>greatly</u> <u>influencing</u> by the <u>Greeks</u>.

   A. that      B. greatly      C. influencing   D. Greeks

5. <u>The</u> vegetable soup tasted so <u>well</u> that we <u>decided</u> to have <u>a</u> second helping.

   A. The      B. well      C. decided      D. a

6. By creating <u>their</u> own beautiful artistic designs, a person <u>can feel</u> a great sense of accomplishment <u>in knowing</u> that the patterns <u>are</u> unique.

   A. their      B. can feel      C. in knowing   D. are

7. <u>There</u> are <u>much</u> books in <u>the</u> library <u>on</u> accounting.

   A. There      B. much      C. the      D. on

8. The students <u>thought</u> that the teacher <u>had given</u> them <u>a</u> unusually <u>difficult</u> homework assignment.

   A. thought      B. had given      C. a      D. difficult

9. Mary's parents <u>disapproved</u> of <u>hers</u> attending the company conference <u>so far away</u> from her <u>home</u>.

   A. disapproved   B. hers      C. so far away   D. home

10. Mrs. Jansen was <u>divorcing</u> <u>from</u> her husband four years <u>ago</u> because of <u>their</u> incompatibility.

   A. divorcing      B. from      C. ago      D. their

11. <u>Although</u> the girl's singing was <u>slightly</u> off-key, her <u>guitar's</u> playing attracted the attention of those who <u>were</u> nearby.

   A. Although      B. slightly      C. guitar's      D. were

12. After a <u>carefully</u> investigation, we <u>soon</u> discovered that the house was <u>infested</u> with termites and <u>other</u> undesirable insects.

   A. carefully      B. soon      C. infested      D. other

13. I was <u>very much</u> surprised at <u>him</u> refusing <u>the</u> position of vice president of the <u>newly-formed</u> corporation.

    A. very much    B. him        C. the         D. newly-formed

14. The <u>witness</u> testimony <u>was</u> essential <u>to proving</u> that the defendant was <u>nowhere</u> near the scene of the crime.

    A. witness       B. was         C. to proving    D. nowhere

15. <u>The</u> Jensens said that their vacation last summer <u>was</u> most <u>enjoyably</u> and <u>relatively</u> inexpensive.

    A. The         B. was         C. enjoyably    D. relatively

16. Since we <u>haven't had</u> too <u>many</u> rain lately, the flowers are <u>rather wilted</u>, and many are <u>dying</u>.

    A. haven't had    B. many        C. rather wilted  D. dying

## EXERCISE 29

Below each sentence, you will see answers marked A, B, C, and D. Select the one answer that best completes the sentence.

1. Many women like to change _____ appearance from time to time because it makes them feel more attractive.

    A. her         B. your        C. their        D. our

2. People think that pandas are _____ than bears, but actually they are rather shy.

    A. friendlier    B. most friendly  C. friendliest    D. friendly

3. Venice is one of _____ cities in Europe.

    A. more beautiful             C. most beautiful

    B. the more beautiful        D. the most beautiful

4. Has _____ seen my gloves and my hat?

    A. anyone      B. anything    C. someone    D. nobody

5. Harry is _____ of all the students in the gym class.

    A.  taller          B.  the tallest     C.  the most tall   D.  more tall

6. The _____ canaries delighted the audience.

    A.  sung           B.  singing       C.  sang         D.  sings

7. Our director's _____ news gave us the incentive to finish our project.

    A.  encouraging  B.  encouraged   C.  encourages   D.  encourage

8. The _____ it rained, the harder we rowed the boat to get to shore.

    A.  as           B.  from         C.  more         D.  than

# Intermediate Grammar

# ESL

## CHAPTER 3

## Adverbs

# Chapter 3
# ADVERBS

Adverbs are words that modify an action verb, an adjective, or another adverb. If the adverb modifies the verb, it usually follows it.

Nan cried **hysterically** as the flames enveloped her car.

Len ran **quickly** to catch the ball.

When an adverb modifies an adjective, it always precedes the adjective.

C. Everett Koop is a **well**-known medical authority.

Saul had died before returning to his **dearly** beloved land.

Some examples of adverbs of intensity modifying other adverbs:

so      very      much      too      really*

*Used more in less formal English to indicate intensity.*

The cars drove **so fast** that we couldn't see the licenses.

Jacob moved the mirror **very slowly**.

The car drove **really** fast as it made its getaway.

Adverbs of time and frequency don't end in **-ly**. They usually precede the verb. Here are some in this category:

| | | |
|---|---|---|
| soon | seldom | anytime |
| sometimes | later | tomorrow |
| often | yesterday | late |
| never | last night | every day |

My cousins *seldom* visit us now that we have moved.

He *never* wants to go there again.

Adverbs of manner are formed by adding *-ly* to the adjective.

    quick > quickly          careful > carefully

However, there are a few forms that have minor changes. With those that end in a consonant +*y*, change the *y* to *i* before adding the *ly*.

    easy > easily          happy > happily

With adjectives ending in *ic*, add *ally* to form the adverb.

    majestic > majestically      angelic > angelically

With other adjectives ending in *ble*, drop the *e* and add **only *y***.

    reasonable > reasonably     noble > nobly

Adjectives look at *how* or *when* something is/was done. An action that happened more than once in the past is indicated by the following expressions:

| | | |
|---|---|---|
| times | frequently | generally |
| dozens of | usually | normally |
| often | sometimes | every day |
| all | many | several |

**Adverbs of frequency** (*often*, *usually*, *frequently*, *sometimes*, *generally*, *normally*) usually come *between* the auxiliary verb ***have*** and the past participle.

We have *often* visited our friends in Atlanta.

The author has *sometimes* written about her personal life in her novels.

Most adverbs end in *-ly*—for example:

rapidly     slowly     quietly     easily     comfortably

## EXERCISE 30

Change the adjectives to adverbs by adding *-ally*. Look up any words you don't know.

**Example:** frantic > frantically

1. basic _____ .       9. cryptic _____

2. historic _____       10. sympathetic _____

3. majestic_____       11. artistic _____

4. economic _____       12. domestic _____

5. comic _____       13. automatic_____

6. strategic _____       14. aromatic_____

7. critic _____       15. organic_____

8. antiseptic_____       16. systematic _____

## EXERCISE 31

Create adverbs by changing the *y* to *i* and adding *ly*.

**Example:** easy > easily

1. sloppy _____

2. heavy _____

3. angry _____

4. clumsy _____

5. ready _____

6. busy _____

7. steady _____

8. merry _____

## EXERCISE 32

Change to the adverb form by dropping the *e* and adding *only* a *y*.

**Example:** notable > notably

1. noble _____

2. able _____

3. capable _____

4. responsible _____

5. feasible _____

6. comfortable _____

# FREQUENCY ADVERBS

These adverbs show the number of times that an action takes place or is repeated. The following are listed in order of occurrence. The graph shows how they relate to one another.

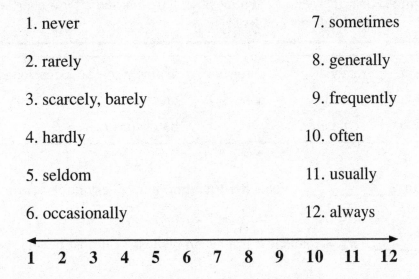

| 1. never | 7. sometimes |
| 2. rarely | 8. generally |
| 3. scarcely, barely | 9. frequently |
| 4. hardly | 10. often |
| 5. seldom | 11. usually |
| 6. occasionally | 12. always |

1  2  3  4  5  6  7  8  9  10  11  12

In a sentence, these adverbs will come directly before a simple verb tense.

James **always** *checks* out his computers before he sells them to his customers.

Margarita **never** *spoke* harshly to her students.

The project **barely** *meets* the federal guidelines.

When these adverbs are used with perfect tenses (***have* + past participle**) they are placed between ***have*** and the **past participle**.

We *have* **often** *visited* that museum.

The director *has* **occasionally** *asked* his employees for suggestions.

Wendy *had* **never** *been* to Niagara Falls before 1993.

If the compound tenses are used as questions, then the frequency adverbs are placed directly before the past participle.

*Have* you **never** *gone* to Stone Mountain near Atlanta?

*Has* Janet **always** *lived* in Vermont?

*Had* Jack **usually** *written* poetry before he decided to write fiction?

## EXERCISE 33

For each sentence, replace the words in parentheses with one of the frequency adverbs in the list that means the same or nearly the same. Some may be repeated.

**Example:** Jeff *barely* knew Mandy when they married after a short engagement. (almost not at all)

| | | | | |
|---|---|---|---|---|
| never | rarely | barely | scarcely | occasionally |
| seldom | usually | generally | often | frequently |
| always | sometimes | | hardly (ever) | |

1. Deborah _____ visits her grandmother. (every day)

2. Allen _____ gets low grades on his tests. (almost never)

3. Leonardo _____ studies in the library. (many days)

4. Has Marina _____ gone to a rock concert? (not one time)

5. Chris and Joe have _____ watched a baseball game on television. (only two times)

6. _____ my friends and I go to the shopping mall. (three times every month)

7. I _____ ever see you anymore. (not very much)

8. Sandy and her husband _____ eat dinner at a restaurant. (maybe once a month)

9. We _____ receive junk mail at home. (almost every day)

10. Mr. Davis _____ travels to Japan on business, but he goes to Europe once a month. (one time every two years)

**EXERCISE 34**

Write the frequency adverb in its proper place in the sentence.

**Example:** Mickey watches sports events on television. (rarely)
**Answer:** Mickey *rarely* watches sports events on television.

1. Football fans watch the games on Sunday afternoons. (always)

2. Pasquale has written a letter to his cousin in Italy. (never)

3. I have seen that program, but I don't like it. (occasionally)

4. We study on Friday afternoons. (usually)

5. Marta prepares a peach pie for special occasions. (generally)

6. They see us on weekends, because we are so busy. (hardly)

7. Monica has gone shopping in the new mall, because it is so far away. (seldom)

8. This neighborhood is quiet, but today it is rather noisy. (usually)

9. Has Jude sung and played for the local dances? (sometimes)

10. Have you thought about writing a novel? (often)

11. The girls take the bus to work, but today it was raining and they got a ride. (generally)

12. I have seen Tom without his wife at the council meetings. (seldom)

13. They talk to us since they moved to the new neighborhood. (barely)

14. We take the children to the park for a picnic on Sundays. (frequently)

15. Have you won the lottery? (never)

# YET, STILL, ALREADY, NEVER, EVER

*Yet* is used with questions and negative answers and indicates a time up to the present. It usually comes at the end of the sentence. It is used mostly with the present perfect tense.

> The plane hasn't arrived *yet*.
>
> Have they finished their report *yet*?

*Still* indicates a continuing action in progress at a given time in the past, present, or future. *Still* follows the verb *be* and precedes other verbs except auxiliaries in questions.

> Marsha is *still* president of the group.
>
> Did the language department *still* offer Russian when you were a student?
>
> He *still* hasn't finished his work. He has *still* not finished his work.

*Never* means "not once"; it is also a negative answer to an *ever* question.

> Have you *ever* met the President?
>
> I have *never* met the President.

*Ever* means "on one occasion"; it is also used for questions. It comes between the auxiliary and the main verb and can be used with a negative.

> Have you **ever** been to a rock concert?
>
> No, I haven't **ever** been to a rock concert.

*Already* is used in affirmative sentences to show that an action has taken place. It usually comes between the auxiliary and the main verb.

> We have **already** seen the movie.
>
> The passengers had **already** left the plane before their relatives arrived.

## EXERCISE 35

Complete each sentence, using one of the words below. There may be more than one correct answer in some sentences.

**Example:** I _**never**_ want to see so much violence again.

| never | ever | already | yet | still |

1. Have you read today's newspaper _____?

2. The Johnsons have _____ visited Switzerland.

3. Kurt is _____ writing his term paper.

4. Are you _____ living in Phoenix?

5. The professor hasn't arrived _____.

6. Has Nancy taken her morning coffee break _____?

7. We have _____ bought tickets for the opera.

8. Martin was _____ working for the airlines when I saw him.

9. Have you reviewed your irregular verbs _____?

10. Have they_____ visited Niagara Falls?

11. Is your friend _____ planning to visit you this month?

12. Has the new trade agreement been negotiated _____?

13. We haven't answered his letter _____.

14. Melanie is _____ reading that novel that she started while she was on vacation.

15. No one has seen the director _____ today.

16. Fifty percent of the project has _____ been completed.

17. Her father was a chemist, but Marleen _____ received good grades in chemistry.

18. Is that team_____ going to win a game this year?

## EXERCISE 36

Complete sentences, using the words below.

| never | ever | already | yet | still |
|-------|------|---------|-----|-------|

1. Susan has _____ written her thesis.

2. I am _____ not ready to discuss that controversial issue.

3. Someone else has _____ taken your seat.

4. Melissa _____ allows her sister to wear her clothes.

5. The physical fitness group is _____ jogging every morning.

6. Did the Pope _____ go to Africa on a visit?

7. Will Valerie _____ marry her childhood sweetheart?

8. I have _____ seen a red butterfly before. Have you?

9. Can you _____ forgive me for making such a mistake?

10. Many Northerners are wondering if spring will _____ arrive.

11. We _____ seem to have time after work to go shopping in the mall.

12. Has Sally _____ flown in a Concorde jet?

13. Rita hasn't graduated from high school _____.

14. Louie's team has _____ won two championships and hopes to win a third.

15. Has anyone else _____ won seven gold medals? I don't think so.

16. Is the store _____ having its big summer white sale?

17. No one has volunteered to accept the chairmanship_____.

# Intermediate Grammar

# ESL

## CHAPTER 4

# Prepositions

# PREPOSITIONS

**Prepositions** are a word or group of words that show the relation between the object and some other word in the sentence. Here is a partial list for you to learn.

| | | | |
|---|---|---|---|
| about | below | in front of | over |
| above | beside | in place of | past |
| according to | between | in regard to | since |
| across | beyond | in spite of | through |
| after | but (except) | in view of | throughout |
| against | by | inside | to |
| ahead of | concerning | instead of | toward |
| along | contrary to | into | under |
| among | despite | like | underneath |
| apart from | down | near | until (till) |
| around | during | of | up |
| as | except | off | up to |
| as far as | for | on | upon |
| at | from | on account of | with |
| because of | in | out | within |
| before | in addition to | out of | without |

**Prepositional phrases** include prepositions usually followed by *the* and a noun and indicate time or location. They answer the questions *when* or *where*.

We study English and math *in the morning*. (when?)

Mr. North prefers to drive *to the office*. (where?)

In terms of location, look at the prepositional phrases as any place a rat can go (under the sink, behind the sofa, between the walls, etc.).

Prepositions except *to* (which may precede the simple form of the verb or gerund) precede a gerund.

Some students put ***off studying*** as long as possible.

Sal is ***against hunting*** deer.

Prepositions can accompany nouns, verbs, and adjectives as an integral part of the phrase. Here is a partial list by category. Please see Appendix D for a more complete list.

### Noun + Preposition

| | | | |
|---|---|---|---|
| absence of | advantages of | amount of | pair of |
| attitude toward | confidence in | degree in | quality of |
| opportunity for | part of | plans for | year of |
| purpose of (for) | bag of | passion for | number of |

### Adjective + Preposition

| | | | |
|---|---|---|---|
| conscious of | contrary to | derived from | consistent with |
| governed by | impatient with | referred to | anxious about |
| worried about | married to | divorced from | interested in |

### Verb + Preposition

| | | | |
|---|---|---|---|
| account for | assign to | bestow on | approve of |
| bound by | confide in | correspond to | break away |
| delight in | exclude from | exempt from | break off |
| have (put) faith in | lead to | regard as | break up |

Prepositions are a difficult concept, and most often the best way to learn them is to listen to how they are used with certain expressions. A more complete of expressions and their appropriate prepositions is located in Appendix D. Look at the following examples:

**In:** years, months, city, state, country, the university, inside a building

In 1990 I lived in San Francisco, in California, while I was in the university.

**On:** specific date, name of a street, day of the week, different forms of transportation (bus, plane), certain floors of buildings, location (on the table/desk/sofa)

> Mary was born on June 14, 1965, in a house on Madison Street.

**At:** exact address, specific time, at home/school/work/the restaurant, with certain expressions such as at first/last/least/once/present/the most/your discretion/your convenience/this moment/this time/a more convenient time

> The party will be held at the Governor's Club at 7:30 p.m.

**Of:** to show possession, pertaining to, used with certain expressions (see Appendix D)

> The parents of John and Mary live in one of the suburbs east of town.

> In the absence of the president, the vice president conducted the meeting.

**From:** origin, out of, giver

> Jan received a letter from her uncle from France.

**For:** during, instead of, intended receiver, because of

> The exam for tomorrow is for the eleven o'clock class.

## EXERCISE 37

From the list of prepositions, select the best one to complete the meaning. Some may be repeated, and some may have multiple answers.

| of | above | after | at | before | by | for |
| --- | --- | --- | --- | --- | --- | --- |
| between | over | with | out of | on | to | |
| from | about | among | because of | off | in | |

The boss said that we must be 1) _____ the office 2) _____ nine o'clock, no later.

I woke up late, jumped 3) _____ the car and drove 4) _____ work.

My mother divided the cookies 5) _____ my friends and me.

We arrived late 6) _____ the rain.

7) _____ you go 8) _____ the house, you must unlock the door.

The birds flew 9) _____ the trees 10) _____ that hot summer day 11) _____ May.

Lucy's sister was born 12) _____ Baltimore 13) _____ June 22, 1970.

Arnold lives 14) _____ 2754 Benton Road.

Scott is 15) _____ love 16) _____ Sandi, and they will marry soon.

The police took the drugs 17) _____ the sellers.

Our plane took 18) _____ an hour late.

We have an agreement 19) _____ us two not to criticize each other.

Harry bought the flowers 20) _____ Peggy 21) _____ her birthday.

Columbus discovered America 22) _____ 1500.

Look for your glasses 23) _____ the shelf 24) _____ the television.

I'm thinking 25) _____ visiting my cousin this summer.

## EXERCISE 38

Supply the correct preposition.

1. The police accused them _____ robbing the bank.

2. You must take _____ account that he was very young then.

3. Don't worry _____ anything. I'll take care _____ everything.

4. Who will pay _____ the damages _____ your car?

5. They are thinking _____ moving _____ California.

6. It's a question _____ finding the right man _____ the job.

7. Does anyone object _____ my smoking a cigarette?

8. He's not interested _____ money _____ all.

9. She really died _____ a broken heart.

10. I asked the pharmacist _____ something _____ a headache.

11. He poured the wine _____ our glasses.

12. He is always _____ a hurry.

13. I asked the waitress to take _____ the dirty dishes.

14. He took me _____ the arm and helped me _____ the street.

15. This is an exception _____ the rule.

16. The sign said, "Keep _____ the grass."

17. Some people have strange ideas _____ bringing _____ children.

18. I dreamed _____ you all last night.

19. There is someone knocking _____ the door.

20. Why was she talking _____ him?

## EXERCISE 39

Circle the correct preposition.

### The *Ra* Expedition

1. (In, On) 1937 while Thor Heyerdahl and his wife were 2. (by, on) a little island 3. (for, in) the Marquesas 4. (on, in) the Pacific Ocean, he began to think 5. (about, to) stories he had heard concerning the great Polynesian sun-god Tiki. This and a series 6. (for, of) events led Thor Heyerdahl, a Norwegian, and five other men to undertake one 7. (for, of) the most daring adventures 8. (of, about) our times—that 9. (of, to) crossing the Pacific Ocean 10. (on, under) a balsa raft as he believed the ancient Polynesians had done.

The *Kon-Tiki*, as the raft was called 11. (to, in) honor 12. (of, for) the sun god, sailed some 4,300 nautical miles 13. (for, from) Peru 14. (for, to) the Polynesian Islands. 15. (On, By) the open sea, they had to withstand many gales and storms, as well as fight 16. (off, of) sharks. When their provisions ran out, they fished 17. (over, for) food and collected rain water to drink.

The 101-day trip proved 18. (for, to) Heyerdahl and the other adventurers that it was possible 19. (by, for) the Polynesians to have traveled 20. (for, from) South America 21. (to, on) their island many centuries before.

## EXERCISE 40

Select the correct preposition to complete the sentence.

1. After jumping _____ the cold pool, the swimmers began to shiver.

   A. into          B. on           C. under        D. beneath

2. Rafael lives in the Eastern part of Venezuela some 200 miles from Caracas at 18 feet _____ sea level.

   A. on top of     B. at           C. over         D. above

3. Jan plans to visit Arizona _____ the middle of spring

   A. at            B. around       C. to           D. for

4. Did you meet the guest speaker _____ the conference?

   A. at            B. in           C. on           D. over

5. The presidential candidate's speech today was inconsistent _____ his remarks made at previous gatherings.

   A. to            B. with         C. about        D. of

6. The assignments were equally divided _____ the five work-study students in the community education department.

    A. among        B. between        C. for        D. into

7. We tried to discourage the students _____ writing on topics that were too difficult for them to complete successfully.

    A. to        B. for        C. from        D. about

8. Both soccer and football teams consist _____ eleven active players for each team on the field.

    A. in        B. on        C. of        D. to

9. Some educators are trying to do away _____ the new mathematics because it has not been as successful as they had hoped.

    A. from        B. to        C. for        D. with

10. As I traveled _____ China on the train, I saw beautiful landscapes, old buildings, and quaint villages.

    A. in        B. on        C. over        D. about

11. Scientists were interested in the radio activity emanating _____ the nuclear power plant located near the ocean.

    A. in        B. to        C. from        D. about

12. Because the committee was anxious to attend the celebration, the president dispensed _____ reading the minutes of the previous meeting.

    A. with        B. from        C. of        D. for

13. At night the sound of the wind intensifies the excitement one feels as he imagines the cries uttered _____ the victims of the Inquisition.

    A. by        B. for        C. to        D. about

# Intermediate Grammar

# ESL

## CHAPTER 5

## Conjunctions

# Chapter 5
# CONJUNCTIONS

A word that connects words or groups of words in a sentence is a **conjunction**. These connecting words can be **relative**, **coordinating**, **correlative**, and **subordinate** conjunctions. Each has a different function and will be studied more in detail in later chapters.

An easy way to remember the coordinating conjunctions is by using the acronym FANBOYS: For, And, Nor, But, Or, Yet, So.

The words *and*, *nor*, *or* can connect nouns, verbs, adjectives, adverbs, or prepositional phrases as a series of elements. Use *nor* in negative sentences.

**Nouns:**    There are pens, paper, *and* pencils on the shelf.

Take the red blouse *or* the green blouse.

I do*n't* like a Porsche *nor* a Cadillac.

**Verbs:**    Joe plays guitar *and* sings well.

The group ca*n't* dance *nor* act.

We will swim *or* ride our bikes on Saturday.

**Adjectives:**    Paul is athletic, studious, *and* generous.

Today is *not* sunny *nor* warm.

Those socks are black *or* blue.

**Adverbs:**    The scouts walked quietly *and* carefully through the woods.

These questions are *neither* neatly *nor* correctly answered.

In ballet jump quickly *or* elegantly, *or* don't jump at all.

**Prepositional phrases:** Look under the bushes *and* among the flowers for the hidden Easter eggs.

You will find your socks under the bed *or* in the closet.

Do*n't* hang the picture over the mantel *nor* above the door.

These conjunctions can connect two main clauses. When they do, use a comma directly before the conjunction.

Lei won a scholarship*, and* she went away to school

I don't have a car*, nor* do I plan to buy one.

My flight leaves at seven*, so* I need to hurry.

We have to leave now*, but* we will return soon.

The conjunction *for* usually means *because*, giving a reason for an action.

Our group moved inside the pavilion, *for* it had started to rain.

Bring your coats along, *for* the evenings are cool in that area that we will be visiting.

## EXERCISE 41

Circle the conjunctions and underline which parts of the sentence are connected. Decide whether they are connecting two complete ideas, just two words of the same part of speech, or a contrast.

**Example:** Tony is out today, but he will return tomorrow. *but*—contrast

The sun is shining brightly, and we are going to the beach.
*and*—two ideas

1. The sky is gray, and it is going to rain.

2. We want to see that new movie, but not tonight.

3. Rudi wants to be a doctor, so he is taking a number of science courses this semester.

4. The doctor can see you Monday, but you have to be here no later than 8:00 a.m.

5. I don't know how to dance, nor do I intend to learn.

6. Maritza doesn't have enough money for the trip, yet she really wants to go.

7. My sister just bought some dishes and glasses for her new house.

8. I wish you a lot of luck, for I know you will need it.

9. The diplomat can't speak Russian nor Italian.

10. Jason ordered the part for his car, but it hasn't come in.

11. We have a test in an hour, and we have to study a lot now.

12. The Howard family is going away for the holidays, but they have not made reservations yet.

13. The team has bought uniforms, helmets, and gloves.

14. Go now and pay later.

15. I will study chemistry or algebra in the fall, but not both.

# Intermediate Grammar

# ESL

## CHAPTER 6

## Verbs

# Chapter 6
# VERBS

There are four principal parts for all verbs, both regular and irregular. They are **present**, **past**, **past participle**, and **present participle**. Except for the verb *be*, the present tense is the form found in the dictionary.

In the present tense, the forms are all the same except for the third person singular (*he*, *she*, *it*) to which you add *-s*.

walk**s**, run**s**, say**s**     (I walk, you walk, he/she/it walks, we walk, they walk)

For verbs that end in *ch*, *o*, *s*, *sh*, and *x*, however, add *-es* for the third person form.

watch**es**, go**es**, pass**es**, wish**es**, wax**es**

For verbs ending in consonant +*y*, change *y* to *i* before adding *-es*

copy > cop**ies**     marry > marr**ies**

For all *regular* verbs in the past tense, add *-d* to forms ending in *E*.

bake**d**, like**d**, revere**d**, quote**d**

For all regular verbs, add *-ed* to forms ending in consonants.

talk**ed**, jump**ed**, wait**ed**, sail**ed**

The **past participle** for regular verbs is the same as the past tense.

Mary *baked* a cake yesterday. (past tense)

Mary *has baked* many cakes for our bake sales. (past participle—regular)

However, for irregular verbs there is usually a different form.

Janet *wrote* many letters to her friends. (past)

Janet *has written* many letters to her friends. (past participle—irregular)

### Regular Verbs

| Past | Past Participle |
|------|-----------------|
| walked | walked |
| planted | planted |
| telephoned | telephoned |

### Irregular Verbs

| Past | Past Participle |
|------|-----------------|
| sang | sung |
| rode | ridden |
| went | gone |

The **present participle** is the form ending in *-ing*. Remember that for verbs ending in either a [vowel + *y*] or a [consonant + *y*], keep the *y* before adding the *-ing*.

marrying, copying, flying

surveying, annoying, portraying

## EXERCISE 42

Write the correct form of the verb in the present tense.

1. the cook _____ (fry)

2. the mirror _____ (magnify)

3. the shoes _____ (pinch)

4. my skin _____ (itch)

5. we _____ (deny)

6. Anita _____ (do)

7. the band _____ (march)

8. Mr. Adams _____ (teach)

9. the students _____ (hurry)

10. the brides _____ (blush)

11. you _____ (wash)

12. my uncle _____ (fish)

13. Ana _____ (study)

14. they _____ (go)

15. the iron _____ (scorch)

16. I _____ (apply)

17. the dress _____ (dry)

18. the airplane _____ (fly)

19. the sun _____ (bleach)

20. the baby _____ (cry)

# AUXILIARY VERBS

Each of these principal parts uses certain **auxiliary** (helping) **verbs** to form different tenses. Look at the following chart to see which auxiliaries accompany the four different forms and the tenses that they create in active voice.

| Present (*see*) | Past (*saw*) | Past participle (*seen*) | Present participle (*seeing*) |
|---|---|---|---|
| do | *No auxillary* | have | is, are, am |
| does | *verbs for* | has | was, were |
| can | *simple past.* | had | can be |
| did | | | could be |
| could | | | may be |
| would | | | might be |
| may | | | would be |
| should | | | should be |
| will/shall | | | will, shall be |
| might | | | ought to be |
| | | | must be |

I *write* my homework every night.

I *can write* my homework every night.

I *would write* my homework every night.

I *will write* my homework every night.

I *may write* my homework every night.

I *wrote* my homework every night.

I *must be writing* my homework every night, or else I wouldn't be passing.

I *wrote* my homework every night.

I *had written* my homework before lunch.

I *have written* my homework every night.

I *am writing* my homework right now.

I *was writing* my homework at 8:00.

# USING AUXILIARY VERBS

Auxiliaries are always followed by the simple form of the verb (infinitive without *to*):

to go      to say      to see      to speak      to work

Auxiliaries cannot be used in combination with each other. When *do* and *have* are the principal verbs of the sentence, the auxiliaries can combine with them.

Tim **does not have** a car.

We **can do** that job in 15 minutes.

The mechanic **could have** the car by tomorrow.

I **will have** these papers for you later today.

Remember the following formulas for word order when using auxiliaries:

| | | | |
|---|---|---|---|
| Affirmative: | subject  +  auxiliary  +  main verb  +  complement | | |
| | She            *WILL*         *WRITE*       the letters. | | |
| Negative: | subject  +  auxiliary  +  negative + v  +  complement | | |
| | She            *WILL*     *NOT WRITE*     the letters. | | |
| Question: | auxiliary  +  subject  +  verb  +  complement | | |
| | *WILL*          she         *WRITE*     the letters? | | |

*Do*, *does*, *can*, and *should* combine with the simple form to express variations in the present. The auxiliaries *do* and *does* are also necessary for asking a question or for forming a negative, as well as for emphasis.

| | | |
|---|---|---|
| They **do need** help. | They **do not need** help. | **Do** they **need** help? |
| I **can play** tennis. | I **cannot play** tennis. | **Can I play** tennis? |
| We **should study**. | We **should not study** now. | **Should** we **study**? |

Remember that *do*, *does*, and *did* are the auxiliary verbs for past and present tenses of all main verbs.

| | |
|---|---|
| Joe plays | > *does play* golf well. |
| Anton sold | > *did sell* his house last year. |
| The students learn | > *do learn* their lessons. |

*Did*, *could*, and *would* (repeated past action) combine to express a variation in the past. *Did* in the affirmative sentences emphasizes the past. Simple past forms also express the same idea. Notice the need for the auxiliary *did* in the negative and question forms.

| | |
|---|---|
| He *did visit (visited)* his cousins. | (for emphasis) |
| *Did* he *visit* his cousins? | (to ask a question) |
| He *did not visit* his cousins. | (to express the negative) |

When I was a child, I *would swim* every summer.

*Would I swim* every summer?

I *would not swim* every summer.

Before his knee injury in 1988, Harry *could run* very fast.

*Could* Harry *run* very fast?

Harry *could not run* fast.

*Could*, *would*, and *might* can express uncertainty based on a condition for a later time. The condition expressed, however, represents something contrary to fact that will probably not change and not materialize later. Remember that these auxiliaries come from three different verbs, and the meaning for each is slightly different.

If we had the money (we don't), we *would buy* a new car.

I *could stop* by tomorrow if you received the document.
(You probably won't receive it.)

She *might be able* to come, but it doesn't look as if she'll get the plane tickets on time.

*May*, *will*, and *shall* are used as auxiliaries to indicate future time. In British English, *shall* is used for *I* and *we* forms, while in American English, *will* is acceptable for all forms.

> She *may* go to New York with us next week.

> I *will* (*shall* for British English) look for a new apartment before the end of the month.

## EXERCISE 43

Underline the auxiliary and/or main verb.

1. The Joneses have just bought a new car.

2. When did you send that package to your sister?

3. When is Tom leaving for California?

4. Can you give me change for this twenty-dollar bill?

5. Will these supplies be enough for your camping trip?

6. How often do you fill your gas tank?

7. The artist painted a portrait of his mother.

8. Nothing seems to matter to them anymore.

9. The president had spoken to the committee before making his decision.

10. The children were playing with their toys all afternoon.

## EXERCISE 44

Change the statements to questions.

1. We can see the movie tomorrow night.

2. Nancy has an appointment for two o'clock today.

3. The landlord might raise the rent again.

4. He would like to visit the United Nations.

5. Susan will be out of town for three weeks.

6. The students should study all the new vocabulary.

7. I had a job in Boston.

8. Enrico bought his new computer last week.

9. Tara paints very well.

10. The carpenters know how to build the house.

**EXERCISE 45**

Oscar is a little confused. He has some incorrect information. Help him change the affirmative statements to negative ones and provide the correct information.

1. Tomatoes grow on trees.

2. The sun shines at night.

3. Roosters can lay eggs.

4. Alligators lived in the desert long ago.

5. My roses could grow without water.

6. The French invented the concept of zero.

7. (Peter has problems with math.) He should study statistics.

8. Most luxury cars get good gas mileage.

9. Bolivia has a large port.

10. Lions have feathers.

## EXERCISE 46

Change the sentences from the present to the future.

1. Grass grows faster in the summer.

2. They serve supper at seven o'clock.

3. The plane arrives late.

4. Nobody sleeps after noon.

5. The play begins on Saturday.

6. It is sunny this afternoon.

7. The Waltons live on a mountain.

8. Nothing interesting happens around here.

9. Poinsettias don't bloom in the summer.

10. The final exams counts for 25 percent of your grade.

## EXERCISE 47: WRITING

Answer the questions, using the correct form of the verb. Write a contrasting idea for the negative.

1. What time does your English class begin?

It _____

_____ not _____

2. Who eats peanut butter sandwiches?

_____

_____ not _____

3. How long does Sarah sleep every day?

She _____

_____ not _____

4. Who runs away from the cat?

_____

_____ not _____

5. Does Badr drive to the university every day?

Yes, _____

No, _____

6. Does Cynthia walk with the children every afternoon?

Yes, _____

No, _____

7. Who sings Spanish songs?

_____

_____ not _____

8. When does Maja dance?

She _____

_____ not _____

9. Who talks on the telephone with the sales department?

_____

_____ not _____

10. Which newspaper does Alia read?

She _____

_____ not _____

11. Does Corazon write letters to her family every week?

Yes, _____

No, _____

12. Does this restaurant serve good food?

Yes, _____

No, _____

# PAST TENSE

Any time before now is considered past tense. The verb tense indicates only that the action took place earlier, with no reference to other actions. While times may be expressed, they are not in relation to other times. Regular verbs form the past tense by adding -*d* to the verbs that end in *e*.

bake > baked            tease > teased            raise > raised

provide > provided  reserve > reserved   rule > ruled

For regular verbs ending in a consonant, add -*ed* to the present tense.

look > looked            fail > failed            wait > waited

Most one-syllable verbs containing one vowel and ending in a single consonant, double the final consonant before adding -*ed*.

stop > stopped            dot > dotted            slam > slammed

Do not double the letters *x* and *w*.

wax > waxed            mow > mowed

When a two-syllable verb ends in a single consonant after a single vowel and the second syllable is stressed, double the final consonant also.

o•mit′ > o•mitted′        con•trol′ > con•trolled′        re•fer′ > re•ferred′

Notice that the stress is on the second syllable for each of the above. Now look what happens if the stress falls on the first syllable.

en′•ter > en′•tered        li′•sten > li′•stened        ri′•val > ri′•valed

For words ending in consonant +*y*, change the *y* to *i* before adding *ed*.

hurry > hurried            copy > copied            fry > fried

\*\*Remember to use *did* as the auxiliary for questions and negatives.

> *Did* you *find* the newspaper?
>
> No, I *did not find* the newspaper.

Unfortunately, there are many verbs in the past tense that do not follow this rule. See Appendix E for a list will help you to learn some of them.

## EXERCISE 48

Circle the correct form of the verb in parentheses.

1. Because we had (forgot, forgotten) to wind the clock before going to bed, we arrived late for work.

2. Have the hikers already (gone, went) to the mountains?

3. Our dog (digged, dug) a hole in the backyard.

4. My cousin (brang, brought) her guitar to the party, and we (sang, sung) many of our favorite songs.

5. Our neighbors (selled, sold) their house last month.

6. Because the laborers were so tired, they (sleeped, slept) an extra hour this morning.

7. After playing tennis for two hours, the players (drank, drunk) two glasses of juice.

8. The airplane (flew, flied) high over the mountain peaks.

9. After the hurricane had hit the area, many beautiful trees (fell, fallen) to the ground.

10. An intense cold wave (freezed, froze) the water pipes, causing them to burst.

11. We had (ate, eaten) so much that we could not ride our bicycles home.

12. Our lunch fell off the boat, and I watched it as it (sunk, sank) slowly into the sea.

13. No one in the audience (understand, understood) the speaker's message.

14. They (telled, told) us what they had planned to do in Washington.

15. Last night we (seen, saw) a great movie.

16. The whistle (blew, blown) loudly as the train approached the station.

## EXERCISE 49

Write the correct form of the verbs, using the past tense or the past participle.

### Garage Saling—A Way of Life

Last week two of my friends and I (1) *were* (be) returning from the shopping mall when we (2) *saw* (see) some "garage sale" signs. It (3) _____ (seem) odd that someone would want to sell a garage, but in the interest of culture, we (4) _____ (decide) to find out what it was. As we (5) _____ (approach) the house, we (6) _____ (see) about ten people leaving with armfuls of things that they had just (7) _____ (buy). We (8) _____ (park) the car and (9) _____ (walk) back to the garage, where two ladies (10) _____ (be) sitting and chatting away. We (11) _____ (look) around and saw some lovely things but could not believe the prices, so we (12) _____ (ask) the ladies about them. We (13) _____ (want) to know why the prices were so low, and they (14) _____ (say) that they were cleaning house and (15) _____ (want) to eliminate many of the things they could not use anymore.

We excitedly (16) _____ (pick) through clothes, books, CDs, kitchen equipment, bedding, and lamps. We recently (17) _____ (move) into dorms on campus, and we did not have very much in our rooms. We

(18) _____ (select) our "treasures" and (19) _____ (can) not believe that we were able to fill a shopping bag for under $10! We asked the ladies about how often people had these sales and how we could find out where they were. They (20) _____ (tell) us that in the nice weather, people had them on Thursdays, Fridays, and Saturdays, and they (21) _____ (advertise) in the newspaper or (22) _____ (put) up their signs on the main road.

We (23) _____ (make) plans to go out again the following week to hunt for more bargains. What a great idea these Americans have for recycling their old things!

# *AGO*

One time expression that indicates a completed past action is the word *ago*. It is sometimes introduced by the following expressions:

> how long ago
> how many days ago
> how many weeks (months, years) ago
> when did

The time that has elapsed is a duration and usually accompanies an expression in the plural, as in the following:

| | |
|---|---|
| three weeks ago | four months ago |
| five minutes ago | hundreds of years ago |
| nine hours ago | a century ago |

> When *did* you *buy* that bicycle?
> I *bought* it *three weeks ago*.

How many years *ago did* Fernando *travel* to Africa?

He *traveled* to Africa *eight years ago*.

How long *ago did* Henry write his book?

Henry *wrote* his book *six months ago*.

*Never* use *ago* when you are trying to relate something in the past to the present. Never use a specific year, day, or date, because it will not show a duration of time.

**INCORRECT:**   We had a test ago on Monday.

**CORRECT:**      We had a test four days ago.

## EXERCISE 50

Answer the questions, using *ago* and the time expressions indicated.

1. How long ago did you paint the house? (two weeks) *I painted it two weeks ago.*

2. When did you begin to study English? (three semesters)

3. Did the plane arrive ten minutes ago? Yes, _____

4. How many days ago did we study the past tense? (five days)

5. When did Janice begin working for the electric company? (eight years)

6. Did you finish your homework two hours ago? No, _____

7. When did they catch the bus? (one hour)

8. How long ago did Carol move here? (seven months)

9. When did this class begin? (20 minutes)

10. How long ago did you meet Mrs. Nelson? (six weeks)

11. When did Waldemar start his weight-lifting program? (four months)

12. When did Nina and Ben get married? (10 years)

13. Did you buy a new car six days ago? No, we _____

14. When did Sandy and Joan send the wedding invitations? (one month)

15. How many years ago did the new museum open? (four years)

# PROGRESSIVE TENSES

Any form of the verb *be*, past, present, or future, when used with the **present participle**, indicates the **progressive** tense—that is, it shows an action in progress at a given time, and the subject is performing that action.

**Present:** Use the present tense of the verb *be* for an action taking place *now*.

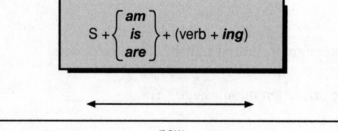

$$S + \left\{ \begin{array}{l} am \\ is \\ are \end{array} \right\} + (verb + ing)$$

```
past                    now                    future
```

These are words that indicate an action is taking place now:

now

right now

at this moment

presently

today

*This semester* (given time) Jess *is studying* English literature.

*Right now* the scouts *are hunting* for their supper.

**Past:** Use the past tense of the verb *be* for an action in progress at a time in the past.

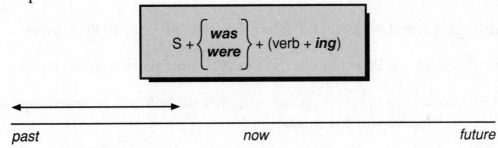

$$S + \left\{ \begin{array}{c} \textbf{\textit{was}} \\ \textbf{\textit{were}} \end{array} \right\} + (\text{verb} + \textbf{\textit{ing}})$$

past                                now                                future

These are words that indicate an action took place in the past:

at that moment

while

as

last semester/month/year

> *While* I ***was watching*** television, my son ***was reading*** a book.
>
> *As* Sarah ***was drinking*** her coffee this morning (given time),
>
> the florist delivered a dozen yellow roses.

**Future:** The future progressive looks at an action that will be taking place at some definite time later than now and uses the **future tense** of the verb *be*.

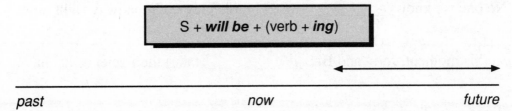

$$S + \textbf{\textit{will be}} + (\text{verb} + \textbf{\textit{ing}})$$

past                                now                                future

These are words that indicate an action that will take place in the future:

tomorrow

next week/month/year

later

after

> *By the end of the year* (given time), you ***will be writing*** longer and better essays.
>
> We ***will be traveling*** in Spain *next summer.*

The adverb *still* indicates that the action continues from past to any other given time.

**Present:** My friend André *is still dating* the same girl after all these years.

**Past:** When we saw Peter last year, he *was still doing* portrait photography.

**Future:** Anita is so in love with her work that she *will still be practicing* medicine when she is 80 years old.

Notice the placement of the adverb in each of the sentences above.

## EXERCISE 51

Using the time expressions as a clue, write the appropriate progressives for each sentence.

1. At 4:00 this morning, I _____ (dream) about something terrible when I suddenly awoke.

2. Our group _____ (meet) again next month to plan the fall festival.

3. No one we know _____ (act) in this play on Broadway right now.

4. At this moment, Jody and Bob _____ (take) their science exam.

5. Right now, Trudy _____ (write) a memo about tomorrow's meeting.

6. Who _____ (run) across the street when you left here this morning?

7. It _____ (rain) very hard when we arrived at the concert last night.

8. We _____ (visit) the Grand Canyon on our vacation next summer.

9. Nancy _____ (marry) her college sweetheart this afternoon.

10. The boss _____ (prepare) the new budget when I entered her office.

11. Jim _____ (sail) to Tahiti at this time tomorrow.

12. Robert _____ (try) to start the lawn mower when it started to rain.

13. Monica _____ (drive) to Philadelphia to attend a conference next Friday.

14. Our director _____ (eat) his lunch now and cannot be disturbed.

15. How many students _____ (graduate) in next Saturday's ceremony?

16. How many paychecks _____ we _____ (get) next year?

17. Sue _____ (program) all the computers in the lab later this afternoon.

18. With all this heavy rain, the grass _____ (grow) higher and higher.

19. Tom _____ (copy) some materials when I passed by his office.

20. Phil _____ (photograph) many interesting sites during his vacation next month.

## PRESENT AND PRESENT PROGRESSIVE

**Present** tense usually refers to habitual actions that started in the past and are still repeated now. Unlike the **present progressive**, these actions are not taking place at this moment. Notice the difference in these two sentences.

Mrs. Dawson *parks* her car in the same spot under the tree every day. (This is a practice she started in the past and repeats every day.)

Mrs. Dawson *is parking* her car under the tree. (This action is in progress at this moment.)

#### Use simple present for:

- repeated or habitual actions
- general truth statements
- all verbs that show mental action
- verbs that pertain to the senses

#### Use present progressive for:

- action in progress now
- *be* + *going* + infinitive to show future action
- to indicate future action

Look at the differences in these sentences.

**Habitual:**   Paul *always writes* his poems in a special book.

**In progress:**   Paul *is writing* a book of poems now.

**General truth:**   The sun *shines* every day in the summer.

**In progress:**   The *sun is shining* right now.

**Mental action:**   I *need* a new tire for the car.

**Mental action:**   We *hate* snow and cold in the winter.

**Appeals to senses:**   The cook *tastes* the food as she prepares it.

**Future:**   My friends *are going to swim* in the pool tomorrow.

**In progress:**   They *are swimming* right now.

**Future:**   All my friends *will be singing* in the festival tomorrow.
    We *will be taking* a test next Monday.

Certain verbs that refer to mental action or that pertain to the senses are usually in the **simple present** and are not normally used in the progressive form as in the following lists:

**Mental Action**

be

| | |
|---|---|
| believe | mean |
| belong | need |
| desire | prefer |
| hate | suppose |
| imagine | understand |
| know | want |
| like | wish |

**Pertain to the Senses**

love

hear

know

see

smell

sound

taste

| | | |
|---|---|---|
| The scientist **believes** his theory is correct. | NOT | The scientist is believing |
| We **hate** going to the dentist. | NOT | We are hating going |

I **understand** how to solve that problem now.

I **hear** that you have a new job.

The soup **tastes** wonderful.

For each of these sentences, the simple form of the verb (*he*, *she*, *it* forms add *-s* or *-es*) is used.

Some examples of words or expressions that show habitual action are the following:

| | | |
|---|---|---|
| every day | always | sometimes |
| every year | usually | frequently |
| on Tuesdays | often | rarely |

Ling ***usually*** *rides* his bike to school.　　　Victor *stops* in my office to chat ***every day.***

My parents **often** *visit* on Sunday afternoons.　We *eat* pizza **on Wednesdays.**

Notice the placement of the time phrases.

For the **present progressive**, use the following:

$$\text{subject} \; + \; \begin{Bmatrix} \textbf{\textit{AM}} \\ \textbf{\textit{IS}} \\ \textbf{\textit{ARE}} \end{Bmatrix} + [\, v + \textbf{\textit{ING}} \,]$$

Remember that the following key words indicate that the action is taking place (in progress):

now　　right now　　at this moment　　presently　　right this minute

The students *are taking* their exams **at this moment.**

I *am* **presently** *living* in a small apartment.

Betty *is waiting* for me in the car **now.**

## EXERCISE 52

Fill in the correct form of the verb in the present or the present progressive.

Even though I (1) _____am_____ (be) a long way from my family, I often

(2) _____ (think) about them. As I (3) _____ (walk) to class, I

(4) _____ (wonder) if they (5) _____ (do) something special at this

moment. I (6) _____ (imagine) that my sister (7) _____ (dance) in her

ballet class while my brothers (8) _____ (play) baseball in the park. Mother

(9) _____ (write) haiku in the garden, and my father (10) _____

(meet) with some important businessmen. Every day my friends (11) _____

(go) to class, and then they (12) _____ (sit) and (13) _____ (study)

near the university. On Saturdays they (14) _____ (swim) in the pool and

(15) _____ (plan) special activities for Sunday. I (16) _____ (know) that all of them (17) _____ (have) fun, and they (18) _____ (do) what they always (19) _____ (like) best. Now it is late and I (20) _____ (need) to hurry to my class and think about my studies.

## EXERCISE 53

Circle the correct form of the verb.

1. While the teacher is explaining the lesson, the students (take, are taking) notes.

2. Every day Peter (calls, is calling) his girlfriend.

3. Nobody (knows, is knowing) the answer to that question.

4. The number of houses for sale (grows, is growing) more and more every day.

5. Neither Mrs. Jensen nor her sons (play, are playing) tennis every day.

6. On Saturdays Mr. Dalton (buys, is buying) his groceries.

7. A boy and two girls (use, are using) the computers at this moment.

8. The students and faculty (park, are parking) in the new lot every day.

9. The Lopez family (prepares, is preparing) dinner now.

10. Andrew (packs, is packing) the suitcases right now.

11. Harry (studies, is studying) all night for the exam tomorrow.

12. Our friends (go, are going) to the beach every Sunday.

13. Tony (eats, is eating) supper at home at this moment.

14. Our professor (talks, is talking) about the space program today.

15. Hugo (works, is working) ten hours every Monday.

16. The bad weather (forces, is forcing) us to stay home today.

17. The rabbit (hops, is hopping) around the yard right now.

18. The chemist always (mixes, is mixing) the chemicals carefully.

19. Anne always (tries, is trying) to finish her projects on time.

20. We (wait, are waiting) now for the letter to arrive.

# INFINITIVES

The basic form of all verbs is the **infinitive**, the simple form of the verb plus *to*. In a sentence, the infinitive consists of two parts: *to* + verb. This form does not indicate *who* is/was performing the action, nor does it show *when* that action took place. It is not a conjugated verb. Examples of the infinitive:

| | | |
|---|---|---|
| to go | to speak | to drive |
| to see | to write | to take off |
| to think | to ride | to realize |

Even though the infinitive is not a conjugated form, there are ways of expressing it in different tenses, depending on the main verb of the sentence.

> subject + verb + infinitive + complement

I **want to visit** Tahiti some day.

Mario **plans to sing** at the concert.

Some verbs that take the infinitive are the following:

| wish    | expect | plan   | refuse  |
|---------|--------|--------|---------|
| want    | need   | try    | request |
| be able | hope   | decide | prefer  |

**Present:** We want *to see* Clint Eastwood's new movie today.

**Present progressive:** I am hoping *to get* tickets for the ballet.

**Future:** Allen will try *to meet* with the president tomorrow.

**Past progressive:** Sandy was willing *to negotiate*, but the company refused.

If you want to express a negative with the infinitive, be sure to use **not** before the infinitive.

> **NOT + TO +** verb

I prefer **not to pay** more taxes this year.

We decided **not to take** a vacation last summer.

They will try **not to drive** more than 400 miles a day.

# LINKING VERBS

Verbs in this special category link or join the subject with its complement. The subject never performs the action, and the verb never takes a direct object. Adjectives, not adverbs, follow these verbs. The following verbs belong to this special group.

| appear | feel* | look* | seem | stay |
|--------|-------|-------|------|------|
| be | get* | prove* | smell* | taste* |
| become | grow* | remain | sound* | turn* |

*Also can be a transitive verb.*

Keep in mind that the verbs *be*, *become*, and *remain* can also be followed by noun phrases. Compare this noun phrase with the adjective.

John **is** *president of the sophomore class.* (noun phrase)

Tony **was** *excited* about winning the prize. (adjective)

Christa MacAuliffe **became** *one of the first women in space.* (noun phrase)

Teddy **became** *tired* after playing several long tennis matches. (adjective)

Mr. Frazer will **remain** *senator* until the end of this term. (noun)

The students **remained** *seated* while the school president distributed the diplomas. (adjective)

The verbs in the list above that are indicated by an asterisk (*) can also be transitive verbs (the subject *does* perform the action and there is a direct object). When they are transitive, they can also be followed by an adverb, not an adjective. Look at the following sentences to distinguish their use as transitive or intransitive verbs. Notice how the subject performs the action in the sentences that contain adverbs and direct objects.

You **will feel** *the effects of the medicine* in a short while. (takes a direct object)

Jason **felt** *uncomfortable* in his three-piece suit. (adjective)

The hikers *cautiously* **felt** their way along the dark mountain trail. (adverb)

Nancy **grew** *a variety of vegetables* in her garden this summer. (takes a direct object)

The weather **grew** *cold* as the front passed over the area. (adj.)

Marcella **looks** very *attractive* with her new hairdo. (adj.)

The little boy **looked** *carefully* before crossing the street. (adv.)

The food in the kitchen **smells** *good.* (adj.)

The customer **insisted on smelling** *the cologne* before purchasing it. (takes a direct object)

Your plan **sounds** *excellent.* (adj.)

Tim *sounded the alarm* when the fire broke out. (takes a direct object)

The hot chocolate **tasted** *good* on such a cold night. (adj.)

The cook **tasted** *the sauce* before pouring it on the vegetables. (takes a direct object)

The mother *hurriedly* **tasted** the food to be sure that it would not burn the baby's tongue. (adv.)

The weather **turned** *hot and muggy.* (adj.)

We had to **turn** *the key* before opening the door. (takes a direct object)

Jill **got** *an A* on her last test. (takes a direct object)

We **got** *tired* of waiting for the bus and decided to walk. (adj.)

The district attorney **proved** *his point* by displaying the evidence. (takes a direct object)

The experiment could **prove** *fatal* if you don't take the proper precautions. (adj.)

Keep in mind that when you are modifying an adjective, you need to use the adverb form. In the following sentences, although you have one of the linking verbs, you are really modifying the adjective, not the verb.

We **felt** *unusually strong* after taking the medicine.
        adv.     adj.

Despite her many problems, Nell **seemed** *unbelievably happy.*
                      adv.     adj.

# USING ADJECTIVES WITH LINKING VERBS

When the above-mentioned linking verbs are intransitive, then the *adjective* form, *not the adverb* form, follows the verb. There is no action involved, and the adjective modifies the subject, not the verb.

We felt **happy** after receiving the good news.

Anita grew **tired** of listening to the same music all day.

No one seemed *pleased* by the new director's remarks.

Peter sounded *excited* when we told him of our plans for the trip.

## EXERCISE 54

Underline either the adjective or the adverb in parentheses to complete the meaning.

1. The lion roared (ferocious, ferociously) in his small cage.

2. Napoleon kept his hand (firm, firmly) placed inside his coat.

3. Ice skating seemed (easy, easily) to the experienced skater.

4. My grandmother's garden smelled (fragrant, fragrantly) as the spring buds opened.

5. President Botha became (angry, angrily) when the voters demanded that he follow their wishes.

6. The program was (exclusive, exclusively) designed for international trade groups.

7. The old cook's chili tasted (delicious, deliciously) as we ate it.

8. Kevin remained (depressed, depressedly) throughout the entire movie.

9. The lawyer is (hurried, hurriedly) looking for his notes on usury law.

10. The fat mouse (zealous, zealously) chewed on his cheddar cheese.

11. Tarzan (courageous, courageously) fought many wild animals in the jungle.

12. The news of a better job (quick, quickly) lifted my spirits.

13. The strong winds in Albany appeared (unbelievable, unbelievably) long lasting.

14. Although the dog was tied up, he thrashed about (mad, madly).

15. Adriane's car looked (good, well) after she brought it back from her long trip.

16. Beethoven's music sounds (wonderful, wonderfully) when compared with today's.

17. The accident victim felt (surprising, surprisingly) good for someone in his condition.

18. The young policeman watched (careful, carefully) as he tried to follow the robber.

19. The jury appeared (unwilling, unwillingly) to deliver its long-awaited verdict.

20. The rose petals felt (smooth, smoothly) as I touched them.

## EXERCISE 55

Circle either the adjective or the adverb in parentheses.

1. Melanie was (grateful, gratefully) to her friend for having rescued her.

2. The contest judge felt (tired, tiredly) after watching 25 dancers perform.

3. No one could speak (quiet, quietly) due to the loud noise.

4. Sandra sounded (excited, excitedly) when I spoke with her on the telephone.

5. The milk in the glass smelled (sour, sourly).

6. Nina looked (beautiful, beautifully) in her wedding gown.

7. The president appeared (uncertain, uncertainly) during his presentation.

8. The table felt (durable, durably) despite its age.

9. The soldiers marched (silent, silently) in memory of their dead comrades.

10. Carmen became (rich, richly) after winning the lottery.

11. The salesman seemed (honest, honestly) when he spoke to us.

12. Julie remained (discreet, discreetly) despite her resentment.

13. The dark clouds in the sky appeared (threatening, threateningly).

14. The prisoner became (violent, violently) when he was recaptured.

15. Joe drove his car (reckless, recklessly) through the dangerous intersection.

16. The weather turned (cold, coldly) after the storm.

17. Holly answered all the questions (correct, correctly).

18. The runner felt (good, well) after he had finished the race.

19. The policeman remained (firm, firmly) while he was writing the ticket.

20. We all got into the car (quick, quickly) as it started to rain.

# *DO* AND *MAKE*

The verbs *do* and *make* cause many problems, because both mean basically the same thing. However, most of the expressions containing these words are idiomatic, and you must learn them as such. When in doubt as to which to use, consult an unabridged (large and complete) dictionary under *do* or *make* to see if you can find the expression you want. On the following page is a list of idiomatic expressions that use *do* and *make*. If you do not understand the meaning of an expression, look it up in the dictionary.

| **Do** | **Make** |
|---|---|
| do a favor | make a difference |
| do justice | make something do |
| do homage | make peace |
| have one's hair done | make trouble |
| do the dishes | make noise |
| do one's hair | make a bargain |
| do . . . miles per hour | make room |
| do one's best | make plans |
| that will do | make a deal |
| do the right (wrong thing) | make a trip |
| do the cooking | make believe |
| do away with | make over |
| do over | make certain |
| do without | make a good impression |
| do housework | make fun of |
| do homework | make a bed |
| do the laundry | make progress |
| have to do with | make one's living |
| do a good job | make friends |
| do it yourself | make a mistake |
| | make a speech |
| | make a stop |
| | make out |
| | make up one's mind |
| | make money |
| | make arrangements |

## EXERCISE 56

Match the expression at the left with the definition at the right. Write your answer in the space provided. One letter is repeated.

1. _____ do a favor

2. _____ do justice

3. _____ do homage

4. _____ have one's hair done

5. _____ do the dishes

6. _____ do one's hair

7. _____ do . . . miles per hour

8. _____ that will do

9. _____ do the right thing

10. _____ do the cooking

11. _____ do away with

12. _____ do over

13. _____ do without

14. _____ do housework

A. eliminate

B. repeat

C. clean up after eating

D. travel at a specific speed

E. go to the beauty shop

F. treat fairly; be favorable

G. wash and set your own hair

H. make a sacrifice; get along not having anything to do

I. prepare food

J. that's enough; something serves the purpose

K. be good or just

L. perform domestic chores

M. praise someone

N. help someone

# EXERCISE 57

Match the expression on the left with the definition on the right. Each answer can be used only once.

1. _____ make a difference       A. ridicule

2. _____ make something do       B. alter; transform

3. _____ make peace              C. plan; put things in order

4. _____ make trouble            D. journey; travel

5. _____ make noise              E. declare a truce

6. _____ make a deal             F. produce a favorable effect

7. _____ make room               G. create unpleasant sounds

8. _____ make plans for a trip   H. pretend

9. _____ make arrangements       I. create problems

10. _____ make believe           J. to matter; influence

11. _____ make over              K. provide extra space

12. _____ make certain           L. agree about something

13. _____ make a good impression M. eliminate a doubt

14. _____ make fun of            N. manage

## EXERCISE 58

Match the expression at the left with the definition at the right. Each answer can be used only once.

1. _____ do homework          A. related to

2. _____ do the laundry       B. perform a task well

3. _____ have to do with      C. not allow someone else to do the job

4. _____ do a good job        D. wash clothes

5. _____ do it yourself       E. make a mistake; break the law

6. _____ do the wrong thing   F. complete assignments

7. _____ make a bed           G. straighten sheet and pillows where one sleeps

8. _____ make progress        H. work

9. _____ make one's living    I. understand; decipher

10. _____ make friends        J. become acquainted with

11. _____ make a mistake      K. commit an error

12. _____ make a speech       L. move forward

13. _____ make a stop         M. to become rich

14. _____ make out            N. to interrupt a journey

15. _____ make up one's mind  O. address an audience

16. _____ make a lot of money P. decide on a course of action

## EXERCISE 59

Supply the correct form of *do* or *make* in each of these sentences. Make sure to use the correct tense.

### Let's Make Plans for the Weekend

TONI:    Beth, what are you planning to (1) ___do___ this weekend?

BETH:    I haven't (2) ___made___ up my mind yet. We had hoped to (3) ___make___ a trip to the state park and go camping.

TONI:    Have you (4) _____ any arrangements yet?

BETH:    No, we have to call ahead and reserve a space, but I can't (5) _____ out the phone number here.

TONI:    Let me see. It's 255-9476.

BETH:    What are you going to (6) _____ with the dog while you are gone?

TONI:    My neighbors said they would (7) _____ me a favor and keep him for us.

BETH:    If we get all of the arrangements (8)_____ , would you and Steve like to join us?

TONI:    Sure, but before I (9) _____ any plans, I have to (10) _____ the beds, (11) _____ the dishes, and get my hair (12) _____ .

BETH:    While you are (13) _____ all that, I will (14) _____ a stop at Gene's office to see what he plans to (15) _____ .

TONI:    You and I can (16) _____ the cooking and (17) _____ the laundry, and we will let the boys (18) _____ a good job of catching and cleaning the fish.

BETH:    Are you sure they can (19) _____ without the television for that long a time?

TONI:  We will have to (20) _____ a deal with them to (21) _____ their best at the campgrounds. Let's not (22) _____ any trouble for them and at least bring a radio along.

BETH:  Okay, Toni, let's (23) _____ certain that this is an enjoyable trip for us, too. Whatever entertainment we plan will definitely (24) _____ a difference on the outcome of our weekend.

TONI:  Call me when you have (25) _____ all the arrangements and we will talk about them. See you later.

## EXERCISE 60: WRITING

After you have looked up these expressions in the dictionary and are sure of their meaning, write an original sentence with each of the following, varying your subjects throughout.

1. do one's best  I always try to do my best.  9. make a deal _____

2. do the cooking _____  10. make believe _____

3. do away with _____  11. make certain _____

4. do without _____  12. make a good impression _____

5. do the laundry _____  13. make progress _____

6. do a good job _____  14. make a mistake _____

7. make a difference _____  15. make out _____

## EXERCISE 61: WRITING

Write a 100-word paragraph describing a typical day in your life. Use five *do* and five *make* expressions.

# AFFIRMATIVE AND NEGATIVE COMMANDS

The **Imperative Mood** (commonly known as commands) is used when you order someone to do or not to do something. The direct commands are addressed to *you* singular and plural. In each of the following, *you* is understood as the subject, the person to whom the command is addressed. Affirmative commands use the simplest form of the verb—that is, the infinitive without *to*. Here are some examples:

~~to~~ go      ~~to~~ eat      ~~to~~ dance      ~~to~~ run

For the negative, each of these adds ***Don't*** in front of the command.

***Speak*** English in this class. ***Don't speak*** Spanish.

***Be*** here at one o'clock. ***Don't be*** here at eleven o'clock.

If the speaker plans to include him/herself in the command, then he/she uses ***Let's*** for the affirmative and ***Let's not*** for the negative.

***Let's go*** to the movies tonight. ***Let's not walk*** in the park.

***Let's talk*** to the professor now. ***Let's not wait*** until later.

## EXERCISE 62: WRITING

Imagine that you were the king, queen, or president for one day. What would you command everyone to do or not to do? Use the verbs below to write commands, or create your own.

**Ex:** *Pay* your taxes before April 15.
***Don't smoke*** inside the library.

| pay | smoke | send | say | drive | talk |
|------|-------|------|---------|--------|-------|
| sing | dance | read | tell | answer | watch |
| walk | go | work | look for | drink | be |

# NEGATIVE COMMANDS

These are commands that instruct a specific person *not* to perform an action. Notice that the negative follows the auxiliary *do*.

Dennis, **don't write** your essay in pencil.

Please **don't litter** the streets with paper.

**Don't let** your gas tank run low, Rita.

**Indirect commands** involve instructions given to someone, but not at the particular moment of speaking. These forms use the word *not* before the infinitive.

The manager asked the employees **not to arrive** late for work.

Our teacher always tells us **not to waste** time.

Please tell your friends **not to park** their cars behind mine.

The park rangers ordered the visitors **not to feed** the bears.

## EXERCISE 63

Change the affirmative commands to negative ones.

1. If you get to the grocery store, buy ice cream. (**Don't buy** ice cream.)

2. Cook the spaghetti for only 10 minutes. (**Don't cook** it for 20 minutes.)

3. We always tell our friends to go to the Hunan restaurant for good Chinese food.

4. My mother always asks me to walk slowly.

5. Tell us what your problem is.

6. Ride your bicycles in the street.

7. Send your letter to the office.

8. Ask them to send the check in the mail.

9. If you cannot solve the equation, ask Ted.

10. The insurance company ordered the client to make payment on the bill.

## EXERCISE 64

Kim is a new student on campus and is somewhat confused about information. Straighten her out by telling her what *not* to do. Use direct commands.

1. Professor Gooding told us to study the new vocabulary in Chapter 3.

2. The secretary in the registrar's office told them to pay fees after June 20.

3. The policeman says to park in the blue zone.

4. Professor Harris said to arrive before 8:15.

5. The librarian asked me to return the books after June 30.

6. The sign in the cafeteria said to eat in the faculty dining area.

7. My friend asked me to ride on the sidewalk on campus.

8. Our teacher requested us to bring a bilingual dictionary to class.

9. In the dormitory we were asked to do our laundry on Friday.

10. The sign in the finance office said to write our Social Security number on the back of all checks.

## EXERCISE 65

Judge Judy is a real judge who has her own television show and meets all kinds of people every week. She is extremely frank and demanding with people. What might be some of her commands to the following people who have appeared on her show recently? Use different verbs throughout. Use affirmative and negative commands.

**Example:** John, your beard is a mess. *Shave your beard. Get a shave.*

1. Marsha, you arrive late for class every day.

2. Preston, your ex-wife can't buy the children's medicine on her salary.

3. Marco, you're too bossy.

4. Ms. Tamuko, your neighbors are complaining about your yard filled with junk.

5. Ms. Davis, your creditors have been patient long enough.

6. Raymond, I won't put up with your outbursts in my courtroom.

7. Mrs. Kaley, your children are too noisy.

8. Vincent, you're a lazy bum.

9. Mandy, you read too many trashy novels.

10. Flo, you're too fat from eating so much junk food.

11. Dennis, you spend more money every month than you earn.

12. Bobby, it's a major crime to steal cars.

13. Ms. Jackson, your food tastes terrible.

14. Dr. Taylor, your patients can't afford such outrageous prices.

15. Mrs. Riordan, your son's an alcoholic at 15.

16. Mario, your grades for a college student are pathetic.

17. Sandy, you are very nasty to your brothers and sisters.

18. Mark, your typing is terrible.

19. Dr. Daniels, your students cannot understand you when you lecture in class.

20. Sue, you need to get a life.

# *USED TO • BE USED TO • GET USED TO*

1. *used to* + **verb** indicates an action (repeated or habitual) in the past, but one that does not take place now.

> Jim *used to ride* his bike to class, but now he drives.
>
> We *used to live* in Oregon, but now we live in Orlando.

2. *be used to* + [**V** + *ing*] indicates an action that has been a common practice for a long time.

> Glen loves to go camping. He *is used to sleeping* on the ground.
>
> Judy is a nurse. She *is used to working* in a hospital.

3. *get used to* + [**V** + *ing*] indicates an action that did not previously take place, but one to which the speaker has accustomed him/herself at a later date.

> Although Toshio never spoke English in Japan, *he's getting used to speaking* it here.
>
> I was very much afraid of the water, but now I *am used to swimming* in the pool.

## EXERCISE 66

Select the correct form for each sentence.

1. Marina is finally getting used to (cook, cooking) in an American kitchen.

2. We thought Perry would never get used to (speak, speaking) before a large group.

3. The towels used to (be, being) in the hall closet, but now they're in the bathroom closet.

4. Lou and the boys are used to (swim, swimming) in the ocean.

5. Scott used to (go, going) to Capital University, but he has graduated and is working in a law firm.

6. The boys are finally getting used to (attend, attending) early-morning classes.

7. Dolly had to get used to (wear, wearing) heavy clothing again after she moved to the North.

8. India used to (belong, belonging) to the United Kingdom, but it is now an independent country.

9. New York used to (be, being) called New Amsterdam.

10. The tennis players are used to (practice, practicing) in very hot weather.

11. Bill is used to (get, getting) to work early every morning.

12. I am finally getting used to (drive, driving) my new car.

13. The ballerina used to (dance, dancing) six hours a day.

14. My neighbors used to (live, living) in Canada.

15. Dr. Nichols will be used to (work, working) in the clinic in a couple of months.

16. The Chinese are used to (eat, eating) with chopsticks.

17. Sherri hopes that she will get used to (type, typing) on her new electric machine soon.

18. Elaine is used to (sew, sewing) six dresses a day.

19. Guy Lombardo got used to (direct, directing) the orchestra when he was very young.

20. After Philippe's accident, he had to get used to (ski, skiing) more carefully.

# 's AND 'd CONTRACTIONS

Distinguishing between the pairs of confusing contractions can cease to be a problem when you follow these simple rules:

The 's rule applies only to forms of **he**, **she**, **it**, and other third-person forms in the singular.

$$\textbf{'s} + [\text{V} + \textbf{\textit{ing}}] = \textbf{\textit{is}}$$

Mary**'s running** now. Mary **is** running.

Who**'s cooking** dinner? Who **is** cooking dinner?

$$\textbf{'s} + \text{past participle} = \textbf{\textit{has}}$$

Vince**'s earned** his raise. Vince **has** earned his raise.

The teacher**'s graded** the papers. The teacher **has** graded....

---
**NOTE**

Do not confuse the contraction for third-person subject + verb with the possessives. Although they may look the same, their meanings are different.

---

$$\text{person} + \textbf{'s} + \text{noun} = \text{possessive}$$

**Ann's** dress is very elegant. (The dress belonging to Ann)

My **mother's** car needs gas. (The car belonging to my mother)

The *'d* rule applies to all forms regardless of the subject.

> *'d* + past participle = *had*

All of our friends said that they*'d gone* camping this weekend.

All of our friends said that they *had gone* camping this weekend.

> *'d* + better = *had*

You*'d better* not eat all of the cookies before supper.

You *had better* not eat all of the cookies before supper.

> *'d* + simple form of the verb = *would*

She*'d visit* Europe if she had the money.

She *would visit* Europe if she had the money.

> *'d* + *rather* + verb = *would rather*

He*'d rather* excavate ruins than take a trip to Las Vegas.

He *would rather* excavate ruins than . . .

---
**NOTE**
For the following expressions, always use *be* as the auxiliary.

---

> accustomed to          supposed to          used to

Mel*'s accustomed to* living alone. = *Mel is* accustomed to . . .

Sam*'s supposed to* turn in his photographs tomorrow. = Sam *is* supposed to . . .

He*'s used to* driving a small car. = He *is* used to . . .

## EXERCISE 67

Decide which of the two forms in parentheses is the correct auxiliary verb.

1. We'd already decided not to go on the field trip. (had, would)

2. Everyone's planning on attending the lecture tonight. (is, has)

3. He's been wondering about that matter for a long time. (is, has)

4. They'd prefer steak to chicken. (had, would)

5. She'd bought the vacuum cleaner before it was on sale. (had, would)

6. Nothing's more unpleasant than to have it rain on a picnic. (is, has)

7. Lisa's playing her guitar for her friends. (is, has)

8. I'd wanted to visit Peru for 15 years. (had, would)

9. He'd better pay his fees before closing time tomorrow. (had, would)

10. The teacher's supposed to show us some slides this afternoon. (is, has)

11. John says that it's snowing so hard that the traffic is not moving. (is, has)

12. Nancy'd like to ride through the scenic area. (had, would)

13. They'd let us borrow the portable electric typewriter, but there are no batteries for it. (had, would)

14. "Something's rotten in Denmark," said Hamlet. (is, has)

15. It'd be easier to correct that paper if you wrote it on the computer. (had, would)

16. We'd appreciate your response as soon as possible. (had, would)

17. Betty's used to driving a long way to work every day. (is, has)

18. How's the team supposed to get here? (is, has)

19. You'd already ordered the pizza before we arrived. (had, would)

20. She's accepted the job that offers more benefits. (is, has)

## EXERCISE 68

Rewrite the sentences, using contractions.

1. Joan has already been to Grand Canyon, but not her brothers.
   *Joan's already been . . .*

2. Who would like to volunteer to be the spokesperson for the rally?
   *Who'd like to . . .*

3. What is happening with the price of oil lately?

4. Mel has been working very hard lately and hopes to be able to relax next month.

5. You would be better off taking the back roads to avoid the rush-hour traffic.

6. Chris said he had ridden his bicycle about 20 miles before it began to storm.

7. Sonya is having her hair done at the new beauty shop today.

8. Mark is surfing in the big contest this afternoon.

9. Brett said that he had already won a trophy in the slalom.

10. I would certainly have considered that offer if they had made it to me.

11. What is in the big green box on the table?

12. When is our plane due to arrive?

13. It has been such a long time since I have gone north to visit my relatives.

14. We had no sooner returned from our vacation than the phone rang.

15. When Billy arrived, Sue had already left for home.

16. Bernie had already accepted the money before he realized why it had been given to him.

17. You would want to read the book if you knew how interesting it was.

18. Kurt is playing ball this evening.

19. You would be surprised how many tourists visit Mount Rushmore every year.

20. Mrs. Hart has taught at Oak Hall School for many years.

## EXERCISE 69

In each sentence, circle the underlined item that is incorrect.

1. It was snowing <u>so</u> hard last night <u>that</u> we <u>can</u> hardly see the road as we <u>were driving</u>.

    A.  so          B.  that          C.  can          D.  were driving

2. The novice player <u>must of</u> tried dozens <u>of times</u> to <u>get</u> the ball <u>through</u> the hoop.

    A.  must of          B.  of times          C.  get          D.  through

3. <u>Because</u> Paul is <u>having</u> trouble with the exam, he <u>finished</u> later than anyone <u>else</u>.

    A. Because     B. having     C. finished     D. else

4. The Declaration of Independence <u>is proclaiming</u> that <u>we</u> are endowed <u>with</u> certain <u>inalienable</u> rights.

    A. is proclaiming     B. we     C. with     D. inalienable

5. Professor Baker was so <u>wrapped up</u> in his presentation <u>that</u> he <u>was deviated</u> from <u>reading</u> his prepared speech.

    A. wrapped up     B. that     C. was deviated     D. reading

6. I asked him <u>who it was</u> who called <u>so late</u> last night and then <u>hanged</u> up just when I <u>answered</u> the telephone.

    A. who it was     B. so late     C. hanged     D. answered

7. Dr. Johnson <u>was taught</u> anthropology <u>and</u> sociology at the university <u>for</u> ten years before <u>retiring.</u>

    A. was taught     B. and     C. for     D. retiring

8. Rosa's wedding <u>was scheduled</u> for August 5, but some unforeseen circumstances <u>forces</u> her <u>to change</u> her plans.

    A. was scheduled     B. August 5     C. forces     D. to change

9. She <u>rose</u> her head <u>from</u> the pillow <u>when</u> she <u>heard</u> the strange noise.

    A. rose     B. from     C. when     D. heard

10. I <u>couldn't</u> sleep last night, so I just <u>laid</u> there <u>thinking</u> about <u>tomorrow's</u> meeting.

    A. couldn't     B. laid     C. thinking     D. tomorrow's

11. If you had <u>thought</u> about it <u>long enough</u>, you <u>will have</u> find a solution <u>to the</u> problem.

    A. thought      B. long enough    C. will have      D. to the

12. If Melanie had prepared <u>a</u> much <u>better</u> speech, the chairman <u>would be</u> <u>impressed</u>.

    A. a           B. better         C. would be       D. impressed

13. <u>All</u> the exhibits we saw <u>represents</u> the Colonial <u>period</u> <u>in history</u>.

    A. All          B. represents    C. period        D. in history

14. <u>Reading</u> many books <u>during</u> the summer <u>are</u> the goal of <u>many</u> young students.

    A. Reading      B. during        C. are          D. many

15. <u>The</u> students, accompanied <u>by</u> their adviser, <u>has</u> lab <u>meetings</u> every Wednesday.

    A. The         B. by            C. has          D. meetings

16. <u>A</u> combination of <u>musical</u> instruments <u>produce</u> an enjoyable and <u>memorable</u> sound.

    A. A           B. musical      C. produce      D. memorable

## EXERCISE 70

Fill in the chart, using the correct tenses. The first two have been done.

| Infinitive | Every day | Yesterday | Tomorrow | Right now |
|---|---|---|---|---|
| go | I go, he goes | went | will go | am, is, are going |
| do | I do, he does | did | will do | am, is, are doing |
| 1. sing | | | | |
| 2. write | | | | |
| 3. fly | | | | |
| 4. think | | | | |
| 5. bake | | | | |
| 6. send | | | | |
| 7. swim | | | | |
| 8. see | | | | |
| 9. dance | | | | |
| 10. run | | | | |
| 11. drive | | | | |
| 12. eat | | | | |
| 13. fry | | | | |
| 14. prepare | | | | |
| 15. carry | | | | |

## EXERCISE 71

Fill in the chart, using the correct tenses. The first two have been done.

| Infinitive | Has/Have (N)Ever | Would/Could | Do/Don't/Let's | Had |
|---|---|---|---|---|
| go | gone | go | go | gone |
| do | done | do | do | done |
| 1. sing | | | | |
| 2. write | | | | |
| 3. fly | | | | |
| 4. think | | | | |
| 5. bake | | | | |
| 6. send | | | | |
| 7. swim | | | | |
| 8. see | | | | |
| 9. dance | | | | |
| 10. run | | | | |
| 11. drive | | | | |
| 12. eat | | | | |
| 13. fry | | | | |
| 14. prepare | | | | |
| 15. carry | | | | |

## EXERCISE 72

Find the error in each sentence, and circle the corresponding letter.

1. A good presentation of merchandise will make a client feel interesting in what is on display.

   A.  A            B.  will make      C.  interesting     D.  what

2. My first and second jobs differed in three major aspects: wages, working condition, and benefits.

   A.  second       B.  in            C.  aspects         D.  working
                                                             condition

3. Once a student is accepted in dental school, he is needing three more years of study before he can graduate.

   A.  accepted     B.  is needing    C.  of study       D.  can graduate

4. There is not many communication among neighbors living in houses as there is among those living in apartments.

   A.  many         B.  living        C.  among          D.  as there is

5. The players try to make as few contact as possible with the opposing team to avoid penalties.

   A.  to make      B.  few           C.  opposing       D.  penalties

6. German shepherds and Dobermans make an excellent pets, protectors, or guides for the blind.

   A.  Dobermans    B.  an            C.  pets           D.  for the blind

7. In football the players are pushing and shoving on both sides, but in baseball there is hardly some contact.

   A.  are          B.  both          C.  there is       D.  some

8. Many people are accustomed <u>to come</u> to Florida for vacation <u>because of</u> the large <u>number</u> of tourist attractions found there and <u>the warm</u> sunshine at the beaches.

    A. to come      B. because of    C. number    D. the warm

9. <u>Driving</u> the speed limit on our nation's highways <u>help</u> save lives, avoid <u>accidents</u>, and <u>reduce</u> gas consumption.

    A. Driving      B. help       C. accidents    D. reduce

10. <u>Us</u> skiers <u>will be leaving</u> for the mountains next Friday <u>as soon as</u> class lets out and <u>we arrive</u> at the station.

    A. Us       B. will be leaving  C. as soon as    D. we arrive

11. My friends are <u>disappointed</u> in <u>me</u> not trying harder <u>to finish</u> the project before the <u>assigned</u> deadline.

    A. disappointed  B. me       C. to finish    D. assigned

12. A cow is a sweet and <u>gentle-looking</u> soul; however, <u>they</u> can be <u>quite</u> stubborn and dangerous <u>when</u> upset.

    A. gentle-looking  B. they      C. quite     D. when

13. Marijuana was <u>once</u> <u>considered</u> less harmful <u>than</u> cigarettes, but scientists have now proved <u>otherwise</u>.

    A. once      B. considered  C. than      D. otherwise

14. He's <u>suppose</u> to <u>arrive</u> at the airport by 2:15, but I heard someone <u>say</u> that the plane had <u>another</u> 45-minute delay.

    A. suppose    B. arrive     C. say      D. another

15. She's <u>used</u> to <u>ride</u> her bicycle <u>to</u> class every day, but she had a flat tire and had <u>to take</u> the bus.

    A. used      B. ride      C. to       D. to take

16. It has been difficult <u>to integrate</u> all the groups <u>to</u> our society <u>due</u> to their <u>different</u> social values and traditions.

    A. to integrate    B. to              C. due             D. different

17. The children <u>were</u> having <u>too good a time</u> playing <u>with</u> their new toys that they forgot <u>to walk</u> the dog.

    A. were            B. too good        C. with            D. to walk
                          a time

18. Peter told <u>us</u> that he <u>finished</u> his project before <u>leaving</u> <u>the house</u> yesterday morning.

    A. us              B. finished        C. leaving         D. the house

19. We <u>would</u> already bought and <u>used</u> the washing machine <u>before</u> the <u>big sale</u>.

    A. would           B. used            C. before          D. big sale

20. Sy's doctor <u>suggested</u> that he <u>takes</u> his medicine <u>with</u> water 30 minutes before <u>eating</u>.

    A. suggested       B. takes           C. with            D. eating

# PART II
# ESL

## Advanced Grammar

# Advanced Grammar

# ESL

## CHAPTER 7

## Pronouns

# PRONOUNS

## POSSESSIVE PRONOUNS

**Possessive pronouns** show ownership (belonging to someone). Notice that there is no apostrophe (') with these forms:

| | |
|---|---|
| mine | ours |
| yours | yours |
| his, hers | theirs |

This book is **his.** That one is **mine.**

We have our books, and they have **theirs.**

### EXERCISE 73

Change these possessive adjectives and nouns to pronouns. Then rewrite the whole sentence.

**Example:** *My* book is very interesting.

*Mine* is very interesting.

1. His sisters live in Kansas.

2. Phil and Quan's store is downtown.

3. Their house has a patio.

4. We bought our tickets.

5. You need your passport stamped.

6. Can he eat his dessert now?

7. We have our passports. Does Sally have her passport?

8. When will you receive your check?

9. Our group took the exams last week. When did you take your exams?

10. Our bill is higher than your bill.

## EXERCISE 74

Look at the following questions and answer them, using the *possessive pronouns.*

**Example:** Where did Rosa put her books? She put **hers** on the desk.

How often do you visit your family? I visit **mine** every Sunday.

1. Do they have their tickets and my ticket?

2. When will your shoes be ready at the shoe repair?

3. Did she pass all her final exams?

4. Where do his parents live?

5. Are those Sara's scissors?

6. Can James identify his car in the parking lot?

7. Did you buy my tickets for the ballet?

8. Have you written your term paper yet?

9. Were your answers correct?

10. When will your checks arrive?

# TRANSFORMATION OF DIRECT AND INDIRECT OBJECTS

There are two ways to write the direct object and the indirect object together in a sentence without changing the meaning.

1. The direct object comes first and is followed by *to* or *for* and the indirect object.

S + V + { direct object } (person/thing) + *to*/*for* + { indirect object } (person/animal)

Bring **the money to Joe** immediately.
        D.O.     I.O.

Shaun will paint **the house for Sheila**.
        D.O.     I.O.

2. The indirect object with no preposition can come before the direct object.

subject + verb + indirect object + direct object

Lend **us twenty dollars** if you can.
  I.O.      D.O.

Vic hands **his mother some dishes**.
      I.O.     D.O.

There is no difference in the meaning between the two placements. Not all verbs can follow this transformation pattern, but here is a list of those that do. Some of these verbs can use both *to* and *for*, while others may use one or the other.

| bring | build | buy | cut | pass | teach |
|---|---|---|---|---|---|
| draw | find | get | give | hand | snow |
| feed | write | promise | read | sail | send |
| lend | leave | tell | pay | make | offer |
| owe | paint | | | | |

If you are using pronouns, you can change both the indirect object and the direct object to the pronoun form.

Tell *the story to me*.          Tell *it to me.*

Bring *the flowers for the girls*.      Bring *them for them.*

If two pronouns are used, follow the first pattern, not the second. In the second one, it sounds repetitive using the same pronouns. If you do not know what they refer to in the first sentence, you will never understand the meaning of the sentence.

It is incorrect to place the prepositional phrase before the direct object.

**INCORRECT:**    The boss sent to them the letters.

**CORRECT:**     The boss sent them the letters.

Keep in mind that in the transformation when you are using the prepositional phrase, the indirect object directly follows the direct object, and it is *not* placed after other parts of the sentence.

Give me the book.           Give the book *to me.*

Nelly found us some tickets.      Nelly found some tickets *for us.*

## EXERCISE 75

Rewrite each sentence so that the indirect object immediately follows the verb, thus eliminating the preposition.

**Example:** Tell the story to us. Tell us *the story.*

1. Get some coffee for me.

2. The teacher read the story to the students.

3. Tim left this gift for you.

4. The artist drew a portrait for me.

5. My son feeds the food to his dog every day.

6. The company will build a house for us very soon.

7. Sally, show your doll to me.

8. Mr. Dixon offered the job to Tracy.

9. Please find my sweater for me.

10. I promised to get a bird for him.

## EXERCISE 76

Rewrite the direct object immediately after the verb, and use a preposition with the indirect object. Make sure that you keep the whole direct object together.

**Example:** Lend us $20.　　　　　Lend $20 **to us**

Mrs. Jones taught them math.　　Mrs. Jones taught math **to them.**

1. Peter owes you many favors.

2. Annette showed her mother the new dress.

3. Alice is making her sister an afghan.

4. Cut them some cake before it disappears.

5. I'll send you the photos as soon as they arrive.

6. Bring me that cart.

7. Janet's grandmother left her a special ring.

8. Sonia paid the ticket agent the money.

9. My father read me the notice in the paper.

10. Nobody bought us anything to eat.

## RECIPROCAL PRONOUNS

These pronouns—*each other* and *one another*—are used only with plural concepts to show that two or more people perform the action on *each other* (two people). Use *one another* when more than two people are involved.

Romeo and Juliet loved *each other.* [He loved her and she loved him.]
We call *each other* every day. [I call him (her, them), and he (she, they) call me.]
They write *each other* frequently.
We visit *each other* every month.
The Greeks and the Persians fought *each other* often.
The ancient civilizations copied *one another* in many ways.
Dress designers are constantly trying to outdo *one another*.
After their divorce, Harvey and Lacy hated *each other* so much that they almost
    killed *each other.*
The children will chase *one another* around the yard until they are exhausted.
Athletes compete against *one another* all the time**.**

## EXERCISE 77

Write sentences that show reciprocal action. Add prepositions and any necessary words to complete the sentences.

**Example:** Actor / actress / kiss / passionately / during / love scene.

*The actor and actress kissed <u>each other</u> passionately during the love scene.*

1. Mr. / Mrs. Smith / sing / often.

2. Chris / Rachel / see / weekends.

3. We / find / in world / great / technological advances.

4. Henry / Joan / look for / in crowd.

5. Marty / his sister / tease / about / pronunciation.

6. Stan / Nancy / their friends / buy / Christmas gifts.

7. My sister / I / give / moral support.

8. The soldier / his wife / hold / tightly / after/ return / Iraq.

9. Tom / Sally / know / for years / before / getting married.

10. Tony / his mother / meet / Thursdays / lunch.

11. Nancy / mother / speak / telephone / every day.

12. Romeo / Juliet / love / very much.

13. John / Paul / not take / seriously.

14. Judy / Christine / tell / secrets.

# WHO, WHOM, WHOEVER, AND WHOMEVER

Because it is often difficult to decide on the correct form of *who*, *whom*, *whoever*, or *whomever*, keep these hints in mind:

- Block out the rest of the sentence and focus on only the relative clause. In that clause, how does the word function—as subject or object?

- Underline *all* subjects and verbs in the complete sentence. Do not forget to include the *you* understood for the commands. If you have an even number (matched pairs of subjects and verbs), then the missing form will be *whom*.

*I told* them to invite (whoever, whomever) *they wanted*.
S + V                                    S  +  V

(Because there are two pairs here, the missing form is the object, *whomever*.)

If there are not an equal number of matching pairs, then use the subject *who*.
*Give* the books to (whoever, whomever) *answers* the door.

(you) give = S + V                      V

Here there is one pair and a verb with no subject, so the correct form is *whoever*. It is the subject of the clause *whoever answers the door*.

S   +   V   +   D.O.

*Who/whoever* and *whom/whomever* are not interchangeable. *Whoever* refers to whatever person, anyone at all, while *who* refers to someone specific.

The girl *who* is wearing the red dress is my cousin. (This refers to a specific girl.)

*Whoever* (any person at all) needs the money should have it.

For the object, use *whomever* to make it the *receiver* of the action in its own clause. There may or may not be a preposition.

Invite *whomever* (any person at all) you choose.

Give the packages to *whoever* answers the door.

Notice that in the second one, the form is the subject, because it performs the action of the clause "whoever answers the door." Don't always assume that because you have the preposition in front of the pronoun, it refers to the object. It refers to the object *only* if it is receiving the action.

I know the boy *to whom* you are speaking.

*Whom* is the object in the first clause as well as in the second clause (you are speaking to *whom*). *Whom* receives the action in both clauses.

Give it to *whomever* you see at the museum.

*Whomever* is the object of the verb give (command form) in the first clause as well as in the second clause (you see *whomever* at the museum). *Whomever* receives the action in both clauses.

Write the letter to *whoever* is the chairman of the committee.

*Whoever* is the subject of the second clause.

Give the money to the man *who* is standing behind the desk.

*Who* is the subject of the clause *who is standing behind the desk*.

## EXERCISE 78

Supply the correct form of *who*, *whom*, *whoever*, and *whomever* in each sentence.

**Example:** Mario knows ***whom*** the committee has chosen for president.

1. It was Terry Schmidt _____ received the golf trophy.

2. The girl _____ the reporter interviewed was the victim of the accident.

3. A secretary _____ has no good communication skills is not an asset to the company.

4. Appoint _____ you choose to fill the position.

5. The scholarship will be given to _____ has the highest grades.

6. To _____ did you wish to speak, sir?

7. I can't decide on _____ to invite to the dinner party.

8. Natalie's mother, _____ you met last night, works in the vice president's office.

9. _____ designed that building certainly knew how to conserve space.

10. Can't you remember the person from _____ you accepted the money?

11. Give the information to _____ answers the telephone.

12. Mr. Hyle, _____ has been our director for 20 years, is retiring in July.

13. Can you guess _____ is coming to visit us tomorrow?

14. The person about _____ you spoke so highly has been offered the job as director.

15. Nancy Wilson, _____ has lived here for 25 years, decided to go to the mountains.

16. I can't imagine _____ would do such a terrible thing!

17. Your successor will be _____ you designate.

18. From _____ did you request the copies?

19. _____ selected those colors has no good taste.

20. _____ has all six numbers will win the lottery.

## PRONOUN REFERENCE

Pronoun reference shows the relationship among pronouns in a sentence or those pronouns that replace nouns previously mentioned. One of the major pronoun errors is found in the relationship of singular nouns later referred to by plural pronouns.

### INCORRECT:

*Everyone* (singular) has to write *their* (plural) own summary before leaving.

*Each student* needs to have permission for *their* trip next week.

*Gun control legislature* will never be successful until *they* are outlawed.

*One* should be very careful before *you* accept dates with people you meet on the Internet.

In each of these sentences, the writer has shifted from singular to plural, or from third personal singular (one) to a second person pronoun (you).

---
**NOTE**

Even though expressions like *each person*, *every teacher*, and *everybody* imply a plural quantity, these all take a *singular* verb and a *singular* pronoun.

---

**EXERCISE 79**

Make all necessary changes in each sentence to reflect pronoun agreement.

**Example:** Every instructor teaches their class differently. Every instructor teaches **his/her** class differently.

1. According to the Constitution, each person is free to do whatever they want as long as they don't infringe on the rights of others.

2. At the beginning of the day, every staff member wore their uniform.

3. Every Girl Scout should carry their cup, name tag, and flash light in a special bag.

4. Each person is convinced that peace is necessary for survival, and they must form a government that will work for the benefit of all.

5. When I arrived at the hotel everyone was carrying their own suitcases.

6. Nobody can get all the things that they want in this life.

7. As he is growing up, each child needs a lot of understanding, or else they will have problems and they will not be good citizens.

8. Each book in the library has their own call letters based on the Dewey Decimal System.

9. Boy Scouts have the responsibility of caring for himself and cooperating with camp counselors and other Scouts.

10. All of the female teachers create her activities and help students work together.

11. We had to take two summer classes, and our teachers told us about it.

12. We needed packing boxes, so we went to the grocery store to get it.

13. Before moving, I used to go to the movies every Saturday, and now I miss it very much.

14. If a person really cares about another, they can find many ways to show their feelings.

15. We all traveled to different parts of the country and decided to write about it.

16. Each of the teams has their own project to finish before the end of the semester.

17. A hospital staff member needs to be friendly, because they are the first people who come in contact with patients.

18. Many times during your life we can have an unusual experience.

19. Each house in the neighborhood has their own unique design and appeal.

20. Every weekend one of my friends invites me to their house.

## EXERCISE 80

Read the following, and circle the correct answer.

### Days with My Grandmother

How I remember the days I spent with my grandmother! She was a kind and generous woman who always seemed to have time and energy for many things. **_Her_** house looked like all the other large houses in one of Cleveland's oldest sections. However, my fondest memories are of her working in the kitchen. She looked so happy and comfortable in her crisp white apron as she kneaded the dough for her baking powder biscuits and molded the pie crust in the Pyrex dishes. She never seemed to grow tired of her myriad daily chores. No matter what she prepared, it always tasted wonderful. **_It_** often smelled so good that I'd run in from play and ask, "Is it ready yet? How soon before I can sample it?"

Even though I was only a ten-year-old girl, she made me feel important. We would sit on the porch after lunch and talk and sip homemade lemonade. She added that extra touch of something special that made **_it_** taste so good.

We often went downtown on the old streetcars. This proved to be a real adventure as we walked two long blocks to board the cars and then sat there as ***they*** rocked back and forth on the tracks on the seven-mile trip to town. The conductor sounded the bell when we reached the end of the line. We walked up and down Euclid Avenue, shopping and stopping to eat in a special restaurant.

Three years later, my grandfather died, and ***she*** appeared sad and distant. She became quiet, and I, too, felt her pain. I grew up very quickly that year, but I have never forgotten the joyful days that ***we*** spent in her old house with the large kitchen filled with the aroma of her wonderful cooking, her kind smile, and our animated conversations.

1. The adjective ***her*** in sentence 3, paragraph 1, specifically refers to

   A.  some woman    B.  grandmother    C.  house       D.  Cleveland

2. In paragraph 1, ***It*** often smelled so good, refers to

   A.  biscuits        B.  kitchen       C.  dough       D.  what she
                                                            prepared

3. In paragraph 2, the last sentence, ***it*** refers to

   A.  lunch          B.  extra touch   C.  porch       D.  lemonade

4. In paragraph 3, sentence 2, the word ***they*** refers to

   A.  blocks         B.  street cars   C.  tracks      D.  neighbors

5. In paragraph 4, sentence 1, ***she*** refers to

   A.  grandfather    B.  conductor     C.  girl        D.  grandmother

6. In paragraph 4, the last sentence, the pronoun ***we*** refers to

   A.  girl and grandmother              C.  girl and conductor

   B.  girl and grandfather D.            girl and I

## EXERCISE 81

Read the following, and answer the questions.

### Channeling

Channeling is not the tuning from one television station to another. It is a form of spiritualism or communication between Guides of the Spirit, the astrophysical world and the earthly plane. _**It**_ is a dialogue communication of a Guide speaking through a medium or psychic _**who**_ has put himself or herself in a hypnotic state. The Guide, in speaking expresses, his or her thoughts and not those of the psychic.

The Guides are various spirit _**entities**_, who had supposedly been physical beings at one time, but now _**they**_ exist in a world or plane commonly called the "astral world." Some of these Guides claim to be thousands of years old and have an ancestry way beyond our understanding. Guides have a somber and calm way of expressing themselves and always appear to have a pleasant and understanding personality. Some well-known Guides are Ramtha, Seth, and Raj. Many mediums claim to have regular contacts with _**them**_.

While it is _**claimed**_ that anybody can contact a Guide, it appears that only those with a so-called psychic power have the ability to succeed. The channeling usually begins when the medium goes into meditation and then _**lapses**_ into a self-induced hypnotic state. By some "supernatural means" the Guide is contacted and begins the dialogue. Guides can be either male or female. Besides a general dialogue, Guides will sometimes answer questions and give advice. Also, during the dialogue, the psychic has no control over the words of the Guide, and _**he**_ or she speaks in a different voice other than that of the psychic.

Generally, the Guide ends the dialogue and the psychic quickly returns to a normal state. Channeling is _**analogous**_ to space aliens . . . some believe . . . some do not.

1. What is channeling?

   A.  Sailing through water channels around the world

   B.  Communication between two Guides

C. Contacting aliens in outer space

D. Traveling thousands of years back in time

2. Which of the following statements is *not* true about Guides?

A. They are only males.

B. They were once humans.

C. They express their thoughts and not those of the psychics.

D. They are contacted by supernatural means.

3. What are Guides?

A. Space aliens who communicate with Earth

B. Humans who have contact with the spirit world

C. Female psychics who communicate with aliens

D. Spirit beings living in the astral world

4. What can be inferred about channeling?

A. It's a means of communication with aliens.

B. It provides answers to supernatural mysteries.

C. It's a way of putting oneself into a hypnotic state.

D. It's a way of communicating with the dead.

5. What happens when Guides finish their communication with psychics?

A. The psychics put themselves in a hypnotic state.

B. Psychics move to an astrophysical world.

C. Psychics converse with Ramtha, Seth, and Raj.

D. Psychics leave their hypnotic state and return to a normal state.

6. How long have some of the most well-known Guides been around?

   A. A few years    C. Hundreds of years

   B. Many years    D. Thousands of years

7. Who can most successfully contact Guides?

   A. Those who speak in another voice    C. Only those who have died

   B. Those with psychic powers    D. Only Ramtha, Seth, and Raj

8. The pronoun *it* in paragraph 1 refers to

   A. spirit    B. channeling    C. communication    D. Guide

9. The pronoun *who* in paragraph 1 refers to

   A. Spirit    B. psychic    C. himself    D. Guide

10. The word *entities* means most nearly the same as

    A. entertainers    B. entrails    C. illusions    D. beings

11. The pronoun *they* in paragraph 2 refers to

    A. beings    B. Guides    C. thoughts    D. years

12. The pronoun *them* at the end of paragraph 2 refers to

    A. mediums    B. entities    C. contacts    D. Ramtha, Seth, and Raj

13. The pronoun *he* in paragraph 3 refers to

    A. Guide    B. psychic    C. anybody    D. male

14. The word *claimed* means most nearly the same as

    A. repudiated    B. disavowed    C. maintained    D. clarified

# *OTHER* AND ITS FORMS

The forms of *other* can be divided into pronouns and adjectives, depending on how they are used in the sentence.

| Pronouns | Adjectives |
| --- | --- |
| others | other |
| the other | the other |
| the others | another |
| another | any other |

Pronouns will replace the adjective forms and the nouns that follow them. While these are all similar, in that they represent a choice between or among elements, they cannot be used interchangeably. *The other* equals a choice between two specifically mentioned elements.

I have two gifts. One is for you, **the other** is for Alice. (the other gift)

There are two cars in the garage. One is my sister's, and **the other** is mine. (the other car)

If there are more than two elements, the expression *the others* is used.

I bought four cakes at the bakery. One is for us; **the others** are for the party tonight. (the other cakes)

Ben found only one pair of his socks, but **the others** must be lost. (the other pairs of socks)

*Other* and *others* are rather general terms, not specifically referring to anything in particular.

Jenny believes in UFOs. **Other** people, however, find it difficult to accept that these objects exist.

After his surgery, Paul had some good days, but **other** days were painful.

In both of these sentences *other* and the noun could have been replaced by *others*, a non-specific group. Both refer to something in the plural form.

other people ⟶ others

other days ⟶ others

*Another* can be both a pronoun and an adjective, and it means *any other*. Whichever element someone chooses will be acceptable. There are only two elements involved.

**Adjective:** Doctor, I can't make my appointment on Friday. Can we make it *another* day? (any other day—Monday, Tuesday, etc.)

**Pronoun:** This pen doesn't write. Please give me *another.* (any other pen)

*The other day* refers to a specific day, but *another day* means any other day, some non-specified day.

## EXERCISE 82

Using the words from the list, write the correct form in the spaces.

**Example:** Because his counselor was absent, Mark had to speak to *another* advisor.

| other | others | another |
|---|---|---|
| the other | the others | any other |

1. Paul is more athletic than _____ boy in his class.

2. There aren't enough books to fill this box. Please get me _____ from on top of the table.

3. _____ day we had visitors from Cleveland.

4. Some students wrote compositions on famous people; _____ wrote on their own personal experiences.

5. Our teacher asked us if there were _____ questions before we began the experiment.

6 and 7. I had to make _____ dress for the party because I gave _____ one to my sister.

8. Here is _____ example of fine Chinese art.

9. Louie made two out of the four goals scored in the game; Chris made _____.

10. Since we don't have time to talk today, we will do it _____ day.

11. We don't accept that theory. _____ people consider it a very important concept.

12. Your experiments are incomplete. Spend _____ day in the lab and finish them.

13. Some of the girls want to wear long dresses to the party; _____ prefer shorter ones.

14. On Mondays, Wednesdays, and Fridays we have literature class, but on _____ days we have science class.

15. Some countries are world famous for their wines; _____ are not so renowned.

16. I can't give you an appointment for _____ time, because the doctor will be on vacation for two weeks.

## EXERCISE 83

In each sentence, decide which of the underlined items is incorrect.

1. One should <u>never</u> lend <u>his</u> car to a reckless driver if <u>they want</u> it <u>returned</u> in <u>good condition.</u>

    A. never        B. his        C. they want    D. returned

2. Talk to <u>any</u> actor and <u>they</u> will tell <u>you</u> that the show cannot <u>go on</u> without him.

    A.  any         B.  they         C.  you         D.  go on

3. Many people become <u>stressed out</u> when financial problems <u>arise</u>, because <u>it</u> can lead <u>to</u> depression, emotional changes, and arguments.

    A.  stressed out     B.  arise         C.  it         D.  to

4. <u>Silence</u> reigned in the courtroom <u>as the jury</u> returned to give <u>their</u> long <u>deliberated</u> verdict.

    A.  Silence         B.  as the jury     C.  their         D.  deliberated

5. <u>Because</u> the blouse that Nancy had <u>bought</u> was <u>too big</u>, she exchanged it for <u>other</u> one.

    A.  Because         B.  bought         C.  too big         D.  other one

## EXERCISE 84

Select the best word(s) to complete these sentences.

1. Each child needs a parental consent form signed by _____ parents.

    A.  one's         B.  their         C.  his         D.  our

2. My brother bought a new car. _____ is the most beautiful thing I've ever seen.

    A.  One         B.  It         C.  He         D.  She

3. _____ day as I was walking down the street, I saw an accident.

    A.  Another         B.  Other         C.  The other     D.  Some other

4. The dentist said that Joel had two cavities and that he needed _____ appointment.

    A.  other         B.  another         C.  the other     D.  some

5. I'm free for lunch on Thursday. Can we meet then?
No, _____ day will be just fine, but not Thursday.

    A.  any other       B.  other         C.  the other     D.  some

## EXERCISE 85

Select the correct form of the pronoun.

1. Have you seen (any, some) of Tom Cruise's movies lately?

2. I can't make an appointment for tomorrow, but (another, the other) day will be fine.

3. Each of the students must turn in an exam with (his, their) name on it.

4. Some people are happy with the new president; (others, any others) are not.

5. Terry doesn't believe in UFOs. (Other, Another) people, however, strongly believe in them.

6. Every book on his desk has (its, their) own special reference number.

7. Phil found two inlaid boxes and a sword. (They, It) were in an antique store.

8. Bring the documents to (him, he) on your way to the office this morning.

9. The committee sent (us, we) the letters, but we haven't answered yet.

10. Each of the figurines comes with (its, their) own certificate of authenticity.

# Advanced Grammar

# ESL

## CHAPTER 8

## Adjectives

## Chapter 8
# ADJECTIVES

## ADJECTIVES ENDING IN -*ly*

Most words that end in -*ly* are adverbs and show the manner in which something is done. However, those that have noun roots are adjectives. Most adjectives with a noun root add *y* to form the adjective.

| | | |
|---|---|---|
| wit—witty* | fault—faulty | salt—salty |
| rock—rocky | knot—knotty | wood—woody |
| throat—throaty | chalk—chalky | fish—fishy |
| rain—rainy | leaf—leafy | mud—muddy* |
| wind—windy | fun—funny* | sun—sunny* |

*Double the final consonant before adding* **y**.

Other nouns add **ly** to form the adjective. These include the following:

worldly     heavenly     humanly     motherly     saintly

Observe the following sentences. The underlined words cannot be made into adverbs. You must find another word or phrase to form the adverb. If the -*ly* word precedes a noun, then it is an adjective. If the -*ly* word precedes a verb or an adjective, then it is an adverb.

**Adjective:**     Her *queenly* attire made Elizabeth I stand out from all the other women present.

**Adverb:**     The *magnificently* dressed queen stood out from all the others.

## EXERCISE 86

Replace the underlined words in these sentences with a synonym from the list below. Look up any new vocabulary before you begin the exercise. Then rewrite the whole sentence, using the synonym.

| religious | terrestrial | corporeal | nocturnal | celestial |
|-----------|-------------|-----------|-----------|-----------|
| studious | well-timed | pale | paternal | annual |

1. John's <u>ghostly</u> appearance told everyone that he was a sick man.

2. Despite Lou's powerful strength, he would not render <u>bodily</u> harm to anyone.

3. In many science fiction stories, <u>earthly</u> beings land on other planets.

4. Scientists are trying to figure out how <u>heavenly</u> bodies keep from colliding.

5. Father Peyton's <u>priestly</u> robes helped him gain admission to many restricted areas.

6. Del's <u>scholarly</u> appearance helped him obtain the part in the new documentary.

7. The raccoon's <u>nightly</u> raids of the garbage cans angered the neighbors.

8. Sue's <u>timely</u> entrance saved many of us from enduring a long lecture.

9. Mike's <u>yearly</u> income has already surpassed $50,000.

10. Mr. Corrigan's <u>fatherly</u> advice enabled his son to become a better student.

## EXERCISE 87

Replace the underlined words in these sentences with a synonym from the list below. Look up any new vocabulary before you begin the exercise. Then rewrite the whole sentence, using the synonym.

| organized | amiable | expensive | uncourageous | fraternal |
|-----------|---------|-----------|--------------|-----------|
| diurnal | holy | maternal | materialistic | beautiful |

1. Mona's <u>lovely</u> silk dress was ruined when she spilled chocolate syrup on it.

2. Pam's <u>friendly</u> manner opened many doors for her.

3. Mr. Stevenson's <u>orderly</u> presentation enabled his students to learn more quickly.

4. Mother Theresa of Calcutta was a very <u>saintly</u> and unpretentious woman.

5. The soldier's <u>cowardly</u> behavior caused him to be court-martialed and barred from the military.

6. Henry VIII's <u>worldly</u> ways appalled the clergy of the Middle Ages.

7. The <u>costly</u> construction project at the university received the disapproval of the board of directors.

8. Jogging is an integral part of Dr. Erbes's <u>daily</u> routine.

9. Father Damian's <u>brotherly</u> love led him to work in a leper colony until he, too, died of leprosy.

10. Mrs. Coleman's <u>motherly</u> affection caused her to be loved by all the children in the neighborhood.

# NOUNS AS ADJECTIVES

Many nouns in English can function as adjectives. However, the dictionary will list them only as nouns. Sometimes these "adjective-nouns" are also accompanied by a number. *Always use the singular form of the noun* when it modifies another noun.

---
**NOTE**

Always use a hyphen in the number-noun combination.
Follow this formula for writing "adjective-nouns":
**number-singular noun as adjective + noun**

---

Jerry's new ***ten-speed bicycle*** helps him move quickly through traffic.

My mother has just bought a ***50-piece set of china***.

## EXERCISE 88

Rewrite each sentence, using numbers and "adjective-nouns." Eliminate all unnecessary words.

**Example:** Adam needs to buy six *stamps worth twenty-five cents.*
Adam needs to buy six *twenty-five-cent stamps*.
*(not twenty-five-cents)*

1. Ivan has just bought a station wagon that has five doors.

2. My cousin likes that lovely gray purse with four compartments.

3. Our new computer has a hard drive of 9.6 gigabytes.

4. There is a new television in the lobby that has a screen that is 30 inches wide.

5. Sherry likes her new stereo with its four speakers.

6. When we went on vacation, we took a cooler that had a capacity of 80 quarts.

7. The Empire State Building is a structure with 92 stories.

8. Can you change this bill worth $20?

9. In our English class last week, we had to write a composition of 250 words.

10. We took a trip across America that lasted ten weeks.

11. To get to Gastonia from here, you need to drive for six hours.

12. Angela was very upset because she had spilled a can that contained five gallons of olive oil.

13. For her dress, Susie needs three yards of material that is 60 inches wide.

14. Tom has just bought a bedroom set that has five pieces.

15. Eva lives in a house that has a garage for two cars.

16. Barbara made a new winter coat with five buttons.

17. Paul's new bicycle has five speeds.

18. Monty repairs cars, so he bought a tool set that contains 125 pieces.

19. We need an extension cord that is nine feet long.

20. My new camp light needs a battery that has nine volts.

## EXERCISE 89

Rewrite each sentence, using the [number + noun as adjective] combination.

**Example:** Tony's *bicycle* has *ten speeds.*
Tony has a *ten-speed bicycle.*

1. The battery he needs for his radio is four volts.

2. Our journey through the mountains took six days.

3. I have only ten dollars. Can you change this bill?

4. My cousin has just bought a house on three levels.

5. Nancy just bought a bathing suit which comes in two pieces.

6. Marcella's apartment has ten rooms.

7. The teacher said that each margin used on the composition had to be three inches.

8. The Manleys' color television is 19 inches wide.

9. Harry just bought a tool set that contains 40 tools.

10. My father has a gas can that holds five gallons.

11. That new model typewriter has 44 keys.

12. The flag kit comes with a pole that is 17 feet long.

13. Mandy always uses the platter with the three tiers when she entertains.

14. The salesman tried to sell us a <u>dining room set of five pieces</u>.

15. My new microwave has a <u>timer for 25 minutes</u>.

16. Susan's just bought a new coat <u>made of mink</u> <u>with two gold buttons</u>.

17. Pete always uses <u>film that has a speed of 800</u>.

18. The Nelsons <u>new car has four doors</u>.

19. When the president passed, the soldiers gave him a <u>salute of 21 guns</u>.

20. Veronica received a new <u>tea set that has 15 pieces</u>.

Some times the numbers are eliminated and just the **singular noun** is used as an adjective to modify another noun.

singular noun as adjective + noun

I have a ***dress made of silk.***

I have a ***silk dress***.

## EXERCISE 90

Change these sentences to follow the [noun + noun] pattern. Eliminate all prepositional phrases.

> **Example:** Kevin likes golf clubs made of titanium.
> Kevin likes ***titanium golf clubs.***

1. Ruth has a lot of jewelry made of gold.

2. I like clothes of wool for winter because they are warm.

3. For picnics we always use forks made of plastic.

4. My mother wants a coat of mink for her birthday.

5. Jane never liked flowers made of silk.

6. Beverly has a set of chimes of brass.

7. The Japanese make beautiful flowers out of paper.

8. Nancy just sewed a skirt out of taffeta.

9. The Johnsons live in a house made of bricks.

10. The hostess served her elegant dinner on plates of china.

11. Cindy likes her new red shoes made of eel skin.

12. Billy's new art kit has lots of crayons.

13. Bernadette just received a briefcase made of leather for her birthday.

14. Beth is building bookcases made of wood.

15. Jeff needs a frame made of copper.

16. Michelle tried on a lovely dress made of silk.

17. Pam prefers clothes made of rayon.

18. The children love to play in a house in the tree.

19. The Gilbert family just built a patio made of stone.

20. Cheryl got a ring of diamonds for her birthday.

## EXERCISE 91: WRITING

Change the following to fit the [noun as adjective + noun] pattern. Write one good sentence with each.

**Example: a lodge for skiing ⟶ a ski lodge**
Mario spends his weekends at the *ski lodge*.

**a coat for winter ⟶ a winter coat**
You need a *winter coat* in December.

1. cream for coffee

2. soup of vegetables

3. salad of fruit

4. watch for the wrist

5. lamp for a desk

6. camera to take movies

7. covers for your books

8. factory that makes dresses

9. gloves made of leather

10. a shirt made of cotton

11. a tree for Christmas

12. bag for shopping

13. an album of photos

14. lab for chemistry experiments

15. vacation in the summer

16. window of stained glass

17. ticket for the train

18. station for buses

19. plates made of paper

20. cream for the hands

# PARTICIPLES AS ADJECTIVES

Participles, whether present or past, can function as adjectives in a sentence. It is often difficult for non-native speakers to decide whether to use the [verb + *-ing*] form or the [verb + *-ed*] form when they are writing or speaking.

As a general rule, use the [V + *-ing*] form when the noun performs or is responsible for the action described by the adjective.

> The ***crying*** baby was quieted by her mother.
>   (The baby was crying.)

> The ***tiring*** journey through the mountains seemed endless.
>   (The journey was tiring those who were traveling.)

> Last Friday night we attended an ***exciting*** play.
>   (The play excited us.)

On the other hand, when the noun modified by the adjective is the receiver of that action, use the past participle.

> The ***irritated*** passengers complained to the captain. (Something or someone caused the passengers to be irritated. They did not cause the action.)

> After winning the grand prize, the ***shocked*** contestant just stood there, not knowing what to say or do. (Winning shocked the contestant.)

> After devouring its prey, the ***satisfied*** lion lay under a shady tree to take a nap.  (Eating satisfied the lion.)

> The ***boring*** teacher left the room. (The teacher is responsible for boring the students.)

> The ***bored*** teacher left the room. (Someone or something was responsible for her leaving.)

## EXERCISE 92

Circle the correct form of the participle (past or present) for each sentence.

1. After the onslaught, the (raided, raiding) village tried to clean up the debris.

2. Despite a long delay, our (requested, requesting) materials finally arrived.

3. The kindergarten teacher read an (interested, interesting) story to her students.

4. Once the colonists were (settled, settling), they began to organize a new government.

5. The newly (explored, exploring) territory was named "Louisiana" in honor of King Louis of France.

6. The (paid, paying) bill was filed away.

7. Unfortunately, it is up to the (worked, working) class to support the poor.

8. After a careful investigation, the (stolen, stealing) property was returned to its owners.

9. The day of the (dreaded, dreading) exam had finally arrived, causing much anxiety.

10. The (escaped, escaping) refugees managed to reach safety before they had been missed.

11. The (hated, hating) emperor was violently attacked by the peasants.

12. Maria's (missed, missing) locket was finally found in her sister's drawer.

13. The (planned, planning) committee has unanimously approved the company's proposal.

14. The (postponed, postponing) concert was rescheduled for the following week.

15. All of the (wandered, wandering) hikers were found in good health, not too far from their wrecked plane.

16. Carlos's (fought, fighting) spirit has enabled him to survive in this uncaring society.

17. Senator Hawthorne addressed the college (graduated, graduating) class.

18. The (frozen, freezing) temperatures during the holidays wiped out the citrus crop.

19. Because Nell had no keys, it was impossible for us to get through the (locked, locking) doors.

20. The police asked all the (invited, inviting) guests to remain seated until the investigation had been completed.

## EXERCISE 93

Select the correct participle in each sentence.

1. Dane's (admiring, admired) glances reassured Nathalie that she was doing a good job.

2. The police officer tried to resolve the problems created by the witnesses' (conflicting, conflicted) reports.

3. The oddly (shaping, shaped) bright ball in the sky caused great concern among the townspeople.

4. The (warping, warped) door was difficult to pry open.

5. There was a lovely (climbing, climbed) rosebush outside my bedroom window.

6. The sudden (rising, risen) temperatures made everyone at the ball game very uncomfortable.

7. The teacher's (questioning, questioned) look let Chuck know that she did not believe his excuse for being late.

8. A neatly (lettering, lettered) sign was placed in the window of the drugstore.

9. The (simmering, simmered) stew sent a pleasant aroma throughout the house.

10. Mona Lisa's (smiling, smiled) face is known throughout the world.

11. A (speeding, sped) truck overturned on the turnpike, causing a monumental traffic jam.

12. The (enveloping, enveloped) fog along the coast prevented the aircraft from landing.

13. New York's (littering, littered) streets appear unsightly to our foreign visitors.

14. Tony chased the (bouncing, bounced) ball down the street.

15. The (crushing, crushed) flower fell limply to the floor.

16. All of the gymnasts relaxed for an hour after participating in the (exhausting, exhausted) exercises.

17. The (opening, opened) envelope lay on the table.

18. Monica's (whining, whined) child was upsetting everyone who was waiting in the doctor's office.

19. The (returning, returned) letter did not bear enough postage.

20. Cleveland's (polluting, polluted) river has been the source of concern among its citizens for many years.

# COMPARISONS OF ADJECTIVES

## Double Comparisons

There are several ways of expressing double comparisons. With this type there is a comparison form in the main clause as well as in the dependent clause. The main clause always comes first in the sentence. Both clauses use the word *the*, a comparison, a subject, and a verb.

> **THE** + comparative + S + V, + the comparative + S + V

The *older* you get, the *slower* you move.

The *longer* we wait, the *more tired* I get.

The *faster* I read, the *more interested* I become.

### EXERCISE 94

Finish the double comparisons.

1. The faster you drive, the _____ .

2. The harder the player hit the ball, the _____ .

3. The higher the sun rose, the _____ .

4. The sooner you finish your job, the _____ .

5. The longer Ray left the photo paper in the developer, the _____ .

6. The larger the car engine, the _____ .

7. The higher the temperature, the _____ .

8. The darker the sky became, the _____ .

9. The nearer we came to my mother-in-law's house, the _____ .

10. The farther you live from me, the _____ .

Other double comparisons always use *the more* as the comparative in the main clause.

> **THE MORE** + S + V + [**THE** + comparative] + S + V

*The more* toys the children see, *the more* they want.

*The more* you water the grass, *the taller* it will grow.

*The more* that dog eats, *the fatter* it gets.

---
**NOTE**

There are also some shorter idiomatic expressions
that use the double comparatives.

---

The more, the merrier.

The sooner, the better.

# Multiple Comparisons

Comparisons can also be expressed in multiples to indicate a much greater or lesser amount of difference. These can include fractions and whole numbers (one-half, one-third, one-tenth).

| number | + TIMES | + AS MANY + plural noun | + AS |
| fraction | + AS MANY + plural noun | | + AS |
| number | + TIMES | + AS MUCH + singular noun | + AS |

Mexico City has approximately **three times as many people as** Tokyo.

In the French classes there are **one-quarter as many students as** in the Spanish classes.

The Davidsons earn **four times as much money as** the Duricas.

Other ratings or fractions can be calculated as the following:

100 percent more or less

two-thirds more or less

four times as much/many as

much more/less than

one-third as much/many as

twice as much/many as

double, triple the amount

## EXERCISE 95

How good is your math? Look at the information in each sentence and write an appropriate comparison.

1. Students in Costa Rica study 40 hours per week. Students in the United States study 30 hours.

2. It is 90 degrees in Phoenix and 45 degrees in Butte.

3. Nevada was a territory for only 3 years when it was admitted to the United States as a state. Washington state was a territory for 36 years.

4. Peru has 20 national public holidays. The United States has about 10.

5. England and Wales produce about 56 major products, while the Falkland Islands produce about 7.

6. On the foreign market, the exchange rate is 12,570 Turkish pounds per American dollar. In Indonesia it is 2,095 rupiahs per dollar.

7. The continent of Africa has an area of about 11,850,000 square miles. Iceland has about 39,709.

8. The diameter of the earth is about 7,927 miles. That of the moon is 2,160.

9. The Nile River is approximately 4,149 miles long. The Snake River in Idaho is 1,038 miles long.

10. The Anapurua Mountains, in Nepal, are 26,492 feet above sea level. Mount Mitchell in North Carolina is at 6,684 feet.

# Idiomatic Expressions with Comparisons —————

In English there are many common expressions that use comparisons. Tell whether the following are equal or unequal comparisons. Because most are idiomatic expressions, look up their meaning in the dictionary. Most are also clichés (overworked expressions), and you should avoid using them in formal writing.

| | |
|---|---|
| light as a feather | dumb as an ox |
| neat as a pin | old as the hills (dirt) |
| the weather took a turn for the worse | skinny as a rail |
| higher than a kite (slang) | smooth as silk |
| nuttier than a fruitcake (slang) | tough as nails (person) |
| wise as an owl | tough as shoe leather (food) |

## EXERCISE 96

Using a dictionary, complete the comparisons.

1. Crazy as a _____

2. Hungry as a _____

3. No sooner said than _____

4. Pretty as a _____

5. Hard as a _____

6. The noisier you are, _____
it is for me to hear you.

7. Wild as the _____

8. Better late than _____

9. As plain as _____

10. As quick as a _____

11. Better safe than _____

12. the sooner _____

13. the bigger_____

14. as stubborn as a _____

15. as white as a _____

16. as red as a _____

17. as sharp as a_____

18. as busy as a _____

19. wise as an _____

20. as strong as an _____

# Illogical Comparisons

Comparisons need to focus on the same elements. When they focus on different elements, they are illogical. Often these illogical comparisons can be corrected by using a possessive form or the expression *that of* or *those of*.

**INCORRECT:**   Linda's wedding dress is more elegant than Janet.
(comparison of a dress and Janet)

**CORRECT:**   Linda's wedding dress is more elegant than Janet's.
(than that of Janet) (comparison of two dresses)

**INCORRECT:**   Badr's car is more expensive than his wife.
(comparison of a car and a wife)

**CORRECT:**   Badr's car is more expensive than his wife's.
(than *that of* his wife) (comparison of two cars)

If you mentally extend the comparison—Janet's dress, that of his wife (his wife's)—you will see the need for the possessive or the *that/those of* forms.

## EXERCISE 97

Correct the illogical comparison in each sentence.

**Example:** The director's salary is higher than his secretary.
The director's salary is higher than his ***secretary's (secretary's salary).***

1. Pharmacists' jobs are different from electricians.

2. Chicago's temperatures are lower than Florida.

3. Susana's coat is prettier than Rosa.

4. Chestnut's supplies are more expensive than Kmart.

5. Eric's sports car is faster than David.

6. Connie's exam was more difficult than her sister.

7. Ralph's new Corvette cost more than his uncle.

8. Painters' lives are more diversified than teachers.

9. Musicians' practice sessions are longer than dancers.

10. The university's faculty is more experienced than the college.

# Other Comparisons and Expressions —————

Other comparisons have different forms. You must learn them as such.

### Words dealing with social classes

high-class = very elegant, related to the highest level of society

low-class = in some cases, not acceptable taste

upper-class, middle-class, lower-class

### Miscellaneous expressions

upper division, lower division

upper torso, lower torso

upper management, midlevel management

high-paying job

high-water, low-water

above water, under water

above sea level, below sea level

high-rent, low-rent district

highly thought of (renown)

high-ranking government official

overall

overrated, underrated

overcoat, underwear

### Ratings of achievement in school or at work

above average, average, below average

overachiever, underachiever

# SEQUENCE OF ADJECTIVES AS NOUN MODIFIERS

Many adjectives in English precede the words that they modify. They also may follow the nouns, but then they are usually set off by commas.

The pine tree, twisted and knotty, was bending in the breeze.

The twisted and knotty pine tree was bending in the breeze.

Our dogwoods, delicate and attractive, added a touch of elegance to our surroundings.

Our delicate and attractive dogwoods added a touch of elegance to our surroundings.

When two adjectives precede a noun and can be interchanged without altering the meaning, or the word *and* can be inserted between them, the first is set off by a comma.

The arid, hot desert climate made it easy to dry our laundry.

The arid and hot desert climate made it easy to dry our laundry.

Notice the difference in these sentences:

Millie's dark green suit accentuated her lovely, long hair.

My new winter coat has long, narrow buttonholes.

It would be wrong to try to say *dark and green* and *new and winter* in the sentences.

Adjectives fit into two basic categories: limiting and descriptive. The former consists of articles, possessives, quantities, and numbers. The latter includes all other adjectives, such as those dealing with size, shape, color, material, quality, and texture.

When you use a series of adjectives to describe the same noun, there is a set pattern for which adjective comes first and which follows that, and what comes next. Here are several examples that are categorized in the chart on the following page:

a big, bright blue circular aluminum object

the small picturesque farming village

a privately owned Japanese tapestry museum

# SEQUENCE OF ADJECTIVES AS NOUN MODIFIERS

In English, when a series of adjectives are used to describe the same noun, they are placed in a set pattern for which adjective comes first, which follows that, and what comes next. The descriptive properties in this table are placed in the order in which they normally appear in English. You can use this chart to decide by category what the word order should be in a sentence.

| 1. Limiting | 2. Size/Age | 3. Description | 4. Intensity | 5. Quality | 6. Color | 7. Form | 8. Texture | 9. Nationality | 10. Religion | 11. Material | 12. Adjective-Noun | 13. Noun |
|---|---|---|---|---|---|---|---|---|---|---|---|---|
| a | big | | bright | | blue | circular | | | | aluminum | | object |
| the | small | picturesque | | | | | | | | | farming | village |
| a | | privately owned | | | | | | Japanese | | | tapestry | museum |
| | | carved | | | white | | | | | wrought iron | | grillwork |
| | | well-kept | | | white-washed | | | | | stucco | | houses |
| some | | world's | finest | | white | | | | | quartz | sand | beaches |
| hundreds of | gigantic | majestic | | historic | | | | | | | | Sequoias |
| a | | | | | red and gray | | woven | | | | | poncho |
| many | tall | neck-craning | | | | | | | | glass | | skyscrapers |
| numerous | | axle-breaking | | narrow | | winding | | | | | hairpin | turns |
| several | large | | | | | | fleecy | | | | baby | lambs |
| five | | | | devoted | | | | Irish | Catholic | | | nuns |
| these | centuries-old, giant | spectacular | | | | | | | | | | trees |
| Sally's | | elegant | | | yellow | cocktail-length | | | | chiffon | prom | dress |

## EXERCISE 98

Categorize each word.

**Example:** Methodist > *religion*     octagonal > *form*     deep > *intensity*

| | | | |
|---|---|---|---|
| 1. false | 9. spiral | 17. tangerine | 25. shallow |
| 2. satin | 10. pine | 18. vast | 26. antiquated |
| 3. purple | 11. young | 19. our | 27. billowy |
| 4. narrow | 12. horseshoe | 20. wide | 28. turquoise |
| 5. copper | 13. convex | 21. dwarfish | 29. imaginative |
| 6. their | 14. rough | 22. oblong | 30. responsible |
| 7. twenty | 15. happy | 23. curved | 31. mechanical |
| 8. oval | 16. fuzzy | 24. interior | |

## EXERCISE 99: Writing

Combine three or four of the following, and add a subject and a verb to complete the sentence. Write three sentences.

**Example:** I bought a *large opaque porcelain vase.*
Harvey loves to make *carved miniature statues.*

| | | | |
|---|---|---|---|
| deep | opaque | porcelain | heart-shaped |
| smooth | gossamer | shimmering | weatherbeaten |
| silky | miniature | large | carved |
| petite | twisted | fluffy | |

# EXERCISE 100

Unscramble the word groups so that the adjectives follow the sequence set up on the preceding pages. The noun to be described is the first word.

1. **Dress:** elegant   the   satin   long   red

2. **Ball:** big   the   round   boy's   beach

3. **Ring:** small   oval   bright   a   diamond

4. **Car:** blue   sleek   sports   new   Rita's

5. **Nights:** winter   cold   many   December's   long

6. **Bears:** little   fat   koala   fifteen   furry

7. **Feathers:** ostrich   big   white   two

8. **Tomatoes:** five   red   ripe   round

9. **Chair:** large   comfortable   a   old   soft

10. **Handle:** ruby-encrusted   delicate   long   the

# EXERCISE 101

In each sentence, decide which underlined item is incorrect.

1. The spy novel I am reading is much more exciting than my sister.

   A. The        B. am reading    C. much more    D. my sister

2. The product you bought at the lower price is the more inferior to the one we sell at a slightly higher price.

   A. bought       B. the more     C. the one     D. slightly

3. The carpenter <u>is making</u> a <u>cabinet of wood</u> that will <u>take</u> six weeks or <u>more</u> to complete.

    A.  is making    B.  cabinet    C.  take    D.  more
                                of wood

4. Lucas won <u>a scholarship for athletics</u> that <u>will</u> pay for four <u>years</u> of study <u>as well as</u> his tuition.

    A.  a scholarship  B.  will    C.  years    D.  as well as
         for athletics

5. Many <u>shivered</u> soldiers stood <u>in</u> line <u>waiting</u> for some hot food <u>to eat</u>.

    A.  shivered    B.  in    C.  waiting    D.  to eat

6. The <u>newly</u> <u>developing</u> plan <u>would</u> be presented to the committee <u>before</u> the end of June.

    A.  newly    B.  developing  C.  would    D.  before

7. A thoroughbred <u>race</u> horse is <u>usually</u> <u>expensiver</u> than a European <u>sports</u> car.

    A.  race    B.  usually    C.  expensiver  D.  sports

8. <u>The sooner</u> you finish <u>your</u> assignment, <u>more quickly</u> we'll be able <u>to leave</u> town.

    A.  The sooner  B.  your    C.  more quickly  D.  to leave

9. Mark <u>won</u> the grant <u>because</u> his grades are <u>higher than average</u> in his <u>academic</u> field.

    A.  won    B.  because    C.  higher than  D.  academic
                                    average

10. Marcy's <u>new</u> shoes cost <u>her</u> twice <u>more than</u> <u>mine</u> cost me.

    A.  new    B.  her    C.  more than  D.  mine

## EXERCISE 102

Below each sentence you will see answers marked A, B, C, and D. Select the one answer that best completes the sentence.

1. In the past, tennis used to be the sport of the _____ class, but that is changing.

   A. higher        B. superior        C. upper        D. mid upper

2. Venice is one of _____ cities in Europe.

   A. more beautiful                   C. most beautiful

   B. the more beautiful               D. the most beautiful

3. The team played _____ game of hockey that the coach was pleased.

   A. better        B. much better        C. so good        D. such a good

4. All of your grades are _____ average. I'm proud of you.

   A. above        B. over        C. super        D on top of

5. Because the freezing temperatures destroyed much of the citrus crop, the prices are _____.

   A. double        B. two times more        C. up two times        D. twice more

6. _____ people in America like to observe as well as participate in sports.

   A. Almost        B. Most        C. Much        D. Too much

# Advanced Grammar

# ESL

## CHAPTER 9

## Conjunctions

# Chapter 9
# CONJUNCTIONS

**Correlative conjunctions** usually come in pairs and join like elements. Be sure that they are placed directly before the words representing the two like elements.

both—and              not only—but also

either—or             whether—or

neither—nor

Larry is a gifted musician who plays **both** the piano **and** the saxophone.

Many movie stars have houses **not only** in California **but also** in New York.

**Whether** you go to the party **or** you stay home is your decision.

---
**NOTE**
Be careful to place these conjunctions directly before the two like elements.

---

**INCORRECT:**  Helen *plays* **both** *music* **and** *sings well.*
                         (noun)     (verb)

**CORRECT:**  Helen **both** *plays music* **and** *sings well.*
                     (verb)         (verb)

**INCORRECT:**  Our team manager is **both** *active in sports* **and** *off the field.*
                                     (adj.)        (prep. phrase)

**CORRECT:**  Our team manager is active **both** *in sports* **and** *off the field.*
                                     (prep. phrase)  (prep. phrase)

While the conjunction *as well as* is not part of a pair, it does join two like elements. Notice that it does not influence the verb in terms of singular and plural.

Nancy, **as well as** her family, **supports** the new proposal.

Teachers, **as well as** students, **plan** to visit the Dali Museum

If, however, you used the conjunction *and* instead of *as well as*, each would have a plural verb.

Nancy **and** her family **support** the new proposal.

Teachers **and** students **plan** to visit the Dali Museum.

Remember that whatever subject follows *or* or *nor* will determine whether the verb is singular or plural.

**Either** Sandy **or** her brothers **drive** to school in the morning.

**Neither** the Johnsons **nor** their son **has** access to the trust.

However, the subject following *as well as* and *including* does not determine the verb. It is the subject that comes before the conjunctions that does. If you cover the clause and work with whatever is left of the sentence, then you won't have any problems with subject/verb agreement.

The *price* of the furniture, *including* the television and sofa, *is* $500.

The *college president*, *as well as* the deans, *is* accountable to the board of trustees.

**Relative conjunctions** introduce clauses that relate to something or someone previously mentioned. These will be studied more in detail in the section "Clauses." The following are relative conjunctions.

| that | which | whichever |
|------|-------|-----------|
| who | whoever | |
| whom | whomever | whose |

I have seen *the movie* **that** you said was so good. (*That* relates to *movie*)

That man **who** is standing by the piano is the new director of the opera.

## EXERCISE 103

Correct each sentence so that the correlative conjunction is in the right place or so that the subject and verb agree.

> **Example:** Ben not only plays the guitar but also the flute.
> Ben plays **not only** the guitar **but also** the flute. (two instruments)
>
> **Example:** Either the soldiers or the captain prepare to march against the enemy.
> Either the soldiers or the captain **prepares** to march against the enemy. (agrees with the subject closer to the verb)

1. Both Annika and Tara is cousins.

2. Neither the boys nor their sister are planning a career in medicine.

3. The band members, as well as the director, goes on tour next month.

4. We not only have cards for baseball but also for football players.

5. Either Friday's concert or Saturday's are fine with me.

6. We are planning not only to go to Switzerland, but also to Austria.

7. John, as well as his friends, hope to be professional writers someday.

8. Neither fats nor sweets is part of a good, healthy diet.

9. The bride's elegant bouquet not only was filled with gardenias, but also lilies.

10. The guests, including the president, pays compliments to the hostess.

11. I both want to buy the stereo and the cabinet.

12. Neither the house nor the doors has to be painted.

13. The flowers, as well as the oak tree, is growing well after the storm.

14. The government both has the power and the authority to raise taxes.

15. Both the plane and the pilot is landing safely.

# Advanced Grammar

# ESL

## CHAPTER 10
## Verbs

# Chapter 10
# VERBS

## PERFECT TENSES

To indicate the **perfect tenses**, use *have*, *has*, or *had* and the past participle. These tenses past, present, and future show the completion (or non-completion) of an action in relation to another action or in relation to a time period or deadline. When you use the **present perfect**, you deal with now (up to this moment) as the deadline and the action has or has not already taken place.

```
    X_____/
    action                now
```

The present perfect is used for the following:

1. An action that took place at some indefinite time in the past:

> We *have* already *seen* that movie. (Sometime in the past in relation to now, that action took place.)

> He *has washed* his hands and is ready to eat. (The hand washing took place at a time before now.)

2. An action that happened more than once in the past:

> I *have visited* Mexico six times.

> Nancy *has written* dozens of letters.

3. An action that began sometime in the past and continues up to this moment:

> Daniel *has studied* here *since 1992*. (He still studies here.)

> Alan *has lived* in that apartment *for six months*. (He still lives there.)

Use the following word order with the present perfect tense:

Question:  $\left\{\begin{array}{l} \textbf{\textit{HAVE}} \\ \textbf{\textit{HAS}} \end{array}\right\}$ + subject + past participle + (complement)

<u>Have</u> you <u>eaten</u> lunch?

Affirmative:  S  + $\left\{\begin{array}{l} \textbf{\textit{HAVE}} \\ \textbf{\textit{HAS}} \end{array}\right\}$ + past participle + (complement)

I <u>have eaten</u> lunch.

Negative:  S  + $\left\{\begin{array}{l} \textbf{\textit{HAVE}} \\ \textbf{\textit{HAS}} \end{array}\right\}$ + **NOT** + past participle + (complement)

I <u>have NOT eaten</u> lunch.

## EXERCISE 104

Each of the following has taken place at some indefinite time. As you look at the sentences, relate them to *now*. Answer each in the affirmative and in the negative.

1. Has the child drunk his milk?

Yes, _____ .

No, _____ .

2. Has Mary sold her house?

Yes, _____ .

No, _____ .

3. Have the directors thought about a solution to the problem?

Yes, _____ .

No, _____ .

4. Have all of you spoken to the teacher?

Yes, _____ .

No, _____ .

5. Charles, have you worn your new shirt?

Yes, _____ .

No, _____ .

6. Have I done a good job on the presentation?

Yes, _____ .

No, _____ .

## EXERCISE 105

Finish each sentence, using the same verb as in the first part. Assume that the events follow a normal, habitual pattern and you are relating these events to today and what has (not) taken place up to this moment.

**Example:** Sally does her homework at night. It's 3:00 p.m. and she **has not done it** yet.

Matt takes two vitamins every morning. Today is Wednesday (afternoon), and he **has taken eight** vitamins so far this week. (number of vitamins)

1. I eat breakfast at 9:00 every day. It's now 8:00 and I _____ yet.

2. It snows a lot in February. It's May 10 and it _____ since _____.

3. Mark works from 8:00 to 5:00, Monday through Friday. It is 2:00 on Thursday, and Mark _____ already _____ hours. (include the number of hours)

4. Peggy types 20 letters every day, Monday to Friday, 8:00 to 5:00. It is 5:00 Friday, and Peggy _____ letters. (number of letters)

5. Mrs. Jones gives her students many tests. This semester she _____ already _____ twelve tests.

6. My bills are due on the 28th of the month, and I pay them on the due day. Today is the 20th, and I _____ yet.

7. Phil visits Mexico once every year. In the past five years he _____ _____ five times.

8. I receive five letters from my family and friends every week. This week I _____

_____ letters. (number of letters also)

## EXERCISE 106

Answer the following questions, using complete sentences.

1. Have you ever traveled to the Grand Canyon?

2. Has your family ever eaten sushi?

3. Have your friends been to an American baseball game?

4. Have your friends visited the Van Gogh exhibit at the museum?

5. Has the plane arrived at the airport yet?

6. Has your best friend ever played a trick on you?

7. Have your teachers helped you with your problems with English?

8. How many exams have you taken this week?

9. What new foods have your eaten here in America?

10. Have you told your parents about your adventures in America?

# PAST AND PRESENT PERFECT

X
_____

1982

I read the book *Aztec* in 1982.

X    X    X    X    X    X    X
_____

1985                                                        Now

Since 1985, I have read many books on the Aztecs.

X

1990

In 1990 the Johnsons lived in Arizona, and then they moved to Ohio.

X ——————————————————————————————————→

1990                                                                    Now

The Johnsons have lived in Ohio since 1990. (still there)

X

1996

I studied English in 1996. (I stopped studying it in 1996.)

X ——————————————————————————————————→

1996                                                      Now (this year)

I have studied English for nine years. (still studying)

X ———————————————————————————————————— X

Yesterday 8:00                                                         5:00

Yesterday I worked nine hours.

X ———————————————————————————————————— X

Today 8:00                                            Now (this time of day)

So far today, I have worked six hours. (still working)

# SIMPLE PAST AND PRESENT PERFECT

## Simple Past

♦ **Single completed action at a *specific* time**
He **drove** to work on Monday.

♦ **Simple past description**
The weather in Hawaii delighted us.

| | |
|---|---|
| yesterday | last week/night |
| last month | in 1998 |
| ago | on Tuesday |
| the day before yesterday | |

## Present Perfect

♦ **Action took place at some *indefinite* time in the past**
We have already seen that movie.

♦ **Action that happened more than once in the past**
She has visited Mexico six times.

♦ **Action that began in the past and continues to this moment**
He has studied English since 2001.

| | |
|---|---|
| already | before |
| ever | since |
| yet | for |

## Sentence patterns

S + [V + **ED**] + C

I studied the new vocabulary.

**DID** + S + simple form + C ?
       verb

Did you pay your tuition on Friday?

S + **did** + **NOT** + simple form + C
       verb

I did not (didn't) watch television last night.

## Sentence patterns

S + { **HAVE** / **HAS** } + past participle + C

I have seen that movie.
Harry has done his homework.

{ **HAVE** / **HAS** } + S + past participle + C ?

Have you eaten in that restaurant?
Has Susan visited the museum?

S + { **HAVE** / **HAS** } + **NOT** + past participle + C

I have not (haven't) read that book.
Ellen has not (hasn't) washed the car.

| Single past definite time | I *parked* in the faculty lot yesterday morning. |
| Indefinite, more than once | I *have parked* in the faculty lot only four times *this month*. |
| Single past definite time | It *snowed* a lot in Cleveland in February. |
| Indefinite, more than once | It *has snowed* fifteen times *since February*. |
| Period in the past | I *hated* snow as a child! |
| Action begun in past | I *have hated* snow *for twenty years*! |
| One definite time | Ray *sang* in the shower last night. |
| Repeated indefinite action | Ray *has sung* that same song *over and over again*. |

Compare the following sets of sentences.

♦ The Davis family *lived* in Orlando for six years, and then they moved to St. Augustine. (They no longer live in Orlando.)

The Davis family *has lived* in St. Augustine for six years. (The family still lives there.)

♦ Marty wrote five letters last week. (one definite time, finished action)

So far this week, Marty *has written* ten letters. (He may write more before the end of the week.)

♦ It *rained* hard last night. (one completed past event)

It *has rained* hard five nights this week. (It may rain again this week.)

♦ We *worked* late Friday night. (one completed action)

We *have worked* late every night this week. (We may continue to work late every night.)

♦ I *paid* $25 for last Saturday's concert ticket. That was too much money! (one event)

I *have paid* $25 for all my concert tickets. (I still am paying $25 per ticket.)

## EXERCISE 107

Write the correct form of the verb.

1. He (wrote, have written) the exercise many times before turning it in.

2. Mark (wore, has worn) his new suit to the party last night.

3. No one (thought, has thought) it would rain yesterday.

4. Larry (read, has read) each of the Harry Potter books this year.

5. Paul (quit, has quit) smoking since his heart attack.

6. While Neal was cutting the bread, he (hurt, has hurt) his finger.

7. Last summer we (took, have taken) a trip to the Great Smoky Mountains.

8. We (waited, have waited) since 2000 to visit my family in China.

9. The sun (set, has set) earlier every night this summer.

10. No one (saw, has seen) the new Mel Gibson movie yet.

11. Luis (finally received, has finally received) his tax refund last Tuesday.

12. After her death, Mother Theresa (left, has left) us a wonderful legacy.

13. José (danced, has danced) very well. Did you see him glide across the room?

14. Hugo (ran, has run) five miles every morning last summer.

15. The wind (blew, has blown) so hard last night that our awning came off.

16. Bart (sang, has sung) in concert ten times this month.

17. The children (ate, have eaten) the apples on their way to the cafeteria.

18. We (heard, have heard) the good news and are glad that you received the award.

19. Mark Spitz (swam, has swum) in many international competitions.

20. The baseball player (caught, has caught) the high fly ball after leaping into the air.

## EXERCISE 108: WRITING

Make a list of 10 things that you and your family did last summer. Change the subjects to use all forms of the verbs. Use 10 different verbs. Contrast this by making another list of what you and your friends have done so far this semester. Again, use 10 different verbs, and change the subjects. Notice the difference in the verb forms.

**Example:** Last summer my family *went* to the beach.

We *walked* along the shore.

This semester my family *has visited* me at school three times.

My friends and I *have walked* in the park many afternoons.

## EXERCISE 109: WRITING

Get a partner and interview him/her, using question words: *who, what, why, when, where,* and *how.* Ask your partner eight questions about his/her life since he or she came to the United States. When you have finished, rewrite the answers in paragraph form, and be prepared to introduce your partner to the class, telling everyone what you have learned about him/her.

**Example:** Adam *has lived* here for eight months. He *has studied* at the university for two semesters. . . .

# PAST AND PAST PERFECT

With the **past perfect** (sometimes called the **pluperfect**), use *had* and the past participle. In relation to a past time or action, this action had already taken place. The verb using *had* and the past participle is always the first of the two actions.

```
X                   X                              X
```
first action    time or second action                      now

*Before 1500* (time reference past) Christopher Columbus *had discovered* America.

```
X                   X                              X
```
discovered       1500                              now

The defendant *told* his lawyer that he *had been* out of the country at the time of the crime.

```
X                   X                              X
```
*had been* (first action)   *told* (second action)          now

Remember the following formula:

> ***BEFORE*** + time past (verb in simple past tense)
> ***AFTER*** + ***HAD*** + past participle

***Before she came*** (second action) to this school, Monique ***had not studied*** (first action) English.

We ***had bought*** (first action) a new car before my wife ***got*** (second action) her new job.

After the student ***had sat*** down (first action), the teacher ***distributed*** (second action) the exams.

Elvis Presley ***had not been discovered*** (non-existent first action) ***before 1950*** (past time).

## EXERCISE 110

Circle the correct form of the verb.

1. Before 1990 Anthu (visited, had visited) her friends in Holland.

2. After I (arrived, had arrived) at the party, everyone began to sing and dance.

3. I (read, had read) the letter after the mailman had delivered it.

4. Saul (told, had told) me that his family had gone on vacation.

5. Sandy (prepared, had prepared) a wonderful party before her friends moved to Arizona.

6. Jose (improved, had improved) his grades after his teacher had sent him a warning.

7. After the committee had made its decision, the chairman (made, had made) an announcement.

8. My package arrived shortly after I (ordered, had ordered) it

9. Terry (waited, had waited) for three hours before he left.

10. I remembered that I (promised, had promised) to send the gift to Rita.

11. Before the party ended, Burt (danced, had danced) with all the girls.

12. After I (mailed, had mailed) the package, I remembered the correct address.

13. Our teacher (gave, had given) us the test results after she had graded them.

14. No one (understood, had understood) the lesson before Professor Sobieski explained it.

15. Before he (went, had gone) to Greece, Dana did not speak a word of Greek.

## EXERCISE 111

Decide whether each sentence requires the simple past or the past perfect tense, and write the correct form.

**Examples:** The landlord **_raised_** (raise) the rent after he had sent us a notice. The papers blew off the table after Mary **_had opened_** (open) the window.

1. Janice Lawson _____ (win) the lottery before she bought her new car.

2. Vera told her friends that she _____ (return) from vacation only a few days ago.

3. The mechanic _____ (repair) Dane's car after he had damaged the motor.

4. We _____ (remain) in Seattle after the conference had ended.

5. Dave _____ (drive) 40 miles out of the way before he realized his mistake.

6. All of the students _____ (pay) their tuition before July.

7. The fishermen had removed their equipment before the boat _____ (sink).

8. I _____ (go) to Kansas before the tornado struck.

9. The pipes _____ (*negative of* freeze) before we turned off the water.

10. I _____ (ring) the bell after I had seen the sign.

11. The carpenters _____ (build) the house after the crew had poured the foundation.

12. The police _____ (catch) the thief after he had escaped.

13. Marcy _____ (*negative of* take) the medicine before she read the label.

14. The airplane _____ (land) after the pilot had spoken with the control tower.

15. Margaret _____ (*negative of* buy) the house before she married Jim.

16. Before the bank manager closed the safe, he _____ (put) in the sacks of money.

17. Before Jennie left for school, she _____ (*negative of* eat) anything.

18. Not many people _____ (fly) with that airline before 1988.

# PRESENT PERFECT PROGRESSIVE

It is also possible to use the progressive to express an action begun in the past that still continues at this moment. Use the following formula:

S + { **HAS** / **HAVE** } **BEEN** + [V + **ING**] + **FOR** + period of time

I **have been living** here for three years.
   (Three years ago I came here to live and continue to live here.)

Frank **has been studying** English since 1989.
   (Frank started in 1989 and still continues to study English.)

**HOW LONG** + { **HAS** / **HAVE** } + S **BEEN** + [V + **ING**] + complement

**How long have you been** working at the Acme Textile Company?

I **have been working** there for 10 years.

**How long has Jody been singing** opera?

**Jody has been singing** opera for 10 months.

## EXERCISE 112

Using the following situations, indicate how long this activity has been taking place.

**Example:** I came to Florida in 1978, and I am still here in 2005. (live)
   I **have been living** in Florida for 27 years.

1. Luis started his classes at the university three semesters ago. (study)

2. Mandy started skiing at 9:00 a.m. It's now 3:00 p.m.

3. Phil started his final exam at 11:00 a.m. and it's now 2:30 p.m. (take)

4. The conference began on Monday and we are still here on Saturday. (attend)

5. Harry and I began dancing together on February 1. Today is May 1.

6. They started to eat at 7:30 and it's now 9:30.

7. I started to speak Spanish six semesters ago.

8. Noel Phelps started to write novels when he was 25. He's now 46.

9. Jack started to drive a truck when he was 30. He's now 44.

10. Paul and Dorothy start to build their house on April 1. It's now September 30.

11. Kent started to play baseball in 1989. It's now 2003.

12. My favorite television program started in December. It's now April. (watch)

13. You started to play the role of King Arthur in 2000. It's now 2005.

14. I started taking my summer vacations in Europe in 1979. It's now 1987.

## EXERCISE 113: WRITING

Answer these questions based on your personal experiences.

1. How long have you been studying English?

2. How long have you been living in your apartment (house)?

3. How long has your family been writing letters to you?

4. How long has your best friend been working at his/her job?

5. How long have your classmates been studying in the library?

6. How long have you and your friends been eating in the cafeteria?

# PAST AND PAST PROGRESSIVE

While both of these tenses indicate a time before now, they cannot be used interchangeably. **Past tense** indicates a simple completed action with no relation to any other action before or after it.

I *ran* to the store for some milk.

We *studied* for three hours last night.

It *rained* yesterday afternoon.

However, when the past action was in progress at a given time or prior to another sudden single action, the verb is in the **past progressive**.

I *was running* to the store when I *met* Bob.

We *were studying* for the exam when the lights *went* out.

It *was raining* yesterday when I *left* the library.

Each of the above sentences shows a past action in progress before another took place. Look at the idea in this chart:

running ~~~~~~~~~~~~~~~~~~~ / met ~~~~~~~~~~~~~~~~~~~~~~ / now

studying~~~~~~~~~~~~~~~~~~~ / went out ~~~~~~~~~~~~~~~~~~ / now

raining ~~~~~~~~~~~~~~~~~~~ / left ~~~~~~~~~~~~~~~~~~~~~ / now

Compare the following sets of sentences.

♦ My father *drove* to work at 8:00 yesterday. (one time)

My father *was driving* to work at 8:00 this morning when he got a flat tire. (action in progress)

♦ We *talked* about our plans for the party before the class. (one time)

We *were talking* when the teacher arrived. (action in progress)

♦ Terry and Monica **played** tennis last night. (one time)

Terry and Monica **were playing** tennis when it started to rain. (action in progress)

♦ I **swam** in the pool this morning. (one time)

I **was swimming** at 10:00 when Maritza arrived. (action in progress)

♦ Patty **read** a book last night. (one time)

Patty **was reading** a book by the fire when I walked into the room. (action in progress)

Look for these key words to help you decide whether to use past or past progressive.

| Past | Past Progressive |
|------|------------------|
| once | always |
| never | every day (night, week, etc.) |
| immediately | many times |
| suddenly | often |
| at once | frequently |
| unexpectedly | mental action verbs |
| finally | while/when (two simultaneous actions = at the same time) |

## EXERCISE 114

Read the following paragraph and write the correct form of the past or past progressive for each verb.

This morning I (1) __was walking__ (walk) to the bus stop when the bus suddenly (2) __pulled__ (pull) away. I (3) _____ (look) at my watch and (4) _____ (see) that it was not late. How strange! I (5) _____ (wait) when my friend Jung (6) _____ (appear). She (7) _____ (carry) a lot of books, so I (8) _____ (move) over so that she could sit down. We (9) _____ (talk) when the next bus (10) _____ (arrive) about 15 minutes

later. On the bus she (11) _____ (read) her book while I (12) _____
(write) some notes and we (13) _____ (*negative of* pay) attention.
Suddenly, I (14) _____ (realize) that we had missed our stop. When we
(15) _____ (get) off the bus, it (16) _____ (begin) to rain and neither of
us (17) _____ (have) an umbrella. We (18) _____ (be) very wet when we
(19) _____ (enter) the library. This Friday the 13th, (20) _____ (be)
terrible! Next Friday the 13th I will stay home all day.

## EXERCISE 115

Circle the correct form of the verb.

Last week I (1) (went, was going) shopping as I do every Friday. When I
(2) (arrived, was arriving) at the parking lot, I (3) (found, was finding) no place
to park. Suddenly, I saw that a blue Toyota (4) (left, was leaving) a spot close
to the entrance. I (5) (parked, was parking) my car when someone suddenly
(6) (jumped, was jumping) in front of me. He (7) (didn't pay, wasn't paying)
attention and I almost (8) (hit, was hitting) him. I finally (9) (got, was getting) into
the store and (10) (started, was starting) my shopping. I (11) (looked, was looking)
for some fruits when the produce person suddenly (12) (brought, was bringing) out
some fresh grapes and bananas. He (13) (said, was saying) that they had just been
delivered. I (14) (picked, was picking) out a few and (15) (put, was putting) them
in my cart. In the meat department the butcher (16) (cut, was cutting) some lamb
chops, so I (17) (decided, was deciding) to wait a few minutes for him to put them in
the display case. I had found most of my groceries and (18) (pushed, was pushing)
the cart to the check out when suddenly one of the wheels (19) (fell, was falling) off.
The manager (20) (helped, was helping) me unload the cart, pay, and get out of the
store. What a shopping nightmare!

## EXERCISE 116

Fill in the correct form of the simple past or past progressive.

1. He __was traveling__ in Europe when he met Sally. (travel)

2. I ___wrote___ six letters today. (write)

3. She _____ her hair when they called. (brush)

4. Marta _____ her dress and couldn't answer the telephone. (change)

5. The boys _____ a bookcase yesterday. (make)

6. She _____ dinner when John arrived. (cook)

7. Paul _____ his mother last night. (call)

8. They always _____ to work in the morning. (walk)

9. They _____ about James when he came in. (talk)

10. People always _____ nice things about him. (say)

11. The girl _____ the butter to the table immediately. (bring)

12. He _____ to France when his father died. (go)

13. Ian _____ his bags and went away. (pack)

14. The audience _____ a lot of questions after the speech last night. (ask)

15. Just as I _____ the store, someone tried to walk in. (close)

16. As the waitress _____ the water, someone bumped into her. (pour)

17. Jim _____ football yesterday when he hurt his knee. (play)

18. I _____ as much as I could but I missed the bus. (hurry)

19. Mike _____ a letter when you called. (type)

20. While Mary _____ the car, her boyfriend was eating. (wash)

# VERBS FOLLOWED BY INFINITIVES

Instead of using a noun as a complement, certain verbs use an infinitive. The following verbs *always* require the infinitive (*to* + base form of verb) if the complement is a verb.

| | | | |
|---|---|---|---|
| agree | expect | learn | seem |
| appear | fail | mean (intend) | want |
| care | hesitate | plan | wish |
| decide | hope | promise | |
| deserve | intend | refuse | |

The director **agreed to raise** his employees' salaries.

My son **will learn to swim** this summer.

Kahn **deserves to receive** the award for his hard work.

# VERBS FOLLOWED BY GERUNDS

Another group, however, requires a gerund (V + *ing*) as a complement. The following fit this pattern:

| | | | |
|---|---|---|---|
| admit | dread | keep | report |
| appreciate | enjoy | mind | resent |
| avoid | escape | miss | resist |
| consider | finish | postpone | risk |
| deny | imagine | practice | suggest |

The thief **admitted taking** the jewelry.

The students **continued writing** the exam despite the power failure.

I **miss seeing** you every day. Please hurry home.

The following expressions require the gerund. In English the gerund usually follows a preposition.

| | | |
|---|---|---|
| accustomed to | count on | it's no use |
| approve of | feel like | keep on |
| be against | forget about | look forward to |
| be a question of | get used to | object to |
| be better off | give up | opposed to |
| be fond of | go on | put off |
| be tired of | interested in | succeed in |
| can't help | it is worth | think about (of) |

I **don't approve of your walking** late at night.

Thomas **is fond of driving** in the mountains.

We just **feel like sitting** home this weekend.

Manuel **succeeded in passing** all of his tests.

There are certain verbs that can be followed by either the infinitive or the gerund without changing the meaning of the sentence. Here is a partial list of those verbs:

| begin | hate | love | remember |
|-------|------|------|----------|
| continue | like | prefer | start |

Tom continues **to study** despite his job.    Tom continues **studying** despite his job.

I prefer **to travel** in the summer.    I prefer **traveling** in the summer.

Ana loves **hates** to study math.    Ana hates **studying** math.

## EXERCISE 117

Circle the correct form for each.

1. The politicians agreed (debating, to debate) on public television.

2. We intend (going, to go) to the mountains on our vacation.

3. The weather seems (being, to be) better today.

4. Many people reported (seeing, to see) unidentified flying objects over the lake.

5. The doctor will postpone (performing, to perform) surgery until the patient feels stronger.

6. The dissidents refused (obeying, to obey) the police.

7. If you leave now, you will avoid (driving, to drive) through rush-hour traffic.

8. Our mother refuses (allowing, to allow) us to see that movie.

9. We hope (buying, to buy) a new television this week.

10. Rita dreads (going, to go) to the dentist's office.

11. Enid decided (repairing, to repair) her car herself.

12. The policeman said that the driver had failed (yielding, to yield) the right of way.

13. I promise not (eating, to eat) any more chocolate.

14. Ruth resisted (spending, to spend) all of her money in the same store.

15. The painters plan (painting, to paint) the house early this morning.

16. Why don't you consider (going, to go) to the beach with us.

17. They enjoy (singing, to sing) in the shower.

18. The bride hopes (having, to have) beautiful weather on her wedding day.

19. We expect (entertaining, to entertain) many family members.

20. My cousin practices (playing, to play) the piano every day.

# TROUBLESOME VERBS

Because of their similarities, three sets of verbs—*rise/raise*, *sit/set*, and *lie/lay*—create problems even for native speakers. If you can remember this simple diagram and one sentence for each example, you will have no problem with these verbs.

| Transitive verbs take a direct object | Intransitive verbs take no direct object |
|:---:|:---:|
| raise | rise |
| lay | lie |
| set | sit |

You can *raise* your test score by studying harder. (*score* is the direct object)

The government *has raised* taxes again. (*taxes* is the D.O.)

Paula *laid* her new dress on the bed. (*dress* is the D.O.)

After *laying* the bricks for the patio, the workers took a long break. (*bricks* is the D.O.)

*Set* the package on the table. (*package* is the D.O.)

The doctor will have *to set* that broken bone so that it heals properly. (*bone* is the D.O.)

--- **NOTE** ---
The subject of the verbs *rise*, *lie*, and *sit* performs the action on itself, never on anyone or anything else.

Hot air *rises* faster than cold. (no D.O.)

The temperature *rose* quickly in the auditorium. (no D.O.)

The abandoned town *lies* in the middle of the desert. (no D.O.)

The sun bathers *lay* on the beach all day. (no D.O.)

Although we *sat* near the window, we still could not feel the breeze. (no D.O.)

Our dog loves *to sit* under the old oak tree. (no D.O.)

--- **NOTE** ---
The verbs *lay* and *set* can take a direct object that is a thing and can also take an object that is a person when another person performs an action on the second person.

The doctor *laid* the trembling child in bed so that he could examine her.
(The child is *lying* on the bed.)

Mrs. Lucas *set* her child in the high chair at dinnertime.
(The child is *sitting* in the chair.)

| Present | Past | Past Participle | Present Participle |
|---------|------|-----------------|--------------------|
| rise | rose | risen | rising |
| raise | raised | raised | raising |
| sit | sat | sat | sitting |
| set | set | set | setting |
| lie | lay | lain | lying* |
| lay | laid | laid | laying |

*Notice the spelling change to avoid writing three vowels (iei) together.*

Here are some idiomatic expressions with troublesome verbs:

| | |
|---|---|
| lay an egg | set about |
| lay away | set aside |
| lay down the law | set back |
| lay into | set out |
| lay off | set a broken bone |
| lay out | set gelatin |
| to be laid up | set the table |
| take it lying down | set the clock |
| all set | |
| hair-raising experience | |
| raise your voice | sit still |
| raise cain | sit in |
| sit in | on |
| give rise to | sit through |
| early riser | sit tight |
| sit up | |

## EXERCISE 118

Use the correct form of *rise* or *raise* in these sentences.

**Example:** Students need **_to raise_** their hands in class.

1. While the movers _____ the desk, one of the drawers fell out.

2. Yesterday morning the sun _____ at 6:12.

3. My mother has _____ early every morning for the past 15 years.

4. Cecilia asked us not to _____ our voices because the baby was sleeping.

5. The office manager happily _____ the salaries of his employees last June.

6. When the judge enters the courtroom, the bailiff says, "Will everyone please

_____ ."

7. No one knows when the government _____ taxes, but it will be soon.

8. The heavy overnight rains forced the river level to _____ .

## EXERCISE 119

Use the correct form of *lie/lay*.

**Example:** The patient **_lay_** on the bed for three hours after his surgery.

1. My dog _____ in the sun every morning.

2. Those old books have _____ in the corner for years.

3. Jane, please _____ your essay on my desk.

4. I can't find my keys; I know I _____ them on the table just a few minutes ago.

5. After I _____ down for a nap, I always feel better.

6. Because Sheila _____ on the beach all day in the hot sun, she had a terrible sunburn.

7. The hen has _____ five eggs this week.

8. The hospital orderlies _____ the patient in bed after his surgery.

## EXERCISE 120

Use the correct form of *sit/set*.

**Example:** No one knew why Harry **_was sitting_** in the back of church after the wedding.

1. Every week Chris _____ aside some money to buy a stereo next Christmas.

2. Millie _____ her hair this morning so that it would look nice for the party tonight.

3. When the fire bell rang, the chemistry students _____ down their test tubes and silently left the lab.

4. Karen, please _____ the table for dinner.

5. While we were _____ around watching television last night, my aunt came to visit us.

6. Secretaries must _____ all day at their desks.

7. Since you are on a diet, I have _____ some gelatin for dessert.

8. Marvin _____ patiently in the lobby and waited for news on his brother's condition.

9. Mrs. Dale told her children to_____ up straight and to listen to the speaker.

# CONDITIONAL TENSES

In this type of construction, which contains the word *if*, the completion of one action is dependent on another. If the existence or performance of an action is hypothetical (not real) or cannot be fulfilled, then that condition is said to be unreal.

If the team *lost* the game, the members *would be* unhappy.
   (The team will win the game; therefore, the members will be happy.)

If the store *were* open now, I *would buy* some groceries.
   (The store is closed; therefore, I cannot buy the groceries now.)

The *if* clause provided an unreal situation, one that could not materialize, because it was contrary to fact or hypothetical. Therefore, the result clause idea could not occur either. The situation could have taken place in the past, the present, or the future if the stipulated condition had been met. Unreal conditions can be present or past.

To express present unreal conditions, follow this formula:

$$IF + \text{verb in past} + \left\{ \begin{array}{l} WOULD \\ COULD \\ MIGHT \end{array} \right\} + \text{verb}$$

If I *saw* Tim on my way to class now, I *would stop* to talk.
   (I won't see him because he doesn't have classes today.)

If it *snowed* very hard, we *could go skiing* in the mountains.
   (It's too warm to snow; therefore, we can't go skiing.)

Each of these sentences presents an unreal condition in the present.

```
┌─────────────────── NOTE ───────────────────┐
│  When using the verb *be* in unreal clauses, remember that only │
│         *were* is the correct form with present conditions.     │
└─────────────────────────────────────────────┘
```

If today **were** Saturday, we **could sleep** later.
(Today's Wednesday and we have to get up early.)

If I **were** you, I **would study** harder.
(I'm not you.)

However, if we look at how past situations *could have been* different, we would use the following formula to express past unreal conditions:

$$IF + HAD + \text{past participle} + \begin{Bmatrix} WOULD \\ COULD \\ MIGHT \end{Bmatrix} + HAVE + \text{past participle}$$

If I **had remembered** to bring my checkbook this morning, I **could have done** all my grocery shopping. (I left the checkbook at home and didn't have enough money to shop.)

```
┌─────────────────── NOTE ───────────────────┐
│         Never use *would* in the *if* clause.        │
└─────────────────────────────────────────────┘
```

**INCORRECT:**   If we would have known how to swim, we could have learned to surf.

**CORRECT:**    If we had known how to swim, we could have learned to surf.

Another form of the past conditional expresses the same idea but omits the *if* from the sentence. Follow this rule:

$$HAD + \text{subject} + \text{past participle} + \begin{Bmatrix} WOULD \\ COULD \\ MIGHT \end{Bmatrix} + HAVE + \text{past participle}$$

**Had we played** against your opponent, we **could have won** easily.

**Had they known** you were in town, Curt and Diana **would have visited** you.

Now that we have seen how the unreal works, let's take a look at the real conditionals, those that will almost certainly materialize. At the time of speaking, there is nothing hypothetical or contrary to fact. These conditionals fall into two categories: the habitual and the factual. The former represents that which always occurs when a certain condition is present.

To express habitual conditions, follow this formula:

*IF* + verb in present, + present

If Susie **comes** to town, we always **have** a party.

If Andrew **goes** dancing, he always **has** a good time.

The *if* in these sentences has the meaning of **when**. When one thing happens, another is certain to happen also.

To express factual conditions, follow this formula:

$$IF + \text{present} + \begin{Bmatrix} WILL \\ MAY \\ CAN \end{Bmatrix} + \text{verb}$$

If the weather **stays** nice, we **can take** a trip.

If Pam **has** all the ingredients, she **will bake** us a chocolate cake.

We can also use these factual conditions with command forms in the result clause. The subject of the result clause can only be **you**.

If you **do** any sewing today, please **mend** my blue corduroys.

If you **get** to the drugstore, *have* my prescription refilled.

Although the *if* clause usually comes first in the sentence, you do not change the meaning by placing the result clause first and following it by the *if* clause.

Notice, however, that the *comma is eliminated* when the *if* clause does not appear first in the sentence.

If we miss the bus, we will have to walk.

We will have to walk if we miss the bus.

If Selena has any more problems with her registration, she will drop the course.

Selena will drop the course if she has any more problems with her registration.

## EXERCISE 121

Write the correct form of the conditional and wishing.

1. If I had known you were arriving today, I _____ (go) to the airport to meet you.

2. No one would have complained if Joe _____ (do) a good job.

3. Mary would have visited her friend in the hospital if she _____ (*negative for* leave) work so late.

4. If you get to the library, please _____ (pick) up that book that I need.

5. We will not be able to hear you if you _____ (speak) so softly.

6. If I _____ (take) this test now, I would not be well prepared.

7. If Sherry _____ (see) him, she would have given him the book.

8. If you take this course this semester, you _____ (graduate) in June.

9. If Sid _____ (have) enough film, he would have taken more pictures.

10. We _____ (attend) the party if we had found a ride.

11. We wish that we _____ (go) to the mountains with you tomorrow.

12. She wishes that she _____ (*negative for* eat) so much for dinner.

13. They wish that they _____ (have) time to go to the lecture.

14. Sarah wishes that she _____ (study) harder last night for today's test.

15. Paul wishes that he _____ (catch) a big fish next week.

16. Bill wishes that his golf score _____ (*negative for* be) so bad.

17. All of us wish that the rain _____ (stop).

18. She wishes that she _____ (win) the prize in yesterday's lottery.

19. Andy wishes that he _____ (lose) more weight before June.

20. I wish my friend _____ (be) here right now.

## EXERCISE 122

Read each situation and, using the conditional, tell what you would do.

1. You have just won the million-dollar lottery.

2. You have finally graduated after long years of study.

3. You had made plans for a picnic or outdoor event, but it's raining and will continue to rain all day.

4. Classes have been canceled for one week.

5. Some relatives of whom you are not too fond are planning to visit your town for one week and would like to spend several days with you.

6. It's raining very hard, and it's cold. You are not in the mood to get out of bed and go to class.

7. You have just seen someone steal some merchandise from a store where you are shopping.

8. You are walking down the street and find $80 on the sidewalk.

9. You have an important test tomorrow for which you are not well prepared. A movie you have been wanting to see is on television in 45 minutes.

10. Your girlfriend (boyfriend) wants to go to the beach this weekend, but you need to finish your term paper for a 9:00 class on Monday.

11. Your best friend has bought you a sweater that fits perfectly, but you hate the colors and design.

12. Your parents offer to take you shopping, but they want to select all your purchases.

13. You are attending a party with all of your friends who are drinking. They try to persuade you to drink also, but you know that you have to drive and that you need to get up early the next morning to go to work.

14. You have a job that you do not like that pays $40,000 a year. You have an offer of a much more enjoyable one that pays only $25,000.

15. The doctor tells you that you need to lose 25 pounds if you want to feel better and have more energy. You hate dieting, but you really do not feel good as you are.

## EXERCISE 123: WRITING

Read the following story about a shopping trip, and then complete the sentences, using the conditional perfect form of the verb. All sentences are past unreal conditions.

### Carlos's Bargain Hunting in the Supermarket

Last Friday Carlos, a Spanish architecture student, went grocery shopping as usual. Only this time, he was not with his American friend. He wanted to prove that he could manage on his own. He even wrote a list so that he would not forget anything. He started with the produce section and put lettuce, carrots, onions, big bananas, grapes, and apples in his cart. Then he found the aisle with all the canned goods. He was excited to find tuna at four cans for one dollar, so he put eight cans in his cart. He also bought some canned peas and green beans and a package of rice.

In the meat section, he selected small packages of sausage and hamburger. Finally, in the diary section, he picked up a bottle of milk and found a loaf of bread nearby.

Proud of his accomplishment and great savings, Carlos left for home to prepare dinner. Because he had a class and didn't have much time to make supper, he decided to eat a tuna sandwich. He thought the tuna had a "different" taste, but he was in a hurry and paid no attention to that small detail.

The next night Carlos prepared some vegetable soup and cut the lettuce, carrots, and onions and put them in a pot to boil. Five minutes later he looked at his soup and realized that he had very soggy lettuce and not cabbage!! Another strange meal!! The next morning, he cut a banana in his dish of cornflakes, only to find that the banana was a plantain, and it had to be cooked before eating!!

He was in a hurry once again at lunchtime, so he ate another tuna sandwich, again with the strange taste. Finally, after eating seven of these sandwiches, Carlos looked closely at the label and realized that he had been eating cat food for one week!!

Carlos's solo shopping venture had turned into a disaster, and he decided that he needed to shop with his American friend a few more times before going solo again.

1. If Carlos had not gone shopping alone, <u>he wouldn't have made so many mistakes</u> .

2. If Carlos had not written a list, he _____ .

3. If Carlos had looked closely at the bananas,_____.

4. If Carlos had gone shopping earlier,_____.

5. If Carlos had not been in a hurry at suppertime,_____.

6. If Carlos had read the labels on the cans,_____ .

7. If Carlos had looked closely at the lettuce,_____.

8. If Carlos had eaten the plantain,_____ .

9. If Carlos had taken his time to fix lunch,_____.

10. If Carlos's friend had gone with him, the shopping venture_____.

# UNLESS

The conjunction *unless* functions the same as *if . . . not* in conditional sentences.

Look at the construction of these sentences:

♦ Unless we finish the project soon, our clients will be angry.

If we don't finish the project soon, our clients will be angry.

♦ Unless Bill had all the ingredients, he wouldn't try the recipe.

If Bill didn't have all the ingredients, he wouldn't try the recipe.

Whatever forms correspond to real and unreal conditions will also be used here. *Unless* is usually followed by an affirmative clause, not a negative clause. Avoid using negative clauses such as this:

We'll have the party here, unless you don't approve.

Say the following instead:

We'll have the party here, unless there is a problem.

**INCORRECT:**   Unless I don't pay the bill, the electric company will turn off my lights.

**CORRECT:**   Unless I pay the bill, the electric company will turn off my lights.

## EXERCISE 124

Supply the correct form of the verb in each sentence.

1. Unless we pay the rent soon, the landlord __will evict__ (evict) us.

2. We _____ (attend) the lecture unless it is canceled.

3. No one will believe you unless you _____ (show) him the evidence.

4. He wouldn't have offered to help unless he _____ (have) the time.

5. Unless my friend learns to budget his money, he _____ (be) in debt.

6. Unless Sam _____ (get) the contract signed, he can't provide the services.

7. Unless Mr. Sanders _____ (find) an assistant soon, he will not finish his report.

8. You will have to pay a fare increase unless you _____ (purchase) your ticket before Monday.

9. My teacher _____ (*negative for* read) this paper unless I type it.

10. Unless the electrician _____ (arrive) soon, we will have to sit in the dark tonight.

11. Unless you _____ (try) on the pants, I will not be able to hem them.

12. Unless I _____ (prepare) supper soon, we will not eat until very late.

13. Unless you _____ (answer) the phone, the caller will think that we are not home.

14. Unless you are more careful, the company _____ (*negative for* insure) you in the future.

15. You will not _____ (receive) your check unless you fill out a time card.

16. Unless we _____ (leave) soon, we will arrive too late for the first act.

17. Unless they hurry, they _____ (miss) the train.

18. Unless a stranger _____ (try) to enter the house, my dog will not bark loudly.

19. Unless you _____ (put) the trash near the curb, the city won't collect it.

20. Unless Sandy _____ (ask) Terry, she will never know why they broke up.

# POSSIBILITY AND PROBABILITY

## Possibility

*May* and *might* are usually interchangeable, but *may* seems to be stronger or shows more emphasis. *Might* is ordinarily used for a future time in a noun clause after a past-tense verb.

| For present or future time | MAY<br>MIGHT } + simple form |
| --- | --- |

She *may* change her mind before she leaves.

She *may* be able to go later.

Andrea thought that she *might* transfer to another university this fall.

He said he *might* have to move to Chicago next year.

*May* and *might* are combined with *to be able to* and *have to* but *never* with *can* or *must*.

We *might have to* postpone the picnic because of the rain.

Ginger *may be able to* speak at our luncheon this week.

| For past time | MAY HAVE<br>MIGHT HAVE } + past participle |
| --- | --- |

The boys *may have tried* to call you yesterday.

I *might have left* my keys at home.

*May not* and *might not* express lack of possibility or probability.

I *may not go* to the party after all.

They *might not be able to visit* us this year.

*May* and *might* are *not* ordinarily used in questions unless *may* asks for permission to do something.

*May I see* that photograph? (asks permission)

He *may* be here at 5:00. Is he likely to be here at 5:00?

Can he possibly be here at 5:00?

# Probability

**Probability** represents what we guess will happen because of a certain set of circumstances, but we are not sure of the outcome:

John hasn't eaten for 24 hours. One of the ideas that we might guess is that *he must be very hungry.* This probability in the present is expressed by *MUST BE* + adjective. We can also use *must be* + [verb + *ing*].

He *must be* looking for a restaurant.

Rita has spent the whole day in the sun. She *must be* sunburned.

Stuart is drinking his third glass of water. He *must be* thirsty.

Look how dark it is outside. It *must be raining*.

Terry's laughing a lot. He *must be having* a good time.

Look at the following sentences and at the probable action that would result from this set of circumstances.

Mehrdad hasn't slept in three days. He *must be* very tired.

Kim has been in the rain all night. She *must be* all wet.

John travels 25 miles to work every day. He *must have* a car.

Mary has won $100. She *must be* happy.

They have bought an expensive house. They *must be* rich.

*Should* and *ought to* express strong possibility that approaches expectation equals probability:

| For present or future | *SHOULD* *OUGHT TO* } + simple form |
|---|---|

You *should (ought to)* receive the package by Wednesday.

The committee *should (ought to) be* announcing the decision by tomorrow.

| For unfulfilled expectations in the past | *SHOULD HAVE* *OUGHT TO HAVE* } + past participle |
|---|---|

Henry *should (ought to) have arrived* on the 8:00 train, but he didn't.

You *should (ought to) have bought* the car when it was on sale.

## EXERCISE 125

Read these sentences and make logical conclusions, using the present or the future of probability.

1. Tom swam the English Channel last week.

2. John has failed his exams.

3. Hal has lost $500.

4. Nobody wants to help him with his homework.

5. John has a slight fever.

6. There are many dark clouds in the sky. It's 80 degrees outside.

7. There are many dark clouds in the sky. It's 30 degrees outside.

8. Xian and Mai have been going together for five years.

9. He is laughing very hard.

10. Tom is very fat.

11. They spend a lot of money at the butcher's.

12. The Simpsons own a big car.

13. It is very hot and Jenny and her friends are at the beach.

14. Jose is very sad.

15. It's 8:00 and the play begins at 8:15. We have far to drive.

16. Mel works very hard. He needs more money.

17. They left New York for Madrid last night. They _____ by now.

18. The director has just offered James a better job.

19. Today is Mary's birthday. She _____ old.

20. Jake is giving a speech this afternoon in class.

**Past probability** guesses at a logical conclusion about a situation in the past, but it does not relate to actions in the present.

I can't find my wallet. I *must have left* it at home.

Peter received a 65 percent on his test. He **must *not have studied.***

Mrs. Thomas paid $1.29 a pound for chicken on Monday. Today it costs $1.59 a pound. They *must have raised* the price.

Peter didn't attend the meeting last night. He *was probably* busy.

It's been 10 days since you wrote the check. It *has probably cleared* by now.

## EXERCISE 126: WRITING

Make logical conclusions to these situations in the past.

1. Mrs. Kenley was talking with a very distinguished gentlemen at the party last night.

   He _____ must have been someone very important _____.
   (He was probably someone important.)

2. What time was it when he arrived? It_____ .

3. The Duricas won the lottery last year. They_____ .

4. Tommy swam the race in record time. He _____ .

5. James failed all of his final exams. He_____ .

6. Bob went to New Mexico last week. He _____ .

7. They bought a yacht last month. They _____ .

8. Nancy left the party early last night. She _____ .

9. Ted and his brother weren't in class yesterday. They_____ .

10. Last week Gary saw a movie starring his favorite actor. _____ .

11. There was a large puddle in the yard this morning. It _____ .

12. Paul studied very hard for all of his tests and he knew the material well.
    He _____ .

13. Val walked 12 miles after her car had broken down. She _____ .

14. I deposited your check in the bank last week. The cashier didn't say anything
    to me today. Your check _____ .

15. What time did you arrive last night? It_____ .

16. How many people attended the lecture on Tuesday? There_____ .

17. Where did Cindy and Leo go on their honeymoon? They _____ .

18. How many times did Louie see that movie? He _____ .

19. How old were you when that picture was taken? I _____ .

20. When did they announce the winners? They _____ .

# SUBJECT/VERB AGREEMENT

One of the biggest problems in writing correctly is that of getting the subject and verb to agree.

Singular subjects take singular verbs:

***The cat chases*** the mouse.

***Nobody wants to listen*** to that song any more.

Plural subjects take plural verbs. Nouns ending in a vowel or a consonant except *ch*, *sh*, *s*, and *x* add *-s* to form the plural:

   ***Those girls*** sing and dance very well.

   ***Roses*** are red; ***violets*** are blue.

Nouns ending in *ch*, *sh*, *s*, and *x* add *-es*:

   These pretty ***dishes*** were my grandmother's.

   Our ***taxes*** are going up again.

Not all words ending in *-s* are plural. The following words are always singular and have no plural form:

| | | |
|---|---|---|
| news | mathematics | arthritis |
| politics | mumps | sinusitis |
| measles | billiards | appendicitis |
| economics | chess | tennis |
| physics | checkers | bliss |

Tonight's ***news*** **is** very interesting.

***Politics*** **plays** an important role in our lives.

***Measles*** **is** a contagious disease.

***Mathematics*** **seems** difficult at first, but it can be easy if you study.

News can become a countable noun only by using the words stories or items, i.e. *news stories* or *news items*. *Measles* can become plural by saying *cases of measles*.

There are many interesting **news items** in today's paper.

Fifteen new **cases of measles** were reported last week.

The other words can be used only as adjectives accompanied by other nouns.

Our **physics professors** explain the experiments very well.

Three **economics classes** are offered during the fall semester.

# IRREGULAR PLURALS

Some words form their plurals without adding *-s*. These irregular words are the following:

| | | | |
|---|---|---|---|
| mouse—mice | louse—lice* | child—children | ox—oxen |
| foot—feet | tooth—teeth | man—men | woman—women |

*A louse is an insect that gets in your hair and makes you scratch your head. You never get only one.*

My **tooth** hurts. My **teeth** hurt.

A **louse** is a parasite. **Lice** are parasites.

─────── **NOTE** ───────
Compound words, such as football and toothbrush, form their plurals according to the rules. Add *-s* and *-es*.

All five **toothbrushes** have the same shape.

The team had to buy new **footballs**.

The following words, however, always indicate a plural concept and require a plural verb:

scissors        glasses (eye)

pants           both

many            people

several

The *scissors* on the table <u>are</u> mine.

Many *people* <u>attend</u> the concerts every week.

However, if *a pair of* precedes scissors, pants, and glasses, use a singular verb.

That *pair of pants* on the bed <u>needs</u> pressing.

An extra *pair of glasses* <u>is</u> helpful in an emergency

*Every* and *any* and their forms (*everyone*, *everything*, etc.) and *each* are always singular and take a singular verb and singular possessive adjectives.

Every student *has his/her* book.

Each of the boys *is* presenting *his* own work.

# PROBLEMS WITH PREPOSITIONAL PHRASES

Prepositional phrases are *not* subjects, so when you have a word group that includes a prepositional phrase other than those mentioned below, look at the noun *before* the phrase to determine whether the verb will be singular or plural.

The *size* ~~of the shoes~~ *makes* a difference in the comfort factor.

His *ability* <u>to speak three languages</u> *increases* his chances of getting the job.

When no prepositional phrase follows *some*, then the word is plural and requires a plural verb.

Many of the graduates are going to college. ***Some plan*** to study medicine.

However, when a prepositional phrase follows the word *some*, it is the object of the preposition; the number of the object determines whether the verb is singular or plural.

I hope that ***some of the dessert*** <u>is</u> still left for me.

***Some of the girls*** <u>are</u> planning a picnic.

Whether *either* and *neither* are singular or plural depends on how they are used in the sentence. When *either . . . or* and *neither . . . nor* are used together, whatever follows *or* and *nor* determines the number of the verb.

<u>Neither</u> **Sid** <u>nor</u> **his buddies** <u>live</u> in a fraternity.

(*His buddies* follows *nor* and is plural; therefore, the plural form of the verb is required.)

<u>Either</u> **Sue's sisters** <u>or</u> **she** <u>is planning</u> to work this week.

(*She* follows *or* and is singular; singular is required.)

--- **NOTE** ---
When a prepositional phrase follows *either* or *neither*, the verb is always singular. Remember that prepositional phrases cannot be subjects.

<u>Either</u> of the girls <u>is</u> capable of doing the job.

<u>Neither</u> of the musicians <u>has</u> the equipment necessary for the type of presentation we are planning.

Expressions like *along with*, *accompanied by*, *together with*, and *as well as* should be treated as if they were prepositional phrases.

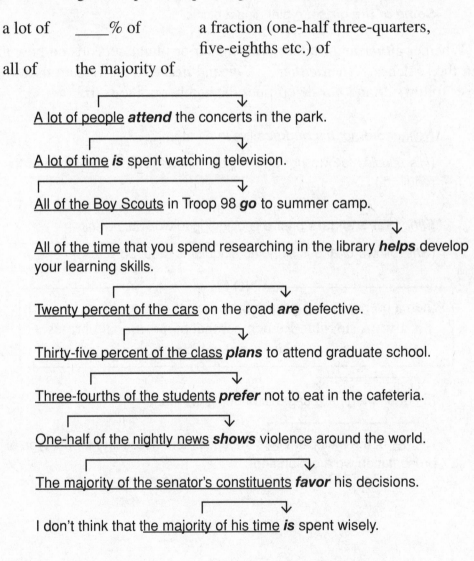

**The waiter**, *as well as the customers*, **is** responsible for being honest.

**The students**, *accompanied by their teacher*, **are** going to Atlanta for the speech contest.

Although objects of prepositions cannot be subjects, in a few exceptional cases they can determine whether the verb will be singular or plural. The following phrases can be singular or plural depending on the word that follows them:

a lot of        ____% of        a fraction (one-half three-quarters,
                                 five-eighths etc.) of
all of        the majority of

A lot of people **attend** the concerts in the park.

A lot of time **is** spent watching television.

All of the Boy Scouts in Troop 98 **go** to summer camp.

All of the time that you spend researching in the library **helps** develop your learning skills.

Twenty percent of the cars on the road **are** defective.

Thirty-five percent of the class **plans** to attend graduate school.

Three-fourths of the students **prefer** not to eat in the cafeteria.

One-half of the nightly news **shows** violence around the world.

The majority of the senator's constituents **favor** his decisions.

I don't think that the majority of his time **is** spent wisely.

The expression *a number of* is always followed by a plural verb.

A number of women **are wearing** long dresses.

However, the expression *the number of* requires a singular verb.

The number of days until graduation **is dwindling**.

When using the *-ing* form of the verb (gerund) as the subject, always use the singular form of the verb.

**Jogging is** good exercise.

**Reading** adventure novels **pleases** Jack.

Subjects of the expressions using [*there* or *here* + a form of the verb *be*] always follow the verb. Find the subject first, and then determine whether the verb should be singular or plural.

**There were** a pen, two books, and a notebook on the table.

**There is** a list of topics at the end of the chapter.

**Here are** the books that you ordered.

**Here is** the money that they owe you.

The word *one* always requires a singular verb.

Two of the employees are on vacation; **one is** in Tahiti; the other is in Rome.

**One** of the bottles on the table **contains** vinegar.

## EXERCISE 127

In this exercise, circle the correct form of the verb for each sentence.

### Feeding the Birds

Many people [pass (1) passes] through Memorial Park every day.
Everybody [talk (2) talks] to Mr. Parsons, an old man who [sit (3) sits] on a
park bench and [feed (4) feeds] the birds. They [fly (5) flies] near and
[peck (6) pecks] at the bread that he [throw (7) throws] to them. The
majority of the people who [come (8) comes] here [know (9) knows]
Mr. Parsons. Today a pair of beautiful blue jays [approach (10) approaches]
and he [give (11) gives] them some wild-bird seed from his hand. A local
journalist [see (12) sees] the kind old man and [decide (13) decides] to talk
with him. He says, "The news [is (14) are] not always good, but some
[has (15) have] more appeal than others." Neither the man nor the journalist
[speak (16) speaks] for a while. A little boy, accompanied by his sisters,
[ride (17) rides] by and [say (18) says] hello. The number of people passing
by to talk with Mr. Parsons [is (19) are] increasing, so the journalist
[take (20) takes] his notebook to interview someone else.

## EXERCISE 128

Circle the correct form of each of verb.

1. The color of those pants (clash, clashes) with that of your blouse.

2. Arthritis (is, are) a serious disease.

3. Every person in this room (has, have) a ticket for the door prize.

4. Neither Christie nor her sisters ever (walk, walks) to school.

5. Some of the flowers (is, are) wilted.

6. The students, accompanied by their parents, (is, are) leaving for a field trip.

7. A number of similar types of plant (grow, grows) well in this climate.

8. Many of the graduates already (has, have) summer jobs.

9. Either the manager or his secretary (distribute, distributes) the employees' paychecks.

10. This dictionary, as well as those travel books, (is, are) on sale this week.

11. A lot of new students (come, comes) to class expecting a great deal of homework.

12. Sixty percent of the foods that we eat (contain, contains) preservatives.

13. The number of days in the billing period (is, are) only 20.

14. Two-thirds of the corn crop (was, were) saved after the drought.

15. (Was, Were) either of you in the building at the time that the alarm sounded?

16. Nobody (look, looks) at bacteria with the naked eye.

17. Neither the investigators nor the scientist (offer, offers) a satisfactory explanation for that occurrence.

18. The majority of the news reports (say, says) that the crash was due to engine failure.

19. One of the machines (break, breaks) down at least once a month.

20. Neither professionals nor amateurs (photograph, photographs) without checking the lens first.

## EXERCISE 129

Fill in each blank with the correct form of the verb.

1. Neither the boys nor their coach _____has_____ (have) seen the captain of the team.

2. A large number of fish _____ (be) swimming down the river.

3. No one _____ (like) to write such long assignments.

4. Either of them _____ (be) a worthy candidate for the award.

5. These scissors _____ (need) to be sharpened.

6. There _____ (be) several books on the desk.

7. The planning committee _____ (want) to adopt the new measures very soon.

8. Reading horror stories _____ (frighten) many people.

9. The Navy _____ (train) many new sailors every year.

10. Every athlete _____ (excel) in one sport or another.

11. Mathematics _____ (require) a lot of time and practice.

12. My teeth _____ (hurt) since I had surgery.

13. Every day _____ (seem) like an eternity since you went to Atlanta.

14. Many people _____ (spend) too much money on junk foods.

15. A pair of new glasses _____ (cost) about $80.

16. Each of the gifts _____ (represent) a symbol of my love.

17. Some of the money _____ (go) for living expenses.

18. Many of the problems _____ (solve) themselves after you learn more about computers.

19. Neither Sandy nor her brothers _____ (drive) to school.

20. Forty percent of all accidents _____ (occur) close to home.

# ACTIVE AND PASSIVE VOICE

Verbs in English can be in either the active or the passive voice, depending on how the writer chooses to present the action. In the active voice, *the subject performs* the action, whether it is past, present, or future. The following sentences show a variety of tenses.

The sun *is shining*.

The child *ran* after the ball.

We *will be visiting* our relatives in Ohio.

Has Joel **received** his package yet?

If we hurry, we **can see** the parade.

In all of the above, the subject performed the action. Here it was important to know who was responsible for the action.

However, in the **passive voice**, the subject does not perform the action but rather receives it. Basically, the passive emphasizes the action itself, rather than the performer of that action. In most cases the performer, known as the agent, is either unimportant or unknown.

The magnificent Taj Mahal *was built* in 1646 A.D.

Do we know who the architect was? No. Does it matter? No.

Active: subject + verb + direct object

Shakespeare wrote *Romeo and Juliet*.

Passive: subject + verb + *BY* + agent
(*BE* + past participle)

*Romeo and Juliet* was written by Shakespeare.

Notice how the subject of the active voice became the agent of the passive voice, and how the direct object of the active voice became the subject of the passive voice. In changing from active to passive, follow the same pattern. Often we are interested in only the year and the purpose and not in the person who performed the action. The following are common constructions using the passive voice.

| | | |
|---|---|---|
| book | was written (by) | in |
| painting | was painted (by) | in |
| organization | was founded (by) | in |
| candidate | was elected (by) | in |
| land, technique | was discovered (by) | in |

*Utopia* **was written** in 1516.

*La Primavera* **was painted** by Botticelli in 1478.

The American Red Cross **was founded** in 1881.

George W. Bush **was elected** president in 2000 and **was re-elected** in 2004.

The printing press **was invented** in 1450.

Notice the elements necessary for this kind of construction.

subject + **BE** + past participle + (**BY** + agent)

The last element is in parentheses because there may not always be an agent (the one responsible for the action) expressed.

**America was discovered in 1492**. (no agent indicated)

**America was discovered by Christopher Columbus in 1492**. (Here the agent is mentioned.)

Only transitive verbs can be used with the passive voice. A form of the verb (**be** + the past participle) must accompany each verb, regardless of the tense.

Your application *is being processed* right now.

The flag *is raised* over the Capitol every morning.

Our new governor *will be inaugurated* next Monday.

The committee *has been appointed* by the chairman.

Amy's house *had been built* before the oil crisis.

When the auxiliaries *must*, *can*, and *may* are used, the passive voice is formed with **be** plus the past participle of the main verb.

```
MUST        ⎤
CAN (COULD) ⎬ + BE +   past
MAY (MIGHT) ⎦          participle
```

The letter *must be typed* this afternoon.

Your loan *can be approved* quickly if you have a good credit rating.

We *may be invited* to a wedding next month.

Look at how the active and passive voice are contrasted. Both of them say basically the same thing, but grammatically they are different.

| Active Voice | Passive Voice |
|---|---|
| The teacher *rings* the bell. | The bell *is rung* by the teacher. |
| The teacher *is ringing* the bell. | The bell *is being rung* by the teacher. |
| The teacher *rang* the bell. | The bell *was rung* by the teacher. |
| The teacher *had rung* the bell. | The bell *had been rung* by the teacher. |
| The teacher *will ring* the bell. | The bell *will be rung* by the teacher. |

## EXERCISE 130

Change each sentence from the active voice to the passive. If the subject is in parentheses, eliminate it in the passive.

**Example:** The teacher rang the bell.

The bell **_was rung_** by the teacher.

(The director) called the meeting to order.

The meeting **_was called_** to order by the director.

1. (Arthur Miller) wrote *Death of a Salesman* in 1949.

   _____

2. The attacking troops captured the fort.

   _____

3. Thomas Jefferson designed Monticello.

   _____

4. (Many people) signed the Declaration of Independence in Philadelphia.

   _____

5. (The weatherman) is predicting rain for tomorrow.

   _____

6. The forest fire destroyed most of the prairie.

   _____

7. The lumberjacks will cut down many trees in order to build 12 new houses.

   _____

8. The altar server lit the candles before the ceremony had begun.

   _____

9. (Everyone) sang songs after the discussion.

_____

10. Thousands of viewers watched the final episode of the program.

_____

11. (No one) knows the author's name.

_____

12. Mel Gibson directed *Passion*.

_____

13. (The government) signed the treaty in 1863.

_____

14. (The police) issued 500 speeding tickets yesterday.

_____

15. (They) will close the Stock Market on July 4.

_____

16. Channel 5 will feature a program on Spain on Wednesday.

_____

17. The committee has made plans for a celebration.

_____

18. (The group) had torn down the old church before 1875.

_____

## EXERCISE 131

Change each sentence from passive to active voice. If no agent is given, then invent someone responsible for the action.

**Examples:** A bill requiring everyone to use seat belts will be signed by the governor.
*The governor will sign* a bill requiring everyone to use seat belts.

The medication was prescribed by the doctor.
*The doctor prescribed* the medication.

Federal employees were evacuated from the buildings during the riots.
*The police evacuated* federal employees from the buildings during the riots.

1. A new car was ordered by the salesman.

2. The water was analyzed by the technician to see whether it was polluted.

3. Your package is being sent air freight.

4. The national anthem will be sung before the soccer match.

5. Frank's house is being painted this week.

6. The fish are being caught in large numbers.

7. Much treasure from the sunken ship *The Atocha* has been discovered by Mel Fisher.

8. My favorite song was played by the orchestra.

9. St. Augustine was occupied by the French at one time.

10. Nancy's dress had been bought in Atlanta two weeks before the wedding.

## EXERCISE 132: WRITING

Because the agent or person responsible for each of these actions is mentioned, it would have been better to write the whole paragraph in the active voice. Rewrite this so that all the verbs are in the active voice.

### Beautiful Hawaii

The planeload of tourists was flown out of Los Angeles toward Hawaii by the pilot. A wonderful meal was served on board by the flight crew. The beautiful scenery en route to the island paradise was enjoyed by the passengers. Upon arrival, the tourists were greeted by native women wearing grass skirts. They were swaying to Hawaiian melodies of the traditional music that was played on ukuleles by local musicians. These musical instruments are considered by many to be native to the islands. Each of the tourists was given a colorful lei of tiny orchids by one of the lovely women. The visitors were warmly received by the citizens of this Pacific island.

## EXERCISE 133: WRITING

Read the following paragraph and change the sentences from passive voice to active voice. Rewrite the whole paragraph.

### Stonehenge

Stonehenge, a megalithic structure located in England, was built by an agricultural tribe of sun worshipers in 2750 B.C. A number of theories about the purpose of such a structure have been proposed about the mystery of Stonehenge. The most accepted theory regarding its significance was devised in 1963 by a British astronomer, Gerald S. Hawkins. It was believed that Stonehenge was a giant stone calendar and observatory. The point at which the sun rose during the midsummer solstice was marked by "heel stones" in the center of the complex. According to anthropologists, religious rites dating back to the time of Atlantis were performed by a religious sect called Druids. It was discovered by scientists, however, that historically and chronologically the Druids and Stonehenge were from different eras.

Most writing will be in the active voice rather than in the passive. However, if you are writing a lot about historical events or scientific accounts, you will find that the passive is preferred, mainly because those responsible for the action are unknown or else unimportant. These written accounts are usually less forceful than those described in the active voice.

# SUBJUNCTIVE

In English there are three moods or ways to express the action of the verbs, a writer or speaker uses. They are **indicative** (all of the tenses already studied in this unit) which indicates the real world, that which is happening, has happened, or will happen. The **imperative** or commands in which the speaker orders someone to do or not to do something. The **subjunctive** represents the unreal, contrary to fact, or form whereby the speaker wants someone else to do something. The **subjunctive** is not used as often as the other two moods in English. Sentences using the subjunctive *always* contain two clauses, one main and one dependent, two different subjects, and the conjunction ***that***.

$$S_1 + V_1 + \textbf{\textit{THAT}} + S_2 + V_2 \text{ (subjunctive)}$$
$$\text{(main clause)} \qquad \text{(dependent clause)}$$

The verb in the subjunctive is always the simple form, one that *does not* show time or agreement. There is no sequence of tenses between the main clause and the dependent clause.

The doctor ***suggests*** that I ***take*** vitamins.    (that he/she/we/you ***take*** . . . )

The doctor ***suggested*** that I ***take*** vitamins.    (that he/she/we/you ***take*** . . . )

The doctor ***will suggest*** that I ***take*** vitamins.    (that he/she/we/you ***take*** . . . )

The main clause is always the first of the two and must contain one of the following verbs:

| | | | |
|---|---|---|---|
| advise | demand | prefer | require |
| ask | insist | recommend | suggest |
| command | order | request | urge |

The general **commanded** that his troops **stand** at attention.

Mother **will insist** that we not **go** camping this weekend.

The nutritionist **prefers** that Abdul **drink** eight glasses of water each day.

Rather than use the subjunctive, many people prefer to eliminate the conjunction *that* and use an indirect object and the infinitive. It is understood that the indirect object will be responsible for performing the action of the infinitive.

> subject + verb + indirect object + infinitive

The university **requires us to take** four math courses.

The police **ordered the demonstrators to leave** at once.

The director **will request all musicians to arrive** early.

I **urge them to stay** another week or two.

A number of impersonal expressions (*it* + *be* + **adjective**) can be used in the main clause with the subjunctive in the dependent clause. Again, the main verb (be) can be in any tense and there is no sequence of tenses.

> *IT* + verb **BE** + adjective + **THAT** + $S_2$ + $V_2$ (subjunctive)

The following adjectives can be used in the impersonal expressions:

| | | |
|---|---|---|
| advised | mandatory | recommended |
| better | necessary | required |
| desirable | obligatory | suggested |
| imperative | preferable | urged |
| important | proposed | urgent |

It **was advised that** all residents **leave** the storm area.

It **is better that** the professor not **discuss** his controversial theory in class.

It **will be preferable that** tourists not **drive** through the jungle.

It **is obligatory that** Marta **pay** her fees at once.

If the *it* phrase is replaced by a person responsible for the action, then the infinitive is used with these adjectives:

advised          recommended          required          urged

This is the new sentence pattern:

> S (person) + verb **BE** + adjective + infinitive

You **were advised to register** immediately.

We **are required to wear** a shirt and shoes in there.

Esther **will be urged to study** economics this year.

Another way to get around using the subjunctive is to eliminate the change of subject and the conjunction *that* and use the infinitive.

> **IT** + verb **BE** + adjective + infinitive

It **will be imperative to study** every night.

It **is obligatory to pay** taxes every year.

It **was urgent to discuss** your medical problem immediately.

It **is better to wait** for a lower interest rate.

## EXERCISE 134

Write either the subjunctive or the infinitive form of the verb.

1. Anissa asked her brothers not _____ (tease) her so much.

2. The dean requests that you _____ (see) him this afternoon.

3. I demand that they _____ (apologize) immediately.

4. The teacher will recommend that we _____ (take) the exam on Friday.

5. It was necessary _____ (write) to the admissions office.

6. It is imperative that Saud _____ (drive) to class.

7. It is better _____ (eat) three good meals every day.

8. We urged them _____ (visit) the museum this week.

9. My parents insisted that I _____ (live) close to campus.

10. You are requested _____ (appear) at graduation ceremonies.

11. Dana was advised _____ (be) cautious on her trip abroad.

12. You will be urged _____ (accept) the new position.

13. It will be desirable that the Murphy family _____ (move) to a larger house.

14. I was advised _____ (give) up smoking for my health.

15. Mandy required us _____ (arrive) no later than 8 p.m.

16. It is preferable _____ (study) in the library rather than in the cafeteria.

17. It will be important _____ (pay) this bill on time.

18. The old man ordered the reporters _____ (get) off his property before he called the police.

19. Rowena insisted that her boyfriend _____ (dance) only with her.

20. Peter preferred that his friends _____ (swim) in the pool, not in the lake.

Another example of using the subjunctive relates to unreal situations and has the verb *wish* in the main clause. If the situation were real, you would not wish for a change. The conjunction *that* is often omitted in spoken English. The subjunctive here looks like the past tense that you studied before. It really is a form of the subjunctive. The only form of the verb *be* for present wishes is *were*. The pattern for this use of the subjunctive and a wish in the present is as follows:

$S_1$ + **WISH** + **THAT** + $S_2$ + past tense

Tim is in California. I **wish** that he **were** here.

Today is Thursday. The children **wish** that it **were** Saturday.

I don't have time. I **wish** that *I* **had** time.

We can't go surfing. We **wish** that we **could go surfing**.

It is possible to have the same subject for both the main and the dependent clauses.

A wish in the past requires sequence of tenses. It also looks at an unreal situation related either to now or to the past. Follow this pattern:

S + **WISH** {present / past} + **THAT** + **HAD** + past participle

Present wishes related to past actions:

Our friends decided not to visit this week.

We **wish** (now) that they **had visited** us.

The weather was hot and dry all last week.

I **wish** (now) that it **had rained** a little.

The boys went to camp last summer.

Their mother **wishes** (now) that they **hadn't gone** to camp.

Past wishes related to past actions:

Joan didn't study Spanish in college.

After Sally had moved to Mexico, she **wished** that she **had studied** Spanish.

In 1982 my son bought a convertible.

Later he **wished** he **had bought** a practical car.

The Johnsons wanted a lovely house in the valley.

They **wished** that it **hadn't been** so expensive.

## EXERCISE 135

Change each of the following wishes from the present to past. Use a past expression, and then rewrite the whole sentence.

**Example:** We wish you **had** more time to visit.
We wish you **had had** more time last week.

1. I wish that I were going to Switzerland.

2. The students wish that they had more time to study.

3. Nancy wishes that she could cook like her grandmother.

4. We wish Tim were here for the party.

5. They wish that they didn't have to take so many math classes.

6. You wish that we could get together more often.

7. I wish it weren't snowing so hard.

8. We wish that this bus driver didn't have to make so many stops.

9. Margie wishes that she could type faster.

10. My parents wish that someone would buy their house.

## EXERCISE 136: WRITING

Imagine that you have just found an old oil lamp. As you rub off some of the dust, a genie appears and tells you that he will grant 10 wishes that you can make for your friends. Using 10 different verbs, wish something different (past or present) for each of your friends.

## EXERCISE 137

Fill in the correct form of the verb, using the clues.

1. I wish that I _____ (buy) the coat when it was on sale.

2. Dave wishes that he _____ (*negative for* drive) so fast, because he got a ticket.

3. Harry arrived late for the interview and wished that he _____ (got) up earlier.

4. The traffic is terrible right now, and we wish that we _____ (take) another route.

5. John wishes that he _____ (have) the money for some lottery tickets because the jackpot is $20 million.

6. I wish I _____ (know) how to repair cars because mine is always having problems.

7. Jake wishes that he _____ (*negative for* drink) so much at the party last night, because he has a hangover this morning.

8. My mother wishes that the breeze _____ (dry) her clothes in a hurry so that she could get them in before it rains.

9. Elizabeth wishes she _____ (*negative for* be) sick last week because she has so much work to do now to catch up.

10. I wish that I _____ (read) as fast as you so that I could finish this novel tonight.

## EXERCISE 138: WRITING

Melanie and her roommate went to a special birthday party last night, but everything seemed to go wrong for them. Rewrite the paragraph, retelling what they wish had or had not happened.

Solange had to work late. I had to wait for her to shower and dress. We arrived late at the party and missed a lot of the fun. Johnny Durango, a hot new local singer, sang a couple of songs, but we didn't hear him. There had been a lot of great food, but we ate only the leftovers. Pete Sinclair, a handsome guy in my biology class, wouldn't dance with me. I was too shy to ask him to dance. Solange drank too much, and she got sick at the party. She lost her keys, so Tom offered to drive us home. He's such a bore! Solange went to bed at 11, and I watched television. I should have stayed home that night!

# SAY AND TELL

Although both *say* and *tell* mean basically the same thing, they cannot be used interchangeably.

*Say* is used when the word *that* introduces a subordinate clause.

> subject + **SAY** + **THAT** + subject + verb + complement
> (subordinate clause)

The new president **said that** he would not raise taxes.

Paul **said that** he had visited Canada every summer for ten years.

*Say* is used with direct speech—that is, when the words of the speaker are repeated exactly as he said them.

> subject + **SAY**, + "subject + verb + complement"

Ted *said*, "I have finished my work, and I'm going home."

Our guest speaker *will say*, "Now is the time for action."

Say is *never* followed by *to* and an indirect object.

Tony says that he will take a geology course next semester.

Fred said that he had talked with his boss about the raise.

*Tell* is usually followed by an indirect object (the person to whom the words are spoken), *that*, and the subordinate clause.

> subject + **TELL** + indirect object + **THAT** + subject + verb + complement
> (subordinate clause)

Sandra *told her sisters* (indirect object) *that* the party was to be a surprise.

Betty *told us* (indirect object) *that* the class had been canceled.

*Tell* is never used with direct quotations.

*Tell* is used with certain words and phrases in idiomatic expressions.

### Tell . . .

| | | |
|---|---|---|
| time | a joke | someone off (reprimand) |
| the truth | a story | two things apart (distinguish) |
| a lie | a secret | on someone (report secrets) |

Someone *told the secret*, and now everyone knows.

Children usually learn to *tell time* in the second grade.

The judge told the witness to *tell the truth.*

The boys *told a lie* after they had broken the window.

When comedians *tell a joke*, everyone usually laughs.

Mrs. Rosman *told* her kindergarten class a funny *story.*

Tom was so angry that he *told* his boss *off*.

# SEQUENCE OF TENSES

The time relationship that exists between two verbs in a sentence is called sequence of tenses. The verbs *say* and *tell* most commonly deal with this relationship, because they concern themselves with relating past, present, and future events. Observe the following rules for selecting the correct verb tenses:

| Verb in the main clause | Verb in the subordinate clause |
| --- | --- |
| present | present<br>present progressive<br>present perfect<br>future |
| past | past<br>past progressive<br>past perfect<br>conditional |

*Say*

Joe *says* that he *plays* tennis every day.

Joe *says* that he *is playing* tennis now.

Joe *says* that he *has played* in a number of tournaments.

Joe *says* that he *will play* at Wimbledon next year.

Phyllis *said* that she *drank* a cup of coffee for lunch every day.

Phyllis *said* that she *was drinking* a cup of coffee when the doorbell rang.

Phyllis *said* that she *had drunk* some coffee in the cafeteria before coming to class.

Phyllis *said* that she *would drink* a lot of coffee while studying for her exams.

*Tell*

Joe *tells* us that he *plays* tennis every day.

Joe *tells* us that he *is playing* tennis now.

Joe *tells* us that he *has played* in many tournaments.

Joe *tells* us that he *will play* at Wimbledon next year.

Phyllis *told* him that she *drank* a cup of coffee for lunch every day.

Phyllis *told* him that she *was drinking* a cup of coffee when the doorbell rang.

Phyllis *told* him that she *had drunk* some coffee in the cafeteria before coming to class.

Phyllis *told* him that she *would drink* a lot of coffee while studying for her exams.

## EXERCISE 139

Circle the correct form.

1. Todd (said, told) us that he was planning a hunting trip.

2. "Supper is ready," (said, told) the hostess.

3. Barry (says, tells) that there is a good movie on television tonight.

4. When did the photographer (say, tell) you that the photographs would be ready?

5. Lecturers usually (say, tell) a story before they begin to speak.

6. The witness has (said, told) the truth about the accident.

7. "Don't point your finger at me," (said, told) Helen.

8. Can anyone (say, tell) me what happened last night?

9. Mrs. Mullens is (saying, telling) her grandson about her life as a child.

10. Nobody has (said, told) anyone the details of the proposed trip.

## EXERCISE 140

Decide whether each sentence requires *say* or *tell*. Make your verb choice agree with the tense of the other verbs used.

1. The children in the first grade were learning _____ time.

2. Tony always _____ that he will arrive on time, but he never does.

3. Nothing Sheila ever _____ made any sense until recently.

4. Last week Dick _____ his students that they would have to write a term paper this semester.

5. Andy _____, "It is certainly a lovely day for a picnic."

6. The government won't _____ us anything more about the project.

7. How long will it be before the interviewer _____ us the results?

8. Did Carl _____ you that he was going to buy a boat?

9. Ed _____ that he plans to go fishing this weekend.

10. The girls _____ that their exhibit is better than the boys'.

In going from direct to indirect speech, many changes take place. The quotation marks are eliminated. The word **that** is used. The verb in the quotation usually changes tense to agree with the verb in the main clause. Pronouns also change in the indirect speech. Observe these pronoun changes:

| Direct speech | Indirect speech |
|---|---|
| I | → he/she |
| you | → I/they/we |
| him/her | → him/her |
| we | → we/they |
| me | → him/her |
| your (adj.) | → my (adj.) |

The boss says, "I want everyone here at 8:00 sharp."
The boss says that he wants everyone here at 8:00 sharp.

My mother said, "You need to wear your coat."
My mother said that I needed to wear my coat.

Our mother said, "You need to wear your coats."
Our mother said that we needed to wear our coats.

The verb in the subordinate clause, too, will differ according to whether the verb is in a quotation or in indirect speech.

The examples below demonstrate how using indirect speech affects the tense of the subordinate verb. The first three pairs use present-tense main (or speaking) verbs, and the rest use past-tense main verbs. (The words in parentheses are the names of the tenses of the subordinate verbs, which are underscored.)

Olga always says, "I have to study in the library." (present)

Olga always says that she has to study in the library. (present)

Pedro says, "I will be home late tonight." (future)

Pedro says that he will be home late tonight. (future)

Dio says to the class, "Study the irregular verbs." (command)

Dio tells the class to study the irregular verbs. (infinitive)

Beverly said, "I am learning to play the guitar." (present progressive)

Beverly said that she was learning to play the guitar. (past progressive)

Dolly said, "I will bake a cake for the party." (future)

Dolly said that she would bake a cake for the party. (conditional)

Silvano said, "We have investigated the matter thoroughly." (present perfect)

Silvano said that they had investigated the matter thoroughly. (past perfect)

Pavel said, "You owe me twenty five dollars for the painting." (present)

Pavel said that I owed him $25 for the painting. (past)

The doctor said to the patient, "You can play tennis again if you are careful." (present)

The doctor told his patient that she could play tennis again if she was more careful. (conditional)

Marvin said, "We have a chemistry test today." (present)

Marvin said that we had a chemistry test today. (past)

Eleanora said, "I <u>read</u> that book last year." (past)

Eleanora said that she <u>had read</u> that book last year. (past perfect)

Jane said, "<u>Write</u> your name on your time sheet and <u>turn</u> it in." (command)

Jane said <u>to write</u> my name on the time sheet and <u>hand</u> it in. (infinitive)

---

**NOTE**

When you use verbs requesting information (ask, inquire), the pattern for indirect speech usually uses *whether* or *if* instead of *that*. The yes/no questions now become embedded in the sentence. Do not use a question mark unless the whole sentence is a question. The word order for the embedded question also changes.

---

Direct speech:

> Normal question: auxiliary + S + V

We asked, "***Will there be*** enough snow on the mountains for skiing?"

Ponce is asking the travel agent, "***Will we make*** a stopover in Madeira?"

Indirect speech:

> Embedded question: ***WHETHER/IF*** + S + V

We asked ***whether (if) there would be*** enough snow on the mountains for skiing.

Ponce is asking the travel agent ***if (whether) we will make*** a stopover in Madeira.

The following sentences are questions and require the use of a question mark. Notice the embedded question.

Are you sure that Daddy will ask me ***what I want for my birthday***?

Did he say ***when Glen would arrive***?

Has anyone told you ***where the party will be***?

Didn't we tell him ***how he had to dress for the interview***?

---

**NOTE**

Often in spoken English and sometimes in written form,
*that* is omitted with *say* constructions.

She says (*that*) he is here. I can feel his presence.

Henry said (*that*) you would be happy to see us.

When you see two clauses like these joined without a conjunction, mentally insert *that* for indirect speech.

## EXERCISE 141: WRITING

Rewrite these sentences, changing from direct speech to indirect speech. Refer to the table on page 280 if you are having problems deciding on the correct form. Make any necessary changes as well.

**Example:** Hank said, "I *will see* you on Friday."
Hank said that he *would see* me on Friday.

1. Helen asked, "Where is he going at this hour?"

2. The project director said, "We will raise enough money to finish construction of the new recreation center."

3. Dr. Jansen said, "Your case is unusual."

4. No one moved when the president said, "I am resigning my office."

5. Yolanda inquired, "What kind of job is it?"

6. Columbo said, "I wonder where the murder weapon is."

7. In tomorrow's speech, the ambassador will say, "We need to negotiate this treaty."

8. Danny asked his teacher, "When will the exam be?"

9. Mark Antony said, "I have come to bury Caesar, not to praise him."

10. "Does Harlan know how to fill in these tax forms?" asked Saundra.

11. "What can we do to improve the park?" asked the mayor.

12. The strikers said, "We will not return until working conditions improve."

13. "How silly Debra looks in that dress!" said the old lady.

14. "There's nothing left for us to do," said the unhappy flood victims.

15. Flora insisted by saying, "I will discuss this matter with your supervisor immediately."

16. Milo always says, "Nobody understands me."

17. The policeman said, "I'm afraid I will have to give you a ticket for speeding."

## EXERCISE 142

If an indirect object is indicated in parentheses, change the verb to *tell* and incorporate the indirect object into the sentence.

**Example:** Solange said, "I will be returning to my country next month." (classmates)
Solange told her classmates that she would be returning to her country next month.

1. Jane said, "I plan on attending the meeting?" (me)

2. A famous American patriot said, "Don't fire until you see the whites of their eyes." (his soldiers)

3. The customs inspector said, "Open that large suitcase." (us)

4. The boss replied, "If you work very hard, you will be promoted soon." (Thomas)

5. The witness replied, "I have nothing more to say." (judge)

6. Trudy is saying, "The judges' decision will be final." (contestants)

7. The restaurant manager said, "I am sorry that you did not enjoy your veal cutlet." (customer)

8. Kerry said, "The company has to concentrate on finding a solution to the problem." (a group of physicists)

## EXERCISE 143: WRITING

Change the following paragraph to indirect speech. Make any necessary tense and pronoun changes. Change *said* to *told* if followed by *to* + indirect object.

Yesterday Carlos and I went to visit some friends of ours. While we were there, our host said, "I want to make an addition to my house, and I am looking for someone to help me with the project." Carlos replied, "I am interested in your project, and will gladly help you with it."

After hearing that, our host said to Carlos, "I will show you exactly what I plan to do, and you can give me some suggestions on how to do it."

While the men were looking at the house, our hostess took me into their greenhouse and showed me her lovely collection of plants. She said to me, "This is the first year that all of my plants have bloomed." I then asked her, "Doesn't the cold bother them?" She replied, "I had a small gas heater installed to use on cold nights."

We all went inside to discuss plans for the new project.

## EXERCISE 144

Circle the correct answer.

1. The painter (said, told) my mother that he would paint the door green.

2. Victor (said, told) that he had already given his brother the keys to the car.

3. The mailman (said, told) us not to put big packages in the box.

4. Jose's coach called and (said, told) him that the baseball game had been canceled.

5. Pasquale (said, told) his daughter a secret that she kept for ten years.

6. Jody (said, told), "I have a dental appointment in one hour."

7. The Spanish teacher can't (say, tell) a joke in English.

8. The tourist (said, told) a lie that the customs official detected at once.

9. Many little children can't (say, tell) time.

10. The lecturer (said, told) that a slide presentation would follow is talk.

11. Cory (said, told) us a true story about one of his expeditions to Guatemala.

12. Bridget (said, told) the truth despite the consequences.

13. Now Rufus (says, tells) that he wants to go to the movies.

14. The anthropologist always (says, tells) his audience a joke before beginning his lecture.

15. Someone (said, told) me that we would be moving to another office soon.

16. Randy (said, told) that he was out of breath because he had run so fast.

17. Allison (said, told), "I wish I had my own telephone."

18. Bruce's parents (said, told) that they were very pleased with their son's grades.

19. Liana (said, told) that her daughter was getting a doll for Christmas.

20. Michael's uncle (said, told) him that he would help him buy a car.

## EXERCISE 145: WRITING

Change each sentence to a direct statement. Remember the rules for sequence of tenses.

**Example:** Glen told his friends that he was having a party on Saturday night.
**Answer:** Glen *said*, "I *am having* a party on Saturday night."

1. The professor told Tom that the class would meet at 11.

2. My friend said that they were going to Europe for the spring.

3. John said that he always felt better in the morning.

4. Mary said that she was going to the dance tonight.

5. The secretary told Mr. Jones that she remembered mailing the letter.

6. Frank's daughter told him that her friend had graduated with honors.

7. The doctor told the nurse that he needed her help.

8. John asked where we had gone on our vacation last month.

9. The lawyer asked where the courthouse was.

10. The students asked when the class would begin.

## EXERCISE 146: WRITING

Change each sentence to indirect speech.

**Example:** The teacher said, "Class, there will be an exam next Wednesday."
**Answer:** The teacher *told the class* that there *would be* an exam on Wednesday.

1. Our neighbors said, "We are going to buy a new car."

2. The politician said, "Poverty will be abolished."

3. The professor said, "The students are all present."

4. The lawyer says to Mr. Green, "I think I can help you."

5. The senator will say to his constituents, "I am interested in conservation."

6. The guest said to the hostess, "Your dinner is delicious."

7. The coach said to the players, "You have to practice more."

8. Mary asked John, "Do you enjoy classical music?"

9. The waitress asked me, "Are you ready to order?"

10. The diplomat asked, "Has the meeting begun yet?"

## EXERCISE 147

Decide which of the underlined items is incorrect.

1. Although the organization be self-sufficient, it is in need of volunteers to help carry out its new projects.

   A. be          B. in need of     C. to help carry    D. its

2. The cause of the airplane crash can have been a malfunctioning right propeller.

   A. The cause    B. can          C. a              D. malfunctioning

3. Having went on a picnic yesterday, we picked wild flowers in the park.

   A. went         B. a            C. picked          D. the

4. It must be raining last night, because there are large puddles around the yard.

   A. be raining    B. there        C. large           D. around the yard

5. The director was depend on his staff to get all the reports to the stockholders before the deadline.

   A. was depend    B. to get       C. to the          D. the
                                       stockholders

6. We heard that our friends won the dean's award for excellence in contributions to the educational program.

   A. that          B. won          C. for             D. to the

7. Marta told <u>her teacher</u> that she <u>already read</u> the <u>assigned</u> book and asked her for another assignment.

    A. her teacher    B. already read    C. assigned    D. another

8. Pete <u>was having</u> the equivalent of a <u>college degree</u> with all his <u>work experience</u> in that field and his on-the-job training.

    A. was having    B. college    C. work    D. on-the-job
                            degree            experience

9. If <u>the</u> musicians <u>wouldn't have played</u> so <u>loudly</u>, the audience would have <u>enjoyed</u> the presentation more.

    A. the    B. wouldn't    C. loudly    D. enjoyed
                    have played

10. When a cat is happy, <u>it</u> will <u>lay</u> down with its front paws tucked <u>under</u> its chest and purr with its eyes <u>closed</u>.

    A. it    B. lay    C. under    D. closed

11. The players try <u>to make</u> as <u>few</u> contact as possible with the <u>opposing</u> team to avoid <u>penalties</u>.

    A. to make    B. few    C. opposing    D. penalties

12. Houses look <u>especially</u> nice <u>when</u> they have been <u>builded</u> at the foot of the mountains or close to a <u>flowing</u> stream or river.

    A. especially    B. when    C. builded    D. flowing

13. Neither the boys nor their soccer coach <u>have</u> seen the captain or the members of the <u>opposing</u> teams <u>since</u> they <u>arrived</u>.

    A. have    B. opposing    C. since    D. arrived

14. Before we can <u>lay out</u> the pattern and <u>cut</u> this material, someone needs <u>sharpen</u> <u>these</u> dull scissors.

    A. lay out    B. cut    C. sharpen    D. these

15. Would Ted have <u>done</u> that if he <u>knew</u> the consequences before he <u>started</u> to campaign <u>for the presidency</u>?

   A. done      B. knew      C. started      D. for the presidency

16. The children promised <u>their</u> parents <u>to not eat</u> the cake while they <u>were gone</u> and wait <u>until after</u> supper.

   A. their      B. to not eat      C. were gone      D. until after

17. Ellen's accustomed <u>to interpret</u> for her foreign students <u>when</u> they <u>have</u> problems <u>understanding</u> the grammar and vocabulary.

   A. to interpret      B. when      C. have      D. understanding

# Test on Verbs

Read the following story about Hans's hospital visit and decide whether the underlined verb is the one that *best* completes the sentence. Some are correct as written. Multiple choice answers follow the story.

### Visiting the Emergency Room

Last week my friend Hans fell while he <u>played</u> soccer and injured his leg.

(2) He was in so much pain that I suggested that he <u>go</u> to the hospital. (3) Hans was afraid that they <u>would keep</u> him there, and because he could not speak the language well, he would not be able to communicate with the doctors and nurses. (4) I assured him that that was not the case, and that he <u>would get</u> very good treatment in the emergency room. (5) Hans wanted <u>to go</u> to the pharmacy to get some painkillers and then to go home and rest. (6) I explained that he could not get painkillers over the counter, and that he <u>needs</u> a doctor's prescription.

(7) When we arrived at the hospital, there were seven people <u>waiting</u> with various problems: large bleeding cut over the eye, a broken arm, food poisoning, and a few other undisclosed medical problems. (8) I <u>tell</u> Hans that he would have to speak to the receptionist first. (9) Finally, an older reassuring woman called his name, and we <u>go</u> up to her desk.

(10) First of all, she asked <u>to see</u> his insurance card and ID. (11) She asked his name, address, and phone number and what <u>is</u> wrong with him. (12) She <u>gives</u> him a four-page questionnaire to fill out.

(13) Hans was upset because he <u>has</u> to answer so many questions. (14) He didn't think that <u>to have</u> chicken pox, mumps, and past operations when he was little made any difference now. (15) He <u>could</u> not understand why they wanted to know about his family's medical history as well. (16) He laughed loudly when he <u>reads</u> the questions "Are you pregnant or do you think you might be pregnant?" "Are you taking any illegal drugs?" (17) He wondered how many people <u>would</u> honestly <u>admit</u> to taking these drugs!!

(18) Hans returned the questionnaire to the receptionist and <u>was waited</u> his turn. (19) Hans <u>becomes</u> upset after waiting for two hours. (20) Finally, he saw the doctor, who <u>says</u> that he was lucky to have only a sprained knee. (21) The doctor gave him an ice pack and some pain pills and told him <u>to keep</u> his leg elevated and to put the ice pack on to reduce the swelling.

(22) Two weeks later Hans <u>will receive</u> a bill from the hospital. (23) He was glad that his insurance <u>paid</u> the $250 and all he had to pay was $30! What an expensive visit and another lesson in American cultural shock!!

1. A. was playing     B. played     C. plays

2. A. goes     B. go     C. went

3. A. would keep     B. will keep     C. were keeping

4. A. will get     B. would get     C. would have gotten

5. A. go     B. to go     C. going

6. A. would need     B. needs     C. was needing

7. A. to wait     B. waiting     C. was waited

8. A. tell           B. was telling        C. told

9. A. go            B. would go         C. went

10. A. to see        B. saw           C. see

11. A. is            B. was          C. had been

12. A. gives       B. gave         C. had given

13. A. has         B. had         C. was having

14. A. to have     B. having       C. had

15. A. can         B. could        C. could have

16. A. reads       B. read         C. will read

17. A. would admit   B. will admit     C. were admitting

18. A. was waited    B. waited       C. waiting

19. A. becomes    B. became      C. will become

20. A. said        B. says         C. had said

21. A. keep        B. keeping      C. to keep

22. A. will receive   B. has received   C. received

23. A. had paid      B. paid         C. will pay

# ESL

## CHAPTER 11

### Test-Taking Techniques

# Chapter 11
# TEST-TAKING TECHNIQUES

Time management is probably the most important thing to consider in preparing for tests. Your review can take place a number of ways: immediate review after class, short daily reviews, and final review. If you review within seven hours of your class, you are more likely to remember the material than if you wait a week or more. Research shows that if you do no review within 24 hours, you could forget as much as 80 percent of what you learned. Ideally you should review all the material for short periods every day in order to keep the ideas fresh in your mind. In addition, try to set up a system of key words that will help you with the different courses you are taking.

You can devise **acronyms**, new words formed by using the first letter of other words, to remember some of the concepts. The following acronyms are used in different classes to help students to remember and to prepare for tests.

ROY G BIV will help in art class to remember the visible color spectrum:

> red, orange, yellow, green, blue, indigo, violet

CHONPS will help in chemistry to remember the gases in the atmosphere:

> carbon, hydrogen, oxygen, nitrogen, phosphorus, sulfur

PIHEC in biology will help with the scientific method:

> state the problem, gather information, create a hypothesis (theory), perform an experiment, draw your conclusion

PEMDAS represents the order for working algebra problems:

> parenthesis, exponents, multiply, divide, add, subtract

IPMAT in biology shows steps to remember in stages of cell division:

> Interphase, prophase, metaphase, anaphase, telophase

FOIL in algebra shows the process of multiplying binomials and trinomials:

> first, outer, inner, last

FACE to remember the notes on a music staff that fall between the lines

WEDDING is a concept used by some Spanish teachers to help students remember which categories of verbs require the subjunctive mood:

> Wishing, Emotion, Doubt, Denial, Impersonal Expressions, Imperative, and Indefinite Antecedents, Negative Antecedents, and Gustar

HOMES helps remember the names of the Great Lakes:

> Huron, Ontario, Michigan, Erie, Superior

Each of the above-mentioned groups spells a word, sometimes a nonexistent word, that will help you remember a concept.

Another memory device is called an **acrostic**. Here sentences are created by making words stand for the first latter of each element you are trying to remember.

KHDODCM is helpful when working with the metric system:

> Kids Have Dropped Over Dead Converting Metrics [Kilometers, Hectares, Decameters, Others (meters, liters, grams), Decimeters, Centimeters, Millimeters]

EGBDF for remembering the notes on the staff lines in music:

> Every Good Boy Does Fine

ARITHMETIC to spell the word correctly, many use this sentence:

> A Rat In Tom's House May Eat Tom's Ice Cream

Repetition is the best review. If you are going to be writing essay-type exams, you need special preparations. In history, art history, or literature exams, where you need to learn many dates, names, or styles, you need to find a better way to study. When you are taking a literature exam, you might want to set up a chart that looks like the following in order to cover all the material studied. From the information on the chart, you could write a good essay to compare, contrast, describe, show cause and effect, or develop a given topic. At a glance you can recall the whole work studied.

| Title | Author | Genre | Location | Time | Characters | Objects | Places |
|-------|--------|-------|----------|------|------------|---------|--------|
|       |        | poetry |         |      |            |         |        |
|       |        | novel  |         |      |            |         |        |

For history, you might set up one that looks like this:

| Date | Person | Event | Location | Consequences |
|------|--------|-------|----------|--------------|
|      |        |       |          |              |

For art history, something like this might be appropriate:

| Period | Artist | Title | Style | Characteristics | Influence |
|--------|--------|-------|-------|-----------------|-----------|
|        |        |       |       |                 |           |

Reviewing these charts every night will help you recall everything studied in class. It will be a lot easier than trying to review paragraph after paragraph on every page.

Another way to prepare for essay exams is to set up **study groups** of no more than five members. Assign different topics to each. This way, individually you will become an expert on your topic, and you can "teach" everyone else. Share your "expert" notes so that everyone else becomes an expert. Meet at least one time per week to share, and two times per week just before the test. Quiz one another.

Ask your instructor what the test will be like (fill-ins, true/false, multiple choice, definitions, essays), and prepare accordingly. If you will be having essay tests, once you create some possible questions, take the time to write essay-type answers. Predicting questions can be easy if you follow these steps. By paying close attention in class, you can pick up on a number of cues that will help to develop techniques for creating your own questions that might appear on the test. Observe your instructors as they present the material. If they repeat material, you should write what they say. When they write information on the board, you know it is important. It could include names, dates, places, formulas, math problems, charts, or diagrams. Writing this information with different-colored inks will make it stand out from the rest of your notes and help you to remember. Also watch your instructors' gestures and movements, because they could be a clue to what is important. If instructors raise their voices, they must want you to note something important. Take notes on what your instructors emphasize in class. Look in your text to see what is written in bold print, in larger print, in a different color, or in a special box or chart and set apart from other material. All of these can help you predict test questions, prepare better, and receive higher grades.

Create **flash cards** (use 3" × 5" cards or pieces of paper) that have questions on one side and answers on the other, vocabulary words for spelling or translation, formulas for math and science, examples of math problems and/or theories. You can always carry them with you and review them when you have a few minutes.

Now that you have studied all the materials, you need to become familiar with the terminology on the test. Some common words are *analyze*, *compare*, *contrast*, *explain*, *define*, *describe*, and *discuss*. Each one asks you to do something different. When your instructor asks you to *contrast* and you *describe*, you probably won't get full credit, if any, for your answer. Look at these terms to see what your instructor would want you to do. Remember that when you are asked to write an essay on an exam, you will probably be writing one or two well-developed paragraphs, not two or three pages, unless you are writing for a composition class.

## Analyze

Break down the main idea into smaller parts and examine each one.

**Example:**   Analyze the causes of the fall of the Roman Empire.

You would list about six or seven causes and explain in more detail how each was responsible for the collapse of the empire.

## Compare

Show similarities in two or more elements.

**Example:** Compare the poetry of John Keats and Lord Byron.

Mentioning several poems that you have studied, you would write specific information that would show how they are the same (theme, location, style, etc.).

## Contrast

Show differences in two or three elements.

**Example:** Contrast the physical geography of Alaska and Hawaii.

After making a short list of the geographical features of both states, you would emphasize the differences between the two.

## Explain

Develop an idea more fully; suggest reasons for specific happenings.

**Example:** Explain some of the theories for the decline of the Mayan civilization in Central America.

After making a short list of reasons, you would write a couple of sentences that would show how each of these reasons was in part responsible for the decline.

## Define

Identify; provide the meaning of certain terms.

**Example:** Define the following terms: binomials, trinomials, and prime numbers.

You need to write a short (usually one or two sentences) definition for each of the terms. This type is different from the others, because the emphasis is on a *short* answer.

## Describe

Provide many details.

**Example:** Describe the most effective way to prepare for your algebra final exam.

Indicate, by using details in a step-by-step process, how you would get ready for the test.

## *Discuss*

Look at favorable and unfavorable aspects of a particular issue.

**Example:** Discuss George W. Bush's political platform for the 2000 presidential election.

You could mention a number of issues presented in the platform and explain why they are good or bad (flawed) or compare and contrast them and their effect on society and how George W. Bush is able to carry them out.

As you can see, there is a certain strategy for answering essay-type questions, and your preparation requires a more detailed review than just knowing a lot of facts. You need to sort your ideas and develop the topic. Make sure that you understand what you have to do. If you do not know, ask your instructor for clarification.

Before you begin to write your essay, do some brainstorming—think about the topic, and write down your thoughts and what you know about it—enough so that you will have sufficient information to develop the topic. Then prepare a brief outline, which will set up a plan for making your ideas flow smoothly and logically. Now you are ready to answer the essay question. Budget your time so that you have enough time to finish and proofread and revise. Skip lines so that you have enough room to add information after you have proofread your answer.

If you have fill-ins, multiple-choice, and essay questions on the same exam, do the first two before writing the essay. Figure out how much time you will need for each section, and stick to those limits. First, do the ones that you know well, and then do the rest. That way you will have a better chance to score higher.

Outside the testing center, when you have finished and while the test is still fresh in your mind, write down the questions to refer to them for future tests in case your instructor allows you to keep your tests. Also review your notes to see whether you have developed the questions as fully as you should have. The more essay-type tests you take, the more familiar you will become with what your instructors want you to do and the better you will perform on this type of test.

# TEST TYPES

There are many types of tests given today, from the most common and widely used multiple-choice type to the more obscure essay type. Each testing instrument requires a different amount of preparation and involves varying degrees of memory recall. Most of the standardized tests given today—such as the College Level Academic Skills Test (CLAST), Test of English as a Foreign Language (TOEFL), GED (Graduate Equivalency Diploma) tests, and other college entrance examinations—are totally or at least partly multiple choice. Understanding the types of tests and what knowledge each is designed to assess will assist you greatly not only in the preparation but also in actually taking the test.

Listed below are the names of some of the most commonly used test types, followed by a brief explanation and suggestions and ideas on how to study for and take each type.

# Multiple Choice

This test type is based upon the memorization of relevant facts, dates, short definitions or clues, statements of fact, brief descriptions, or complex mathematical problem solving. These tests are usually designed to test factual information. The most common questions are those asking for actual answers to the problem/ question given. The other question format provides a statement and your decision as to whether it is true or false. In all multiple-choice test formats, you will see the statement/questions first and then a series of possible answers.

**What is the capital of the United States of America?**

(a) Delaware

(b) Miami

(c) Washington, D.C.

(d) San Antonio                    [Correct answer: (c)]

**Sharks are plant-eating fish found in the ocean.**

(a) True

(b) False                                    [Correct answer: (b)]

In a number of multiple-choice tests, the list of possible answers includes a choice of "none of the above" for questions in which none of the answers listed are correct.

**Which was one of the ships used by Christopher Columbus?**

(a) *La Pinta*

(b) *Voyager*

(c) *Sea Lady*

(d) *Martina*

(e) None of the above                        [Correct answer: (a)]

## Study Guide

Study one-word definitions, rules, mathematical principles, important dates, specific terminology, and statement of facts.

## Test-Taking Hint

Read the question or statement and all the possible answers listed first, and then select the answer.

For true/false tests, identify "catch words," such as ***all***, ***only***, ***occasionally***, ***never***, ***always***. If these words are used, no exception can ever be present.

**The sun never rises in Alaska.**

(a) True

(b) False                                    [Correct answer: (b)]

Examine the statement(s) of fact given for any inconsistencies. Do not guess, if at all possible.

---
**NOTE**

Some multiple-choice tests include a penalty for guessing. That is, the percentage correct is calculated by using the total number of answers divided by the number of correct. Tests that do not penalize guessing are scored according to the total number of possible answers divided by the total number correct.

---

## Matching

This type of testing instrument also provides both the questions and the possible answers. Usually the questions or answers are given in scrambled fashion. You select the answer from the choices given and "match" it to the question. Most matching type tests provide two columns—one with definitions, statements, or clues and the other with all the possible answers. In many tests, more answers than questions are provided, in an effort to challenge the test taker.

The following is a sample of one of the most commonly used matching tests, including the instructions.

Find the name in Column B that best identifies the information in Column A. None of the letters may be repeated, and there will be two extra names. Write your answer on the lines in the margin.

| Column A | Column B |
|---|---|
| _____ 1. discovered America instead of a route to India | a. Father Jacques Marquette |
| _____ 2. claimed the Mississippi Valley for Louis XIV | b. Robert de la Salle |
| | c. Hernando de Soto |
| _____ 3. founded the city of Quebec | d. Christopher Columbus |
| | e. Samuel de Champlain |

[Answers: 1. d; 2. b; 3. e]

A more difficult type of matching provides a statement that contains blanks indicating that some of the information or facts are missing. The answers provide a list of the possible "fillers." The questions are usually answered by the process of elimination.

There are usually a few extras provided; therefore, you must be careful not to confuse any of the answers. Once you use one of the correct answers, you will get another one wrong, because you cannot repeat any one of the choices.

In the column at the right, you will find the answers to these statements. Write in the word(s) in the spaces provided. Do not repeat any answers.

| | | |
|---|---|---|
| _____ | 1. He wrote the tragedy *Romeo and Juliet*. | Voltaire |
| _____ | 2. Famous Italian who was responsible for writing *The Divine Comedy*. | Cervantes |
| | | Goethe |
| _____ | 3. *Candide,* a French play, was written by William Shakespeare. | Dante Alighieri |

[Answers: 1. William Shakespeare; 2. Dante Alighieri; 3. Voltaire]

A more difficult version of the fill-in provides no answer clues and requires students to be well versed in the material in order to write the answers. This type is very common on tests.

In the spaces provided, fill in the answers to the following statements.

1. This curious woman opened a box given her by the gods, and all sorts of evils flew out.    _____

2. Chief and most powerful god of the Greeks.    _____

3. Ruler of the sea in Roman mythology.    _____

[Answers 1. Pandora; 2. Zeus; 3. Neptune]

## Study Guide

Study definitions or descriptions that contain one-word "clues," dates of major events, rules, and titles.

## Test-Taking Hints

First read the question or statement, and then be careful to read *all* of the choices listed as one may be more correct than the other.

As you finish each question, "check off" or "cross out" the choice of the answer you used to make sure you do not repeat that answer.

| | | | |
|---|---|---|---|
| __C__ | 1. capital of the Inca Empire | A. | Lima |
| __D__ | 2. knotted cords for recording data | B. | chuño |
| _____ | 3. freeze-dried potatoes | C. | ~~Cuzco~~ |
| _____ | 4. seaport capital of modern Peru | D. | ~~quipu~~ |

# Short Answer

This form of test involves the use of a fragment of a sentence, a partial fact or a question or questions requiring you to identify or describe relevant facts or information. Many short answer tests use isolated questions based on a particular chapter or story.

Provide a brief sentence or sentences to define or describe the information requested below.

1. How did Louis Pasteur discover a cure for smallpox?

2. Why should you be careful when siphoning a solution in a pipette?

3. What causes weightlessness on the moon?

A more advanced type of test requiring total recall is one in which you must identify different items. These involve names of people with whom we associate dates, places, and events, or terms that we must define. These usually require short answers.

Identify the following musical terms:

    (1) chorus

    (2) cantus planus

    (3) a cappella

    (4) polyphony

    (5) contrapunto

Many short-answer tests require you to read a passage and then answer a series of questions relevant to the information provided in the passage. Here are three questions based on a passage that would have been provided on the test:

1. Why did Christopher Columbus apply the term "Indians" to the people with reddish skin that he met in the New World?

2. Why did Queen Isabella of Spain provide Christopher Columbus with funds, supplies, and men and give her consent to his sailing to the New World?

3. How did Columbus obtain the members of his crew?

## Study Guide

Familiarize yourself with all the relevant facts regarding the main theme or topic you were requested to study.

When reviewing themes, rules or terms, outline the main concepts and identify key words that will assist you in remembering the necessary information.

## Test-Taking Hints

When you answer questions relating to a passage, read all of the questions first, because this will give an idea of the kind of information you will be looking for. As you begin to read the passage, underline key phrases or words that you think the questions refer to or that will aid you in answering the questions.

For short-answer definitions or those listed as "identify," be sure to give only the information you were asked for. Do not provide excessive details, because you may end up not even answering the question.

# Essay

Essay questions are similar to short answer ones in that you are required to write your response. However, essays are usually much longer, require many more details, and involve thought processes such as reasoning, evaluation, or comparison. Unless you know the material extremely well, these test types will be very difficult for you.

Write a short essay on only two of these topics:

1. Compare and contrast the Aztec and Inca civilizations, paying particular attention to social structure, arts and crafts, written language, architecture, and education.

2. Explain why many primitive civilizations died out after a period of time.

3. What made Hagia Sofia in Constantinople such an architectural achievement?

4. Compare the conquests of Alexander the Great in the fourth century B.C. with those of Adolf Hitler.

## Study Guide

Become very familiar with the subject matter being tested.

Think of possible essay questions and possible answers.

Outline major topic areas to make it easier to memorize relevant facts that will assist you in remembering the major points or key issues.

### Test-Taking Hints

First read all of the questions completely. This gives you an idea of the scope of the test. Then reread all questions and underline the key words, such as *list*, *describe*, *Identify*, *compare and contrast*, and *explain*.

Pay close attention to the directions. If you are given an option, choose yours carefully. Answer first the easiest one(s).

Do not begin to write and don't correct your grammar and spelling as you go. First write, and then, only after you have answered all of the required questions, go back and revise and edit.

Determine the weight or points for each question, and use this to gauge the content and length of each answer. Do not write a lot and spend too much time on questions that carry very little weight.

Answer only that which is asked of you; do not fabricate or create answers. Simply answer the question.

## NOTE-TAKING SKILLS

# Before the Lecture

- Learn to take good notes. Do *not* try to write down everything you hear during a lecture.

- Watch a documentary on television and take notes for practice.

- Watch the news and summarize all the information presented.

- Attend lectures in the community and take notes.

- Listen to political campaigners.

- If your library has taped lectures, borrow them, listen to them, and take notes.

- If your instructor distributes a vocabulary list for the next chapter, always look up the words before the next class. That way, you won't have to take so many notes on definitions, and you will be prepared to ask questions during the lecture.

# During the Lecture

- Write only the *most* important words and ideas.

- When you are taking notes in class, pay better attention; concentrate on what the teacher is saying.

- Ask questions to clarify information.

- Participate in discussions.

- Be aware of the teacher's gestures, raising voice, and repetition. These usually indicate that the teacher is giving some important information.

- Copy whatever your teacher writes on the board.

- Use a tape recorder *only* as a backup, because you never know when there will be a mechanical failure, and if you rely totally on the recorder, you will lose all the information presented.

- Keep your notes short and to the point.

- Make use of abbreviations and symbols.

- Organize your notes; use space to show relationships between ideas.

- If your instructor distributes a set of notes, focus on the way they are written.

- Avoid distractions so that you do not miss anything that is being said, or you will misinterpret the information when you write it down.

- Pay attention to graphs and charts, because they contain a great deal of information in capsule format. Be able to elaborate on the chart when you study.

- Leave a lot of room in the margin or skip lines so that you can go back to the notes and insert more information, write memory aids in the margins, or write questions to ask in class the next day.

# After the Lecture

- Reread your notes as soon as possible after taking them.

- Rewrite the notes, expanding your ideas.

- Highlight the most important information.

- If you can type, type your notes so that they will be easier to read. You can also review as you type.

# WAYS TO IMPROVE YOUR STUDY SKILLS

- Find a quiet, well-lit, comfortable place to study.

- If you need music to create a study mood, find softer music with no lyrics. Avoid the temptation to sing along.

- The more you repeat, the longer the information will stay with you.

- Plan many short study sessions, and take breaks to stretch, eat/drink something, or unwind.

- Work on today's notes first, and then review past notes.

- Write questions on material that you do not understand. Then ask your teacher the following day.

- Work in small groups of three or four and discuss materials.

- Create practice tests and quiz one another.

- Create note cards, allowing you to do mini-reviews during planned or unplanned free time (waiting for someone, appointments, etc.).

- Write important vocabulary, information, dates, etc., on note cards, and keep reviewing data.

- Keep a small notebook of *new* vocabulary words from your readings. Review the list often, and make these new words a part of your active vocabulary.

- Preview test material *before* class. That way, you will be prepared to ask and answer questions.

- Not all of us are good artists, but even copying crudely a drawing from a lecture and labeling it will help you remember the information until later, when you can get a better picture for your notes.

- Practice clustering ideas with a graphic. The focal point is the largest circle, and the details are in the smaller ones. See the clustering section in the essay writing part of this book.

- Develop your own strategy. Whatever works for you, use it!

# HOW TO PREVIEW INFORMATION

- What does the exercise/activity/reading include?

- What am I to do with it?

- Is there a glossary that will help me with new vocabulary?

- How is the important information highlighted—bold face, italics, capital letters, footnotes, notes in margins, graphs, diagrams, photographs?

- Do the questions require me to think about a lengthy answer that may also bring in previously learning information?

- Will I find the answers written out, or will I have to make a judgment on my own?

- Read questions of an exercise first so that you have an idea of what to look for in the reading.

- Focus on details.

- Underline important words, not the whole paragraph or page.

- Learn to read faster. Try moving your finger tips across the printed words at a regular pace and get your eyes to follow your fingers. With practice you can increase your reading speed and cut down the time your spend on your assignments. Speed is particularly important in taking timed exams. The faster you read, the faster you will finish. Read a lot and often.

- After you have read a paragraph or two, stop for a moment and, in your own words, write down some of the ideas you remember. This will allow you to see whether you really understand what you have read.

- Read introductory paragraph(s) and summary paragraphs first.

- Read first sentences of paragraphs (usually the topic sentence express the main idea).

# HOW TO PREPARE FOR TESTS

- Study material in depth.

- Self-test in a variety of ways.

- Learn the format of the exam and practice it (multiple choice, fill-in, etc.).

- Review the material out loud. The more senses are involved in the process, the more you will remember the material.

- Do many short reviews with rest breaks or review sessions scheduled over several days to keep the information in your long-term memory. This is better than one long "cram" session.

- Set time limits to see how well you can express your ideas within these limits.

- Review key words so that you can use them in your answers.

- Work *seriously* with one or two other students and test one another on the information. Discuss it. Keep on repeating it until it stays with you.

- Try to simplify your learning through the use of mnemonic devices (tricks to help you remember) or simple drawings that will help you learn a lot in a short period.

- Be able to apply what you have learned in writing your answers. Not all tests will be fill-ins, multiple choice, or matching. Your answers could be *explain* or *compare/contrast* types, which means that you need to provide many details to support your answer.

- Distinguish among the terms in the test-taking section (*explain*, *describe*, etc.).

- If you are doing a series of practice tests, especially computerized ones, keep track of your progress.

- Think out ideas logically before writing essays. As you brainstorm—that is, think about the topic and write down some facts and ideas—use short outlines, to give yourself a better idea of how the essay will flow.

- Stay focused; avoid distractions.

- Set up charts with different categories to remember information at a glance.

- Keep in mind that there are no extra-credit points on standardized tests, so you must answer correctly as many questions as possible.

- Set a timer to practice timed exercises.

## What to Do the Night Before the Exam

- Get a good night's rest.

- If you have studied often for short periods, you should have your material well organized in your mind. Relax and watch your favorite television program or listen to your favorite music to unwind before you go to bed. If you are not stressed when you get to bed, you should sleep well and be refreshed in the morning.

- Feel confident that you will do well.

## Stress-Reduction Techniques

Whether we like it or not, we are surrounded by stress. No one has ever become really happy living with a great deal of stress. How can you relieve some of the stress in your life?

- Practice deep-breathing exercises. Sit, stand, or lie in a comfortable position. Concentrate only on your breathing, very deep breathing at first, and then shallower inhaling and exhaling. This way you can concentrate on only one thing at a time, and you won't feel the anxiety associated with the test.

- Think of something pleasant, like floating aimlessly on a cloud.

- Soak in warm water in a tub.

- Turn on some dreamy music and move gently to the rhythm.

- Plan ahead, and don't wait until the last minute. That causes when stress to set in.

- Eliminate the negative feelings that surround you.

- Take a walk in a quiet area, and concentrate only on nature.

- Swim in a pool when it is quiet, usually later at night.

- Arrive early for the test.

- Tell yourself that you have prepared well and will do your best.

- Don't let other students' behavior distract you (early departure, coughing, nervousness). Realize that many students have not prepared themselves for the test.

# ESL
## GLOSSARY

# GLOSSARY

**Active voice.** Sentence structure in which the subject is responsible for performing the action of the verb.

> He runs.    She reads.    They write.

**Adjective.** Word that describes a noun or a pronoun.

> The **fat** cat climbed the tree slowly.

**Adverb.** Word that modifies a verb, an adjective, or another adverb.

> The ballerina danced **gracefully** across the stage.

**Agreement.** How words correspond to other words in a sentence or phrase.

> That *pair* of slacks *needs* to be washed.

**Clause.** Part of a sentence. Main clauses (independent) can stand alone and convey a complete thought. Dependent (subordinate) clauses do not convey a complete idea even though they may contain a subject and verb. The latter need the main clause to give the whole structure meaning.

> *Because it was raining* (dependent), we arrived late (independent).

**Dangling participle.** Participial phrase (V + *ing* or V + *ed*) at the beginning of a sentence that is not the subject and does not modify the noun or pronoun after the phrase.

> *Pounding the nail,* the picture was finally hung.

**Direct speech.** The exact words of someone, usually written between quotation marks.

> Tom said, "I will attend the meeting at 8:00 tonight."

The opposite is indirect speech: Tom said that he would attend the meeting at 8:00 tonight.

**Fragment.** Part of a sentence that does not convey a complete idea.

> That morning in the park. (no subject, no verb, no complete idea)

**Gerund.** Verb form ending in *-ing* that may be used as a noun.

> *Running* is good exercise.

> *Jogging*, *swimming*, and *dancing* are good exercises.

**Participle.** Form of verb usually ending in *ed* (past) or *ing* (present)

> frightened — frightening        fried — frying

**Passive voice.** Sentence structure in which the subject does not perform the action, but rather receives it; *be* + past participle.

> The play *was written* by Shakespeare.

**Preposition.** Word relating a noun or pronoun to other words in a sentence (for example, *in*, *into*, *on*, and *by*). The tickets are *for* **the afternoon performance**.

**Pronoun.** A word that takes the place of a noun.

**Relative pronoun.** Pronoun that relates to the word that precedes it. Such pronouns introduce a dependent clause (*who*, *whom*, *that*, *which*)

> I know Dane Cameron, *who* is the director of Acme Computers.

**Run-on.** Two complete sentences joined without any punctuation (which is an error in grammar).

> It rained very hard we got wet and had an accident.

**Sentence.** A group of words containing a subject, a verb, and a complete thought.

> Mrs. Davis drove to Chicago on Monday.

**Sequence of tenses.** Relationship in time of verbs used in a sentence.

> The teacher *said* that we *would have* an exam on Friday.

**Voice.** Form of verb that shows whether the subject performs action (active) or receives action (passive).

> Vince *wrote* the poem in 1980. (active voice)

> The poem *was written* in 1980. (passive voice)

# ESL
## APPENDICES

# APPENDICES

## *A* AND *AN*

As a general rule, **a** should be used before words beginning with a consonant sound, and **an** should be used before a vowel sound. The letters **h** and **u** will cause problems. Words in which the letter **h** is pronounced are preceded by **a** (a ham, a heart, a horn), while those in which the **h** is not pronounced are preceded by **an**.

A good rule to follow is that all words beginning with **h** have the first letter pronounced except for the following, in which **h** is not pronounced and which use the article **an**:

| | | |
|---|---|---|
| heir | honest | honor |
| heiress | herb | honorary |
| heirloom | hour | honorarium |

In the following words, the **h** is pronounced, so use the article **a**:

| | | |
|---|---|---|
| helmet | heater | hateful |
| happy | historic | hymn |
| habit | halibut | Hessian |

When words beginning with the letter **u** have the consonant sound **yoo** ($\bar{u}$), they are preceded by the article **a**: a uniform, a university, a utensil.

Those that begin with the **ŭ** sound, as found in **cup**, require the article **an**: an umbrella, an unhealthy uncle.

The prefix **un-**, indicating a negative, always has a vowel sound: unfriendly, unhappy, unusual.

---
**NOTE**
The *yoo* sound does not always mean that the word
will begin with the letter *u*.

---

Other examples of the *yoo* sound are the following:

*a European* vacation

*a eulogy* delivered by her brother

*a euphemism*

She has *a euphoric* glow about her.

*a eucalyptus* in the backyard

Other words that begin with the *yoo* sound and use the article *a*:

| | | |
|---|---|---|
| eunuch | euphemism | euphoria |
| euphonium | euphoric | Eurasian |
| eurhythmic | Euromarket | Euripidean |
| unity | uniform | universal |
| unified | university | utilities |

# THE

The article *the* is used to indicate something specific.

*The* book on the table is mine.

I mailed *the* letter that you gave me yesterday.

*The* is also used for names of mountains, rivers, islands, and oceans; names of musical groups; ethnic groups; specific documents, etc.

Many people spend their vacations in *the Rocky Mountains.*

Mel and Sandy spent their honeymoon in *the Hawaiian Islands*.

*The Beatles* were a famous musical group in the sixties and seventies.

*The Declaration of Independence* was written in 1776.

Non-count nouns can use *the* in some situations and not in others. For example, when referring to an element in general terms, the article is not used.

*Money* is necessary to pay the bills.

Budgeting *time* carefully will make you a better student.

*Food* tastes better when it is fresh.

However, when the element is used in specific terms, the article *the* is necessary.

*The money I gave you* is for the rent. (specific money)

*The time we have together* is precious. (specific time)

I need to *buy the food* for our party. (specific food)

When plural count nouns refer to elements in general, no article is required.

Working *days* is more pleasing to some than to others.

*Grapes* grow in *bunches on vines*.

Some words, unless they restrict the meaning, do not use the definite article.

**breakfast, church, college, dinner, home, hospital** (British)

**heaven, hell, lunch, school, supper**

Some people believe in *heaven* and *hell*, but others don't.

John studies *at school*, and his mother works *at home*.

Mildred is learning a great deal in her art classes *in college*.

Tom had an accident and is *in hospital*. (British)

Tom had an accident and is *in the hospital*. (American)

# APPENDIX B

# VOCABULARY HELP

**I Before E Rule**

*I* before *E*

Except after *C*

Or when sounded as *ay*,

As in *neighbor* and *weigh*.

| I before E | | Except after C | Or when sounded as *ay* |
|---|---|---|---|
| achieve | mischief | ceiling | beige |
| believe | niece | conceit | eight |
| brief | patience | conceive | freight |
| chief | pierce | deceit | neigh |
| conscience | priest | deceive | neighbor |
| conscientious | relief | perceive | reign |
| field | shield | receipt | rein |
| fierce | siege | receive | sleigh |
| grief | yield | receiver | vein |
| | | | weigh |
| | | | weight |

| *There are exceptions to every rule:* | | | |
|---|---|---|---|
| ancient | leisure | seismic | skein |
| either | neither | seismograph | their |
| height | science | seize | veil |
| heir | scientific | seizure | weird |

# APPENDIX C
# PLURAL CONCEPTS

## NON-COUNT NOUNS

Some categories of non-count nouns can be subdivided into count nouns. Some of these include the following:

| | | | |
|---|---|---|---|
| **furniture** | chairs<br>tables<br>sofas<br>lamps | **produce** | fruits<br>vegetables<br>potatoes<br>carrots |
| **money** | dollars<br>cents<br>pesos<br>yen | **literature** | poems<br>short stories<br>tragedies<br>comedies |
| **jewelry** | rings<br>necklaces<br>watches<br>earrings | **information** | data*<br>facts<br>statistics<br>*datum = singular |
| **agriculture** | tomatoes<br>bananas<br>grapes<br>oranges | **scenery** | trees<br>flowers<br>highways<br>houses |
| **transportation** | cars<br>buses<br>bicycles<br>vans | **baggage** | suitcases<br>valises<br>hand bags |

— NOTE —

Many non-count nouns can be used with plural concepts
when a plural unit of measure precedes them.

*pieces of* furniture      *kinds of* produce

*stacks of* money      *categories of* literature

*boxes of* jewelry      *sources of* information

*types of* agriculture      *means of* transportation

Other non-count nouns that are always singular are those referring to intangible or abstract concepts. They include the following:

| air | liberty | anger | intolerance |
|-----|---------|-------|-------------|
| sky | loyalty | euphoria | solitude |
| heaven | arrogance | love | comfort |
| hell | happiness | laughter | satisfaction |
| truth | sadness | hatred | understanding |
| beauty | prejudice | education | knowledge |

# FORMING PLURALS

Words ending in vowels and consonants usually add *-s* to form their plurals.

# Exceptions

1. After *s*, *sh*, *ch*, and *x*, add *-es*

   press—press<u>es</u>     patch—patch<u>es</u>     wish—wish<u>es</u>     tax—tax<u>es</u>

2. For nouns ending in *y* after a consonant, change *y* to *i*.

   fly—fl<u>ies</u>     enemy—enem<u>ies</u>     lady—lad<u>ies</u>     salary—salar<u>ies</u>

3. For nouns ending in *y* following a vowel, add *-s*.

   monkey—monkeys     tray—trays     decoy—decoys

4. Some nouns have irregular plurals. Learn them.

   foot—feet     tooth—teeth     child—children     ox—oxen

   woman—women     man—men     louse—lice     mouse—mice

5. Some words use the same form for singular and plural.

   fish     deer     sheep     moose     reindeer     caribou

6. Compound, or two-part, words pluralize only the entity that could be countable. Remember that the first part of a compound word usually acts as a adjective, and adjectives have no plurals except *these* and *those*. Notice, however, in the word, and sisters-in-law, it is the first part that is pluralized, because it is the entity that can be counted.

   football—footballs   butterfly—butterflies   toothbrush—toothbrushes

7. The plurals of most nouns ending in *f* are formed by adding *-s*.

   brief—briefs   proof—proofs   belief—beliefs

   *Exceptions:* Change *f* or *fe* to *v* and add *-es*.

   life—lives   knife—knives   calf—calves   wife—wives   shelf—shelves

   wolf—wolves        leaf—leaves        half—halves        thief—thieves

8. Follow these rules for plurals of proper nouns and family names.

   Jones—the Joneses        Whitley—the Whitleys        Mixa—the Mixas

   The **Joneses** (the Jones family) are leaving for Puerto Rico on the noon flight.

   Rex Ryan is a tennis star. All the **Rexes** I know are football players.

9. For certain group of nouns ending in consonant + *o*, add *-es* to these words.

   echoes          dominoes          potatoes          tomatoes          heroes

10. For some words that end in *ex* and *ix*, drop the suffix and add *ices* to form the plural.

    index > indices                    codex > codices

    ibex > ibices                      appendix > appendices

11. Another category of irregular plurals relates to words ending in *sis*. Instead of adding *es* to the root word, the *i* in the suffix just changes to *e*. Other words in this category are *chrysalis*, *synthesis*, *dialysis*, *hypothesis*, *antithesis*, and *parenthesis*.

    There are a number of other rules dealing with foreign words that have been incorporated into the language, as well as a variety of other plural forms. Whenever you find a noun and are not sure of the plural form, look it up in your dictionary.

Non-count nouns are those that do not usually have a plural form and cannot be numbered as the ones above.

coffee money energy water knowledge

However, we can place the liquids in containers and count the containers; money is mentioned in monetary units (dollars, cents); time is figured in hours and minutes, etc.

five cups of coffee            twenty dollars

six hours                      fifty minutes

Singular vocabulary dealing with food can also become plural if we mention the units or containers for that food. Examples:

| | | |
|---|---|---|
| gallons | quarts | pints |
| ounces | pounds | tablespoons |
| teaspoons | cups | slices |
| pieces | bottles | jars |
| cans | packages | loaves |

Some adjectives are also limited to count and non-count nouns.

| Count | Non-count | Both |
|---|---|---|
| many | much | some |
| few | little (quantity) | any |
| several | an amount of | no |
| various | the number of | a lot of |
| these/those | not any | |
| a number of | | |

Certain words referring to foods are considered noncountable and have no plural forms. Here is a partial list:

| | | | |
|---|---|---|---|
| lettuce | bread | milk | ketchup |
| cabbage | butter | juice | salt |
| corn | macaroni | tea | garlic |
| fish | spaghetti | mustard | toast |

On the other hand, some foods can be counted and do have plural forms:

| | | | |
|---|---|---|---|
| waffles | beans | pies | carrots |
| peppers | potatoes | donuts | lima beans |
| onions | cakes | relishes | tomatoes |

You might also find it strange to see how some of these foods are measured:

| | | |
|---|---|---|
| *ear* of corn | *head* of lettuce | *clove* of garlic |
| *sprig* of parsley old | potatoes grow *eyes* | |
| *foot-long* hot dogs | *bunch* of grapes | |

## APPENDIX D

# WORD PHRASES WITH PREPOSITIONS

In English there are a number of word groups that contain prepositions. They include combinations with **nouns**, **adjectives**, and **verbs**. Here is a partial list. Practice using them in sentences until they become part of your active vocabulary.

### Noun + Preposition

| | | |
|---|---|---|
| bag of | pride of | (dis)satisfaction with |
| cup of | discussion of | search for |
| passion for | list of | investigation into |
| pair of | chance to | enthusiasm for |
| quality of | reason for | need for |
| year of | penchant for | response to |
| number of | quantity of | in the spirit of |
| dose of | amount of | loss of |
| game of | desire for | hope for |
| exception to | insistence on | type of |
| in addition to | purpose for | importance of |
| book of | in consideration of | |
| declaration of | peak of | |
| source of | gift of | |
| bunch of | opinion of | |
| basis for | love of/for | |
| tale of | hate for | |

## Adjective + Preposition

| | | |
|---|---|---|
| consistent with | taken by/with | famous for |
| anxious about | angry with/at | expelled from |
| worried about | afraid of/for | enrolled in |
| married to | tired of | delayed by |
| divorced from | upset with | weakened by/from |
| guilty of | (dis)satisfied with | saddened by |
| interested in | jealous of | threatened by |
| fond of | fascinated by | encouraged by |
| afraid of | dependent on | dismayed by |
| drawn to | supportive of | responsible for |
| different from | accustomed to | made for/by |
| equal to | interested in | influenced by |
| offended by | concerned about | designed by/for |
| superior to | crazy about | |

## Verb + Preposition

The **verb + preposition** list is far greater than the other lists, because one verb can use a variety of prepositions. With each preposition, the verb takes on a different meaning. Look up these verb phrases in an unabridged (larger, more complete) dictionary.

| | | | |
|---|---|---|---|
| approve of | come across | draw aside | disagree with |
| | come after | draw out | |
| break away | come away with | | fill up |
| break down | come by | come along with | fill out |
| break off | come in | come down with | fill in |
| break up | | figure out | |
| break in | look after | figure on | get across |
| break out | look for | | get after |
| break through | look up | find out | get along |
| break with | look down | find in favor of | get around |
| | look over | depend on | get at |
| call after | look out for | | get along with |
| call away | look about | get by | get away from |
| call on | look at | get over | get back at |
| call up | look back on | get up | get behind |
| call back | look forward to | get through | |
| call off | look in on | get down to | get out |
| call down | look into | get in | |
| call forth | | give up | search for |
| call together | refer to | give out | |
| call off | rely on | give into | drop over |
| | detract from | give away | drop out |
| care about | | give back | drop in |
| care for | count on | give forth | drop off |
| | count down | give over | |
| check into | count out | give off | come out |
| check out | count up | | come over |
| check out of | | cover up | come about |
| check over | do away with | cover for | |
| check up on | do up | cover over | try on |
| check with | do over | cover with | try out |
| | do for | | try for |
| close in on | do about | do without | |
| close down | | do with | |
| close off | draw up | have to do with | |
| close out | draw on | | |

# APPENDIX E

## IRREGULAR VERBS

| Present | Past | Past Participle |
| --- | --- | --- |
| am, are | was, were | been |
| beat | beat | beaten |
| begin | began | begun |
| bite | bit | bitten |
| blow | blew | blown |
| break | broke | broken |
| bring | brought | brought |
| build | built | built |
| buy | bought | bought |
| catch | caught | caught |
| choose | chose | chosen |
| come | came | come |
| dig | dug | dug |
| do | did | done |
| draw | drew | drawn |
| drink | drank | drunk |
| drive | drove | driven |
| eat | ate | eaten |
| fall | fell | fallen |
| fight | fought | ought |
| find | found | found |
| fly | flew | flown |
| forbid | forbad(e) | forbidden |

| Present | Past | Past Participle |
|---|---|---|
| forget | forgot | forgotten |
| freeze | froze | frozen |
| get | got | got (gotten) |
| give | gave | given |
| go | went | gone |
| grow | grew | grown |
| hang (objects) | hung | hung |
| hang (people) | hanged | hanged |
| have | had | had |
| hide | hid | hidden |
| hold | held | held |
| keep | kept | kept |
| know | knew | known |
| lay | laid | laid |
| lead | led | led |
| leave | left | left |
| lie | lay | lain |
| lose | lost | lost |
| meet | met | met |
| read (rēd) | read (rĕd) | read (rĕd) |
| ride | rode | ridden |
| ring | rang | rung |
| rise | rose | risen |
| run | ran | run |
| say | said | said |
| see | saw | seen |

| Present | Past | Past Participle |
|---------|------|-----------------|
| sell | sold | sold |
| send | sent | sent |
| shake | shook | shaken |
| shrink | shrank (shrunk) | shrunk |
| sing | sang | sung |
| sink | sank | sunk |
| sit | sat | sat |
| sleep | slept | slept |
| speak | spoke | spoken |
| spend | spent | spent |
| stand | stood | stood |
| steal | stole | stolen |
| sting | stung | stung |
| strike | struck | struck |
| swear | swore | sworn |
| swim | swam | swum |
| swing | swung | swung |
| take | took | taken |
| teach | taught | taught |
| tear | tore | torn |
| think | thought | thought |
| throw | threw | thrown |
| wake | woke (waked) | waken (waked) |
| wear | wore | worn |
| win | won | won |
| write | wrote | written |

**The following verbs have the same forms for all three parts.**

| Present | Past | Past Participle |
|---|---|---|
| burst | burst | burst |
| cost | cost | cost |
| cut | cut | cut |
| hit | hit | hit |
| hurt | hurt | hurt |
| let | let | let |
| put | put | put |
| quit | quit | quit |
| set | set | set |
| shut | shut | shut |
| spread | spread | spread |

# ESL
## ANSWER KEYS

# ANSWER KEYS

## EXERCISE 1

1. She
2. We
3. me
4. her
5. us
6. them
7. He
8. him
9. us—we
10. her
11. she
12. us
13. they
14. him
15. her
16. her
17. they
18. I
19. he—they
20. he

## EXERCISE 2

1. He
2. us
3. her—me
4. him
5. Whom
6. us
7. them
8. I
9. he
10. me
11. us
12. them
13. they
14. us
15. she
16. me
17. her
18. I
19. I
20. who

## EXERCISE 3

1. yourself
2. himself
3. ourselves
4. themselves
5. itself
6. myself
7. herself
8. yourselves
9. herself
10. himself/herself

## EXERCISE 4

1. We
2. I
3. himself
4. him
5. yours
6. themselves
7. Mine
8. herself
9. them
10. her
11. they
12. I
13. ourselves

## EXERCISE 5

1. I met an actor whose picture won an Oscar.
2. We bought a house, *which* cost $150,000.
3. Sally introduced me to her boyfriend, *who* is a civil engineer.
4. Maureen bought a dress, *which* cost her $45, and had to return it.
5. Jake gave Isabel a ring *that* had diamonds and rubies.
6. Mrs. Duncan is talking to her students *whose* project are due on Friday.

7. Norman lives with his sister *who* is a nurse.
8. The soldiers *to whom* the president is awarding the medal were injured in combat.
   (The president is awarding medals to the soldiers *who* were injured in combat.
9. Mr. Franklin graded the tests *that* we took on Friday.
10. The director knows the candidate *who* was chosen to be manager.

## EXERCISE 6

| | | |
|---|---|---|
| 1. who | 5. whom | 9. that |
| 2. whose | 6. that | 10. whose |
| 3. that | 7. which | 11. which |
| 4. whom | 8. that | 12. which |

## EXERCISE 7

| | | | |
|---|---|---|---|
| 1. are | 6. have | 11. Has | 16. Have |
| 2. are | 7. are | 12. is | 17. are |
| 3. was | 8. wasn't | 13. Are | 18. are |
| 4. have | 9. Were | 14. have | 19. Are |
| 5. Has | 10. was | 15. Were | 20. Was |

## EXERCISE 8

| | | |
|---|---|---|
| 1. to | 8. to | 15. that |
| 2. to | 9. that | 16. that |
| 3. that | 10. that | 17. to |
| 4. to | 11. that | 18. that |
| 5. that | 12. to | 19. that |
| 6. to | 13. that | 20. to |
| 7. that | 14. to | |

## EXERCISE 9

| | | |
|---|---|---|
| 1. It | 8. it | 15. there |
| 2. there | 9. It | 16. It |
| 3. It | 10. there | 17. It |
| 4. It | 11. there | 18. There |
| 5. it | 12. it | 19. It |
| 6. there | 13. there | 20. It |
| 7. there | 14. there | |

## EXERCISE 10

| | | | | | |
|---|---|---|---|---|---|
| 1. C | 2. A | 3. A | 4. B | 5. B | 6. A |

## EXERCISE 11

| | | | |
|---|---|---|---|
| 1. A | 3. C | 5. D | 7. C |
| 2. C | 4. A | 6. A | 8. C |

## EXERCISE 12

| | |
|---|---|
| 1. whom | 4. there |
| 2. any | 5. whomever |
| 3. I | 6. whose |

## EXERCISE 13

| | | |
|---|---|---|
| 1. my | 8. Terry's | 15. Tom's |
| 2. Peter's | 9. my | 16. the group's |
| 3. her students' | 10. your | 17. my |
| 4. their | 11. Kim's | 18. the club's |
| 5. his | 12. our | 19. Ann's |
| 6. your | 13. the workers' | 20. the government's |
| 7. the landlord's | 14. the policeman's | |

## EXERCISE 14

| | | |
|---|---|---|
| 1. his | 8. citizens' | 15. their |
| 2. Helen's | 9. brother's | 16. children's |
| 3. friend's | 10. boy's | 17. Lonnie's |
| 4. clowns' | 11. son's | 18. birds' |
| 5. your | 12. Tony's | 19. neighbors' |
| 6. my | 13. Anita's | 20. their |
| 7. Anne's | 14. Our | |

## EXERCISE 15

| | |
|---|---|
| 1. some | 11. some |
| 2. any | 12. some |
| 3. any | 13. any |
| 4. Someone/Somebody | 14. some |
| 5. any | 15. something |
| 6. anyone/anybody | 16. some |
| 7. anyone/anybody (someone-conv.) | 17. someone/somebody |
| 8. someone/somebody | 18. anyone/anybody |
| 9. any | 19. anything |
| 10. anything | 20. anything |

## EXERCISE 16

| | | |
|---|---|---|
| 1. wider | 6. nobler | 11. later |
| 2. paler | 7. wiser | 12. larger |
| 3. braver | 8. politer | 13. riper |
| 4. cuter | 9. closer | 14. rarer |
| 5. humbler | 10. staler | 15. safer |

## EXERCISE 17

| | | |
|---|---|---|
| 1. cozier | 6. heavier | 11. noisier |
| 2. shier | 7. prettier | 12. friendlier |
| 3. dizzier | 8. uglier | 13. lonelier |
| 4. angrier | 9. merrier | 14. healthier |
| 5. easier | 10. earlier | 15. lovelier |

## EXERCISE 18

| | | |
|---|---|---|
| 1. quieter than | 5. slimmer than | 9. colder than |
| 2. lovelier than | 6. hazier than | 10. coyer than |
| 3. faster than | 7. sleepier than | |
| 4. closer | 8. narrower than | |

## EXERCISE 19

| | | |
|---|---|---|
| 1. more famous | 10. more morose | 18. more alive |
| 2. more helpful | 11. more cutting | 19. more flagrant |
| 3. more pensive | 12. more clever | 20. more fragrant |
| 4. more captive | 13. more normal | 21. more callous |
| 5. more exact | 14. more sheepish | 22. more forward |
| 6. more loving | 15. more festive | 23. more grateful |
| 7. more daring | 16. more glorious | 24. more useless |
| 8. more basic | 17. more childlike | 25. more selfish |
| 9. more fiendish | | |

## EXERCISE 20

| | |
|---|---|
| 1. many more | 6. many more |
| 2. much prettier than | 7. more straightforward than |
| 3. more abundant than | 8. much (far) less |
| 4. less intelligent than | 9. more rapidly |
| 5. far less cramped than | 10. much (far) less interesting |

## EXERCISE 21

1. Mexico City has many more inhabitants than Micanopy. Micanopy has fewer inhabitants than Mexico City.
2. Philip earns much more (money) than Tony. Tony earns much less than Philip.
3. Nancy is younger than her brother. Nancy's brother is older than she.
4. The millionaire has many more cars than I have. I have fewer cars than the millionaire.
5. The art building is taller than the language lab.
6. A chocolate bar has more calories than a banana. A banana has fewer calories than a chocolate bar.
7. It is much hotter in Arizona than in Anchorage. It is much cooler in Anchorage than in Arizona.
8. Rudy studies less than Ralph. Ralph studies more (harder) than Rudy.
9. It is warmer in Cleveland than in Buffalo. It is colder in Buffalo than in Cleveland.
10. Betty learned Portuguese more easily than Arabic. Betty learned Arabic more slowly than Portuguese.

## EXERCISE 22

Answers will vary.
1. Silver costs less than gold. Gold is more valuable than silver.
2. An elephant is larger and stronger than a monkey.
   A monkey is smaller, weaker, and more intelligent than an elephant.
3. Cotton is softer than plastic. Plastic is harder than cotton.
4. Coca-Cola is sweeter than milk. Coca-Cola is less nutritious than milk.
   Milk is more nutritious than Coca-Cola.
5. Spinach is less tasty than cake. Cake is tastier than spinach.
6. Tom Cruise is younger (more handsome) than Paul Newman. Paul Newman is older (more mature) than Tom Cruise.
7. A yacht is more expensive (faster) than a canoe. A canoe is less expensive (slower) than a yacht.
8. An airplane is faster (bigger, more expensive) than a train. A train is slower (smaller, less expensive)than an airplane.
9. Swimming is more active than watching television Watching television is less active than swimming.
10. The North Pole is colder (farther away) than California. California is warmer (closer) than the North Pole.

## EXERCISE 23

| | | |
|---|---|---|
| 1. better | 5. better | 9. worse |
| 2. farther | 6. Farther | 10. better |
| 3. better | 7. better | |
| 4. worse | 8. better | |

## EXERCISE 24

1. Kevin hit as many home runs as Dave.
2. It's as warm in Oahu as in Dallas.
3. Maureen ate as many pieces of pizza as her sister.
4. Brian sleeps as many hours as Rita.
5. Phil weighs as much as Harry.
6. Tracy works as diligently in school as Trisha.
7. This sweater costs as much as the yellow one.
8. Joel runs as fast as his brother.
9. The long dress is as elegant as the short dress.
10. José spends as much time studying English as math.
11. Some high school students do as many homework assignments as college students.
12. Joan Collins has as much jewelry as Liz Taylor.
13. The Andersons have as many pieces of furniture in the dining room as in the living room.
14. There are as few students in the chemistry class as in the physics class.
15. I paid as much for my textbook as Anne did (paid for hers).

## EXERCISE 25

1. Semi-gloss paint is the most expensive. Flat paint is the least expensive (cheapest).
2. The can of corn is the largest. The can of mushrooms is the smallest.
3. Apricots are the most fattening fruit. (Apricots have the most calories.) Cantaloupe is the least fattening fruit. (Cantaloupe has the fewest calories.)
4. Cleveland is the hottest city. Trenton is the coolest city.
5. Bremerton is the farthest (city) from Olympia. Tacoma is the closest (city) to Olympia.
6. The red candle will burn the longest. The white candle will burn the shortest.
7. The kitchen cabinet is the largest (widest). The bath cabinet is the smallest. (narrowest)
8. The quarterback was the hungriest. (The quarterback ate the most hamburgers.) The cheerleader was the least hungry. (The cheerleader ate the fewest hamburgers.)
9. Arthur is the healthiest athlete. Ted is the least healthy athlete.
10. Diane was the thirstiest. (Diane drank the most lemonade.) Suzy was the least thirsty. (Suzy drank the least lemonade.)

## EXERCISE 26

1. farther
2. best
3. hotter
4. more expensive
5. more famous
6. more boring
7. more helpful
8. more interested
9. more frequently
10. worst
11. most quietly
12. most quickly
13. best
14. colder
15. most foolish

## EXERCISE 27

| | | | |
|---|---|---|---|
| 1. from | 5. as | 9. than | 13. from |
| 2. as | 6. as | 10. from | 14. more |
| 3. than | 7. from | 11. more | 15. than |
| 4. than | 8. as | 12. as | |

## EXERCISE 28

| | | | |
|---|---|---|---|
| 1. C | 5. B | 9. B | 13. B |
| 2. C | 6. A | 10. A | 14. A |
| 3. A | 7. B | 11. C | 15. C |
| 4. C | 8. C | 12. A | 16. B |

## EXERCISE 29

| | | | |
|---|---|---|---|
| 1. C | 3. D | 5. B | 7. A |
| 2. A | 4. A | 6. B | 8. C |

## EXERCISE 30

| | | | |
|---|---|---|---|
| 1. basically | 5. comically | 9. cryptically | 13. automatically |
| 2. historically | 6. strategically | 10. sympathetically | 14. aromatically |
| 3. majestically | 7. critically | 11. artistically | 15. organically |
| 4. economically | 8. antiseptically | 12. domestically | 16. systematically |

## EXERCISE 31

| | | | |
|---|---|---|---|
| 1. sloppily | 3. angrily | 5. readily | 7. steadily |
| 2. heavily | 4. clumsily | 6. busily | 8. merrily |

## EXERCISE 32

| | |
|---|---|
| 1. nobly | 4. responsibly |
| 2. ably | 5. feasibly |
| 3. capably | 6. comfortably |

## EXERCISE 33

| | |
|---|---|
| 1. always | 6. Occasionally (Sometimes) |
| 2. rarely (seldom) | 7. hardly (rarely, scarcely) |
| 3. often (usually/frequently) | 8. sometimes |
| 4. never | 9. usually (frequently) |
| 5. hardly | 10. seldom (rarely) |

## EXERCISE 34

1. Football fans always watch the games on Sunday afternoons.
2. Pasquale has **never** written a letter to his cousin in Italy.
3. I have seen that program **occasionally**, but I don't like it. (I have **occasionally** seen . . .)
4. We **usually** study on Friday afternoons.
5. Marta **generally** prepares a peach pie for special occasions.
6. They **hardly** see us on weekends, because we are so busy during the week.
7. Monica has **seldom** gone shopping in the new mall, because it is so far away.
8. This neighborhood is **usually** quiet, but today it is rather noisy.
9. Has Jude **sometimes** sung and played for the local dances?
10. Have you **often** thought about writing a novel?
11. The girls **generally** take the bus to work, but today it was raining and they got a ride.
12. I have **seldom** seen Tom without his wife at the council meetings.
13. They **barely** talk to us since they moved to the new neighborhood.
14. We **frequently** take the children to the park for a picnic on Sundays.
15. Have you **never** won the lottery.

## EXERCISE 35

1. yet
2. never/already
3. still
4. still
5. yet
6. yet (already)
7. already
8. still (already)
9. yet (already)
10. ever
11. still
12. yet
13. yet
14. still
15. yet
16. already
17. never
18. ever

## EXERCISE 36

1. already
2. still
3. already
4. never
5. still
6. ever
7. ever
8. never
9. ever
10. ever
11. never
12. ever
13. yet
14. already
15. ever
16. still
17. yet

## EXERCISE 37

1. in
2. by/at
3. in
4. to
5. among
6. because of
7. Before
8. in
9. above/over
10. on
11. in
12. in
13. on
14. at
15. in
16. with
17. from
18. off
19. between
20. for
21. for
22. before
23. on
24. above/over
25. of/about

## EXERCISE 38

| | | | |
|---|---|---|---|
| 1. of | 6. of/for | 11. into | 16. off |
| 2. into | 7. to | 12. in | 17. about/up |
| 3. about/of | 8. in/at | 13. away | 18. about |
| 4. for/to | 9. of | 14. by/across | 19. at |
| 5. of/to | 10. for/for | 15. to | 20. to/about |

## EXERCISE 39

| | | |
|---|---|---|
| 1. In | 8. of | 15. On |
| 2. on | 9. of | 16. off |
| 3. in | 10. on | 17. for |
| 4. in | 11. in | 18. to |
| 5. about | 12. of | 19. for |
| 6. of | 13. from | 20. from |
| 7. of | 14. to | 21. to |

## EXERCISE 40

| | | | | | | |
|---|---|---|---|---|---|---|
| 1. A | 3. B | 5. B | 7. C | 9. D | 11. C | 13. A |
| 2. D | 4. A | 6. A | 8. C | 10. A | 12. A | |

## EXERCISE 41

1. and—two ideas
2. but—contrast
3. so—two ideas
4. but—contrast
5. nor—two ideas
6. yet—two ideas
7. and—two words of the same part of speech
8. for—two ideas
9. nor—two words of the same part of speech
10. but—contrast
11. and—two ideas
12. but—two ideas
13. and—two words of the same part of speech
14. and—two ideas (commands = two ideas)
15. or—two words of the same part of speech but—contrast

## EXERCISE 42

| | | |
|---|---|---|
| 1. fries | 8. teaches | 15. scorches |
| 2. magnifies | 9. hurry | 16. apply |
| 3. pinch | 10. blush | 17. dries |
| 4. itches | 11. wash | 18. flies |
| 5. deny | 12. fishes | 19. bleaches |
| 6. does | 13. studies | 20. cries |
| 7. marches | 14. go | |

## EXERCISE 43

| | | | | |
|---|---|---|---|---|
| 1. have | 3. is | 5. will | 7. painted | 9. had |
| 2. did | 4. can | 6. do | 8. seems | 10. were |

## EXERCISE 44

1. Can we see . . . ?
2. Does Nancy have . . . ?
3. Might the landlord raise . . . ?
4. Would he like . . . ?
5. Will Susan be . . . ?
6. Should the students . . . ?
7. Did I have . . . ?
8. Did Enrico buy . . . ?
9. Does Tara paint . . . ?
10. Do the carpenters know . . . ?

## EXERCISE 45

1. Tomatoes *don't* grow on trees.
2. The sun *doesn't* shine at night.
3. Roosters *can't* lay eggs.
4. Alligators *didn't* live in the desert long ago.
5. My roses *can't* grow without water.
6. The French *didn't* invent the concept of zero.
7. He *shouldn't* study statistics.
8. Most luxury cars *don't* get good gas mileage.
9. Bolivia *doesn't* have a large port.
10. Lions *don't* have feathers.

## EXERCISE 46

| | | | |
|---|---|---|---|
| 1. will grow | 4. will sleep | 7. will live | 10. will count |
| 2. will serve | 5. will begin | 8. will happen | |
| 3. will arrive | 6. will be | 9. won't bloom | |

## EXERCISE 47

Answers will vary.
1. It begins at 8:00. It doesn't begin at 11:00.
2. The children eat peanut butter sandwiches. They don't eat spinach.
3. She sleeps eight hours every day. She does not sleep late on week days.
4. The dog runs away from the cat. The dog does not run away from the children.
5. Yes, he drives to the university every day. No, he doesn't drive to work every day.
6. Yes, she walks with the children. No, she doesn't walk with the dog.
7. Ingrid sings Spanish songs. She doesn't sing Italian songs.

8. Maja dances at parties. She doesn't dance in class.
9. The manager talks with the sales department.
   He does not talk with the advertising department.
10. Alia reads the *Washington Post*. She does not read *Newsweek*.
11. Yes, she writes letters to her family. No, she doesn't write letters to her students.
12. Yes, it serves excellent food. No, it doesn't serve Japanese food.

## EXERCISE 48

| | | | |
|---|---|---|---|
| 1. forgotten | 5. sold | 9. fell | 13. understood |
| 2. gone | 6. slept | 10. froze | 14. told |
| 3. dug | 7. drank | 11. eaten | 15. saw |
| 4. brought . . . sang | 8. flew | 12. sank | 16. blew |

## EXERCISE 49

| | | | |
|---|---|---|---|
| 1. were | 7. bought | 13. wanted | 19. could |
| 2. saw | 8. parked | 14. said | 20. told |
| 3. seemed | 9. walked | 15. wanted | 21. advertised |
| 4. decided | 10. were | 16. picked | 22. put |
| 5. approached | 11. looked | 17. moved | 23. made |
| 6. saw | 12. asked | 18. selected | |

## EXERCISE 50

1. I painted the house two weeks ago.
2. I began to study English three semesters ago.
3. Yes, the plane arrived ten minutes ago.
4. We (you) studied the past tense five days ago.
5. Janice began working for the electric company eight years ago.
6. No, I didn't finish my homework two hours ago.
7. They caught the bus one hour ago.
8. Carol moved here seven months ago.
9. This class began 20 minutes ago.
10. I met Mrs. Nelson six weeks ago.
11. Waldemar started his weight lifting program four months ago.
12. Nina and Ben got married 10 years ago.
13. No, we didn't buy a new car six days ago.
14. Sandy and Joan sent the wedding invitations one month ago.
15. The new museum opened four years ago.

## EXERCISE 51

1. was dreaming
2. will be meeting
3. is acting
4. are taking
5. is writing
6. was running
7. was raining
8. will be visiting
9. will be marrying
10. was preparing
11. will be sailing
12. was trying
13. will be driving
14. is eating
15. will be graduating
16. will . . . be getting
17. will be programming
18. will be growing
19. was copying
20. will be photographing

## EXERCISE 52

1. am
2. think
3. am walking
4. am wondering/wonder
5. are doing
6. imagine
7. is dancing
8. are playing
9. is writing
10. is meeting
11. go
12. sit
13. study
14. swim
15. plan
16. know
17. are having
18. are doing
19. like
20. need

## EXERCISE 53

1. are taking
2. calls
3. knows
4. is growing
5. play
6. buys
7. are using
8. park
9. is preparing
10. is packing
11. is studying
12. go
13. is eating
14. is talking
15. works
16. is forcing
17. is hopping
18. mixes
19. tries
20. are waiting

## EXERCISE 54

1. ferociously
2. firmly
3. easy
4. fragrant
5. angry
6. exclusively
7. delicious
8. depressed
9. hurriedly
10. zealously
11. courageously
12. quickly
13. unbelievably
14. madly
15. good
16. wonderful
17. surprisingly
18. carefully
19. unwilling
20. smooth

## EXERCISE 55

1. grateful
2. tired
3. quietly
4. excited
5. sour
6. beautiful
7. uncertain
8. durable
9. silently
10. rich
11. honest
12. discreet
13. threatening
14 violent
15 recklessly
16. cold
17. correctly
18. good
19. firm
20. quickly

## EXERCISE 56

| | | |
|---|---|---|
| 1. N | 6. G | 11. A |
| 2. F | 7. D | 12. B |
| 3. M | 8. J | 13. H |
| 4. E | 9. K | 14. L |
| 5. C | 10. I | |

## EXERCISE 57

| | | |
|---|---|---|
| 1. J | 6. L | 11. B |
| 2. N | 7. K | 12. M |
| 3. E | 8. D | 13. F |
| 4. I | 9. C | 14. A |
| 5. G | 10. H | |

## EXERCISE 58

| | | | |
|---|---|---|---|
| 1. F | 5. C | 9. H | 13. N |
| 2. D | 6. E | 10. J | 14. I |
| 3. A | 7. G | 11. K | 15. P |
| 4. B | 8. L | 12. O | 16. M |

## EXERCISE 59

| | | | | |
|---|---|---|---|---|
| 1. do | 6. do | 11. do | 16. do | 21. do |
| 2. made | 7. do | 12. done | 17. do | 22. make |
| 3. make | 8. made | 13. doing | 18. do | 23. make |
| 4. made | 9. make | 14. make | 19. do | 24. make |
| 5. make | 10. make | 15. do | 20. make | 25. made |

## EXERCISE 60

Answers will vary.

## EXERCISE 61

Answers will vary.

## EXERCISE 62

Answers will vary.

## EXERCISE 63

1. *Don't buy* ice cream at the grocery store.
2. *Don't cook* the spaghetti for only ten minutes.

3. We always tell our friends *not to go* to the Chinese restaurant.
4. My mother always asks me *not to walk* slowly.
5. *Don't tell* us what your problem is.
6. *Don't ride* your bicycle in the street.
7. *Don't send* your letter to the office.
8. *Don't ask* them to send the check in the mail.
9. If you cannot solve the problem, *don't ask* Ted.
10. The insurance company ordered the client *not to make* payment on the bill.

## EXERCISE 64

1. Study the vocabulary in Chapter 3. Don't study the vocabulary in Chapter 4.
2. *Don't pay* your fees before June 20.
3. Park in the blue zone. *Don't park* in the red zone.
4. Arrive before 8:15. *Don't arrive* after 9:00.
5. Return the books after June 30. *Don't return* them before June 30.
6. Eat in the faculty dining area. *Don't eat* in your office.
7. *Don't ride* on the sidewalk.
8. *Don't bring* a Spanish dictionary to class.
9. Do your laundry on Saturday. *Don't do* your laundry on Friday.
10. *Don't write* your Social Security number on the front of your checks.

## EXERCISE 65

Answers will vary, but here are some possibilities:
1. Get up earlier and arrive on time.
2. Give your wife more money for medicine. Buy the medicine for your children.
3. Stop being so bossy. Be nicer to everyone.
4. Ms. Tamuko, clean up your yard. Get rid of al that junk in you yard.
5. Ms. Davis, pay your creditors immediately.
6. Raymond, be quiet in my courtroom. Don't talk unless I speak to you.
7. Mrs. Kaley, keep your children quiet. Tell your children to be quiet. Control your children.
8. Vincent, get a job. Get up and go to work.
9. Mandy, stop reading trashy novels. Get a good book. Go to the library and find a good book.
10. Flo, go on a diet. See a doctor about your weight. Stop eating junk food. Eat healthy food.
11. Dennis, stop spending so much money. Control your spending. Spend wisely. Get a better job.
12. Bobby, stop stealing cars. Get counseling.
13. Ms. Jackson, lean to cook. Take this back and fix me something else.
14. Dr. Taylor, lower your prices. Have a heart.
15. Mrs. Riordan, get help for you son. Stop giving him alcohol.

16. Mario, study harder and get better grades. Get a tutor. Talk to your professors and get some help.
17. Sandy, be nicer to your brothers and sisters. Speak kindly to them.
18. Mark, learn to type. Get a professional typist.
19. Dr. Daniels, get a microphone, speak loud and clearly. Use a better choice of words.
20. Sue, get a life. Take up some sports. Join a club. Meet some interesting people.

## EXERCISE 66

| | | | |
|---|---|---|---|
| 1. cooking | 6. attending | 11. getting | 16. eating |
| 2. speaking | 7. wearing | 12. driving | 17. typing |
| 3. be | 8. belong | 13. dance | 18. sewing |
| 4. swimming | 9. be | 14. live | 19. direct |
| 5. go | 10. practicing | 15. working | 20. skiing |

## EXERCISE 67

| | | | |
|---|---|---|---|
| 1. had | 6. is | 11. is | 16. would |
| 2. is | 7. is | 12. would | 17. is |
| 3. has | 8. had | 13. would | 18. is |
| 4. would | 9. had | 14. is | 19. had |
| 5. had | 10. is | 15. would | 20. has |

## EXERCISE 68

| | | | |
|---|---|---|---|
| 1. Joan's | 7. Sonya's | 13. It's been . . . I've gone | 19. You'd be |
| 2. Who'd | 8. Mark's | 14. We'd | 20. Mrs. Hart's |
| 3. What's | 9. he'd | 15. Sue'd | |
| 4. Mel's | 10. I'd . . . they'd | 16. Bernie'd . . . it'd been | |
| 5. You'd | 11. what's | 17. you'd | |
| 6. he'd | 12. When's | 18. Kurt's | |

## EXERCISE 69

| | | | | | |
|---|---|---|---|---|---|
| 1. C | 4. A | 7. A | 10. B | 13. B | 16. C |
| 2. A | 5. C | 8. C | 11. C | 14. C | |
| 3. C | 6. C | 9. A | 12. C | 15. C | |

## EXERCISE 70

1. sing, sings; sang; will sing; am, is, are singing
2. write, writes; wrote; will write; am, is, are writing
3. fly, flies; flew; will fly; am, is, are flying
4. think, thinks; thought; will think; am, is, are thinking

 5. bake, bakes; baked; will bake; am, is, are baking
 6. send, sends; sent; will send; am, is, are sending
 7. swim, swims; swam; will swim; am, is, are swimming
 8. see, sees; saw; will see; am, is, are seeing
 9. dance, dances; danced; will dance; am, is, are dancing
10. run, runs; ran; will run; am, is, are running
11. drive, drives; drove; will drive; am, is, are driving
12. eat, eats; ate; will eat; am, is, are eating
13. fry, fries; fried; will fry; am, is, are frying
14. prepare, prepares; prepared; will prepare; am, is, are preparing
15. carry, carries; carried; will carry; am, is, are carrying

## EXERCISE 71

| | has/ have (n) ever | done | would, could | do | Do! Don't Let's | do. do. | |
|---|---|---|---|---|---|---|---|
| 1. sing | " | sung | " | sing | " | sing | " sung |
| 2. write | " | written | " | write | " | write | " written |
| 3. fly | " | flown | " | fly | " | fly | " flown |
| 4. think | " | thought | " | think | " | think | " thought |
| 5. bake | " | baked | " | bake | " | bake | " baked |
| 6. send | " | sent | " | send | " | send | " sent |
| 7. swim | " | swum | " | swim | " | swim | " swum |
| 8. see | " | seen | " | see | " | see | " seen |
| 9. dance | " | danced | " | dance | " | dance | " danced |
| 10. run | " | run | " | run | " | run | " run |
| 11. drive | " | driven | " | drive | " | drive | " driven |
| 12. eat | " | eaten | " | eat | " | eat | " eaten |
| 13. fry | " | fried | " | fry | " | fry | " fried |
| 14. prepare | " | prepared | " | prepared | " | prepare | " prepared |
| 15. carry | " | carried | " | carried | " | carry | " carried |

## EXERCISE 72

| | | | | |
|---|---|---|---|---|
| 1. C | 5. B | 9. B | 13. A | 17. B |
| 2. D | 6. B | 10. A | 14. A | 18. B |
| 3. B | 7. D | 11. B | 15. B | 19. A |
| 4. A | 8. A | 12. B | 16. B | 20. B |

## EXERCISE 73

 1. *His* live in Kansas.
 2. *Theirs* is downtown.
 3. *Theirs* has a patio.
 4. We bought *ours*.

5. You need *yours* stamped.
6. Can he eat *his* now?
7. Do *hers* work in the office?
8. When will you receive *yours*?
9. All of you took *yours* last week.
10. *ours* is higher than *yours*.

## EXERCISE 74

1. They have *theirs* and *mine*.
2. *Mine* will be ready after 3 p.m.
3. She passed *hers*.
4. *His* live in Greeneville.
5. Those are *hers*.
6. James can identify *his*.
7. *Ours* (*Yours*) have expired (are lost).
8. I've written *mine*.
9. *Yours* come to visit often (seldom, etc.).
10. *Ours* (*Mine*) will arrive tomorrow.

## EXERCISE 75

1. Get *me* some coffee.
2. The teacher read *them* the story.
3. Tim left *you* this gift.
4. The artist drew *me* a portrait.
5. My son feeds *the dog* its food every day.
6. The company will build *us* a house very soon.
7. Sally, show *me* your doll.
8. Mr. Dixon offered *Tracy* the job.
9. Please find *me* my sweater.
10. I promised to get *him* a bird.

## EXERCISE 76

1. Peter owes many favors to *you*.
2. Annette showed the new dress *to her mother*.
3. Alice is making an afghan *for her sister*.
4. Cut some cake *for them* before it disappears.
5. I'll send the photos *to you* as soon as they arrive.
6. Bring that cart *to me*.
7. Janet's grandmother left a special ring *to her*.
8. Sonia paid the money *to the ticket agent*.
9. My friend read the notice in the paper *to me*.
10. Nobody bought anything *for us* to eat.

## EXERCISE 77

1. Mr. and Mrs. Smith sing to each other often.
2. Chris and Rachel see each other on weekends.
3. We find each other in a world of great technological advances.
4. Henry and Joan look for each other in the crowd.
5. Marty and his sister tease each other about their pronunciation.
6. Stan and Nancy and their friends buy one another Christmas gifts.
7. My sister and I give each other moral support.
8. The soldier and is wife held each other tightly after his return from Iraq.
9. Tom and Sally knew each other for years before getting married.
10. Tony and his mother meet on Thursdays for lunch.
11. Nancy and her mother speak to each other on the telephone every day.
12. Romeo and Juliet loved each other very much.
13. John and Paul do not take each other seriously.
14. Judy and Christine tell each other secrets.

## EXERCISE 78

| | | | |
|---|---|---|---|
| 1. who | 6. whom | 11. whoever | 16. who |
| 2. whom | 7. whom | 12. who | 17. whomever |
| 3. who | 8. whom | 13. who | 18. whom |
| 4. whomever | 9. Whoever | 14. whom | 19. Whoever |
| 5. whoever | 10. whom | 15. who | 20. Whoever |

## EXERCISE 79

1. they want > he wants,   they don't > he doesn't
2. their > his/her
3. their > her
4. they > he
5. their > his/her
6. their > he/she come > comes
7. they > he they will be good citizens > he will be a good citizen.
8. their > its
9. himself > themselves
10. her > their
11. it>them
12. it > them
13. it > the
14. they > he, their > his
15. it > them
16. their > its
17. they are > he, she is,

18. we > you
19. their > its
20. their > his/her

## EXERCISE 80

| 1. B | 2. D | 3. D | 4. B | 5. D | 6. A |
|------|------|------|------|------|------|

## EXERCISE 81

| 1. B | 6. D | 11. A |
|------|------|-------|
| 2. A | 7. B | 12. D |
| 3. D | 8. B | 13. D |
| 4. B | 9. B | 14. C |
| 5. D | 10. B | |

## EXERCISE 82

| 1. any other | 7. the other | 13. others |
|--------------|--------------|------------|
| 2. the others/another | 8. another | 14. the other/other |
| 3. The other | 9. the others | 15. others |
| 4. others | 10. another | 16. any other (another) |
| 5. any other | 11. Some (Other) | |
| 6. another | 12. another | |

## EXERCISE 83

| 1. C | 2. B | 3. C | 4. C | 5. D |
|------|------|------|------|------|

## EXERCISE 84

| 1. C | 2. B | 3. C | 4. B | 5. A |
|------|------|------|------|------|

## EXERCISE 85

| 1. any | 3. his | 5. Other | 7. they | 9. us |
|--------|--------|----------|---------|-------|
| 2. another | 4. others | 6. its | 8. him | 10. its |

## EXERCISE 86

| 1. pale | 6. studious |
|---------|-------------|
| 2. corporeal | 7. nocturnal |
| 3. terrestrial | 8. well-timed |
| 4. celestial | 9. annual |
| 5. religious | 10. paternal |

## EXERCISE 87

1. beautiful
2. amiable
3. organized
4. holy
5. uncourageous
6. materialistic
7. expensive
8. diurnal
9. fraternal
10. maternal

## EXERCISE 88

1. Ivan has just bought a *five-door station wagon*.
2. My cousin likes that lovely gray *four-compartment purse*.
3. We have a new *9.6-GB computer*.
4. There is a new *30-inch-screen television* in the lobby.
5. Sherry likes her new *four-speaker stereo*.
6. When we went on vacation we took an *80-quart cooler*.
7. The Empire State Building is a *92-story structure*.
8. Can you change this *$20 bill*.
9. In our English class last week, we had to write a *250-word composition*.
10. We took a *10-week trip* across America.
11. Gastonia is *six-hour drive* from here.
12. Angela was very upset because she had spilled a *five-gallon can of olive oil*.
13. Susie needs three yards of *60-inch material* for her dress.
14. Tom has just bought a *five-piece bedroom set*.
15. Eva lives in a house with a *two-car garage*.
16. Barbara made a new *five-button winter coat*.
17. Paul has a new *five-speed bicycle*.
18. Monty repairs cars, so he bought a *125-piece tool set*.
19. We need a *nine-foot extension cord*.
20. My new camp light needs a *nine-volt battery*.

## EXERCISE 89

1. He needs a *four-volt battery* for his radio.
2. We took a *six-day journey* through the mountains.
3. Can you change this *ten-dollar bill*?
4. My cousin has just bought a *three-story house*.
5. Nancy just bought a *two-piece bathing suit*.
6. Marcella has a *ten-room apartment*.
7. The teacher said that we needed *three-inch margins* on the composition.
8. The Manleys own a *19-inch color television*.
9. We installed an *eight-track tape player* in the car.

10. My friend has a *five-gallon gas can*.
11. There is a new model *44-key typewriter*.
12. The flag kit comes with a *17-foot pole*.
13. Mandy always uses the *three-tier platter* when she entertains.
14. The salesman tried to sell us a *five-piece dining set*.
15. My new microwave has a *25-minute timer*.
16. Susan has a new *two-gold button mink coat*.
17. Peter always uses *800-speed film* for his camera.
18. The Nelsons have a new *four-door car*.
19. When the President passed, the soldiers gave him a *21-gun salute*.
20. Veronica bought a new *15-piece tea set*.

## EXERCISE 90

1. gold jewelry
2. wool clothes
3. plastic forks
4. mink coat
5. silk flowers
6. brass chimes
7. paper flowers
8. taffeta skirt
9. brick house
10. china plates
11. eel skin shoes
12. crayon art kit
13. leather briefcase
14. wood bookcases
15. copper frame
16. silk dress
17. rayon clothes
18. tree house
19. stone patio
20. diamond ring

## EXERCISE 91

1. coffee cream
2. vegetable soup
3. fruit salad
4. wrist watch
5. desk lamp
6. movie camera
7. book covers
8. dress factory
9. leather gloves
10. cotton shirt
11. Christmas tree
12. shopping bag
13. photo album
14. chemistry lab
15. summer vacation
16. stained glass window
17. train ticket
18. bus station
19. paper plates
20. hand cream

## EXERCISE 92

1. raided
2. requested
3. interesting
4. settled
5. explored
6. paid
7. working
8. stolen
9. dreaded
10. escaping
11. hated
12. missing
13. planning
14. postponed
15. wandering
16. fighting
17. graduating
18. freezing
19. locked
20. invited

## EXERCISE 93

| | | | |
|---|---|---|---|
| 1. admiring | 6. rising | 11. speeding | 16. exhausting |
| 2. conflicting | 7. questioning | 12. enveloping | 17. opened |
| 3. shaped | 8. lettered | 13. littered | 18. whining |
| 4. warped | 9. simmering | 14. bouncing | 19. returned |
| 5. climbing | 10. smiling | 15. crushed | 20. polluted |

## EXERCISE 94

Answers will vary.
1. . . . the sooner you will get there.
2. . . . the farther it went.
3. . . . the hotter it got.
4. . . . the sooner you can leave.
5. . . . the darker the photograph got.
6. . . . the more horse power you will have.
7. . . . the thirstier I get.
8. . . . the more it looked like rain.
9. . . . the more nervous I got.
10. . . . the longer it will take you to get here.

## EXERCISE 95

1. Students in the United States study three-quarters as much as students in Costa Rica.
2. It is twice as hot in Phoenix as in Butte.
3. Washington state was a territory 12 times as long as Nevada.
4. Peru has twice as many national holidays as the United States.
5. England and Wales produce eight times as many major products as the Falkland Islands.
6. You need six times as many Turkish pounds as Indonesian rupiahs to equal one American dollar.
7. Iceland is about one-third as large as the continent of Africa. Africa is about 300 times as large as Iceland.
8. The diameter of the earth is almost four times as big as that of the moon.
9. The Snake River is about one-fourth as large as the Nile.
10. The Anapurna Mountains in Nepal are about four and a half times as high as Mount Mitchell in North Carolina.

## EXERCISE 96

| | | |
|---|---|---|
| 1. fox | 4. picture | 7. wind |
| 2. bear | 5. rock | 8. never |
| 3. done | 6. the harder | 9. day/nose on your face |

| | | | |
|---|---|---|---|
| 10. wink | 13. the better | 16. beet/lobster/tomato | 19. owl |
| 11. sorry | 14. mule | 17. tack | 20. ox |
| 12. the better | 15. ghost/sheet | 18. bee | |

## EXERCISE 97

1. Pharmacists' jobs are different from electricians' jobs.
2. Chicago's temperatures are lower than Florida's temperatures.
3. Susana's coat is prettier than Rosa's coat.
4. Chestnut's supplies are more expensive than Kmart's supplies.
5. Eric's sports car is faster than David's car.
6. Connie's exam was more difficult than her sister's exam.
7. Ralph's new Corvette cost more than his uncle's Corvette.
8. Painters' lives are more diversified than teachers' lives.
9. Musicians' practice sessions are longer than dancers' sessions.
10. The university's faculty is more experienced than the college's faculty.

## EXERCISE 98

| | | | |
|---|---|---|---|
| 1. quality | 9. form | 17. noun/color | 25. quality |
| 2. material | 10. material | 18. intensity | 26. quality |
| 3. color | 11. description | 19. limiting | 27. texture |
| 4. quality | 12. form | 20. size | 28. color/noun |
| 5. noun | 13. form | 21. quality | 29. color/noun |
| 6. limiting | 14. texture | 22. form | 30. quality |
| 7. limiting | 15. description | 23. form | 31. quality |
| 8. form | 16. texture | 24. description | |

## EXERCISE 99

Answers will vary.

## EXERCISE 100

1. the long elegant red satin dress
2. the boy's big round beach ball
3. a small bright oval diamond ring
4. Rita's new sleek blue sports car
5. December's many long cold winter nights
6. 15 little fat furry koala bears
7. two big white ostrich feathers
8. five round ripe red tomatoes
9. a large old soft comfortable chair
10. the long delicate ruby-encrusted handle

## EXERCISE 101

| | | | | |
|---|---|---|---|---|
| 1. D | 3. B | 5. A | 7. C | 9. C |
| 2. B | 4. A | 6. B | 8. C | 10. C |

## EXERCISE 102

| | | | | | |
|---|---|---|---|---|---|
| 1. C | 2. D | 3. D | 4. A | 5. A | 6. B |

## EXERCISE 103

1. both are
2. their sister <u>is</u>
3. members <u>go</u>
4. we have cards not only for . . .
5. either <u>is</u>
6. planning to go not only to Switzerland but also
7. John . . . <u>hopes</u> to be a professional writer
8. sweets <u>are</u>
9. bouquet was filled with not only . . . but also . . .
10. guests <u>pay</u>
11. I want to buy both . . .
12. doors . . . <u>have</u>
13. flowers <u>are</u>
14. government has both the power and . . .
15. both . . . <u>are</u>

## EXERCISE 104

1. Yes, the child has drunk his milk. No, the child hasn't drunk his milk.
2. Yes, Mary has sold her house. No, Mary hasn't sold her house.
3. Yes, the directors have thought about a solution to the problem.
   No, the directors haven't though about a solution to the problem.
4. Yes, all of us have spoken to the teacher. No, all of us haven't spoken to the teacher.
5. Yes, I have worn my new shirt. No, I haven't worn my new shirt.
6. Yes, you have done a good job on the presentation. No, you haven't done a good job on the presentation.

## EXERCISE 105

1. I have not eaten breakfast yet.
2. it hasn't snowed a lot since February
3. Mark has already worked 33 hours
4. has already typed 100 letters
5. has already given
6. have not paid my bills yet
7. has visited Mexico
8. I have received five

## EXERCISE 106

Answers will vary, but here are some possibilities:

1. I have (never) traveled
2. My family has (never) eaten
3. My friends have (never) been in
4. My friends have (not) visited
5. The plane has (not) arrived
6. My best friend has (not, never) played
7. My (our) teachers have (not) helped us
8. I have taken _____ exams
9. I (we) have eaten _____
10. I have (not) told my parents

## EXERCISE 107

| | | | |
|---|---|---|---|
| 1. has written | 6. hurt | 11. finally received | 16. has sung |
| 2. wore | 7. took | 12. left | 17. ate |
| 3. thought | 8. have waited | 13. danced | 18. heard |
| 4. has read | 9. has set | 14. ran | 19. has swum |
| 5. has quit | 10. has seen | 15. blew | 20. caught |

## EXERCISE 108

Answers will vary.

## EXERCISE 109

Answers will vary.

## EXERCISE 110

| | | |
|---|---|---|
| 1. had visited | 6. improved | 11. had danced |
| 2. had arrived | 7. made | 12. had mailed |
| 3. read | 8. had ordered | 13. gave |
| 4. told | 9. had waited | 14. had understood |
| 5. had prepared | 10. had promised | 15. had gone |

## EXERCISE 111

| | | |
|---|---|---|
| 1. had won | 7. sank | 13. had not taken |
| 2. had returned | 8. had gone | 14. landed |
| 3. repaired | 9. had not frozen | 15. had not bought |
| 4. remained | 10. rang | 16. had put |
| 5. had driven | 11. built | 17. had not eaten |
| 6. had paid | 12. caught | 18. had flown |

## EXERCISE 112

1. Luis has been studying in the university for three semesters.
2. Mandy has been skiing for six hours.

3. Phil has been taking his final exams for three hours.
4. We have been attending the conference for six days.
5. Harry and I have been dancing for three months.
6. They have been eating for two hours.
7. I have been speaking Spanish for six semesters.
8. Noel Phelps has been writing novels for 21 years.
9. Jack has been driving a truck for 14 years.
10. Paul and Dorothy have been building their house for six months.
11. Kent has been playing baseball for 14 years.
12. I have been watching my favorite television program for four months.
13. You have been playing the role of King Arthur for five years.
14. I have been taking my summer vacations in Europe for eight years.

## EXERCISE 113

Answers will vary; however, the verbs should be the following:

1. I have been studying
2. I have been living
3. My family has been writing
4. He/She has been working
5. They have been studying
6. We have been eating

## EXERCISE 114

1. was walking
2. pulled
3. looked
4. saw
5. was waiting
6. appeared
7. was carrying
8. moved
9. were talking
10. arrived
11. was reading
12. was writing
13. were not paying
14. realized
15. got
16. began
17. had
18. were
19. entered
20. was

## EXERCISE 115

1. went
2. arrived
3. found
4. was leaving
5. was parking
6. jumped
7. wasn't paying
8. hit
9. got
10. started
11. was looking
12. brought
13. said
14. picked
15. put
16. was cutting
17. decided
18. was pushing
19. fell
20. helped

## EXERCISE 116

1. was traveling
2. wrote
3. was brushing
4. was changing
5. made
6. was cooking

7. called
8. walked
9. were talking
10. said
11. brought

12. was going
13. packed
14. asked
15. was closing
16. was pouring

17. was playing
18. hurried/was hurrying
19. was typing
20. was washing

## EXERCISE 117

1. to debate
2. to go
3. to be
4. seeing
5. performing
6. to obey
7. driving

8. to allow
9. to buy
10. going
11. to repair
12. to yield
13. to eat
14. spending

15. to paint
16. going
17. singing
18. to have
19. to entertain
20. playing

## EXERCISE 118

1. were raising
2. rose

3. risen
4. raise

5. raised
6. rise

7. will raise
8. rise

## EXERCISE 119

1. lies
2. lain

3. lay
4. laid

5. lie
6. lay

7. laid
8. laid

## EXERCISE 120

1. sets/is setting
2. set
3. set

4. set
5. sitting
6. sit

7. set
8. sat
9. sit

## EXERCISE 121

1. would have gone
2. had done
3. had not left
4. pick
5. speak
6. took
7. had seen

8. will graduate
9. had had
10. would have attended
11. could go
12. had not eaten
13. had
14. had studied

15. could catch
16. were not/had not been
17. would stop
18. had won
19. could lose
20. were

## EXERCISE 122

Answers will vary.

## EXERCISE 123

Answers will vary.

## EXERCISE 124

1. will evict
2. will (may, can) attend
3. show
4. had (had had)
5. will be
6. gets
7. finds
8. purchase
9. will (may, can) not read
10. arrives
11. try
12. prepare
13. answer
14. will (may, can) not insure
15. receive
16. leave
17. will (can, may) miss
18. tries
19. put
20. asks

## EXERCISE 125

Possible answers:
1. Tom must be a good swimmer. Tom must be strong.
2. John probably didn't study (must not have studied).
3. Hal must be worried.
4. He must be obnoxious.
5. John must be sick.
6. It will probably rain. It must be going to rain.
7. It will probably snow. It must be going to snow.
8. Xian and Mai must be very good friends. They will probably get married someday.
9. He must have heard a funny joke.
10. Tom must not get too much exercise. Tom probably eats too much.
11. They must like meat.
12. They must have a lot of money. They probably have a large family.
13. They must be having fun. They will probably going swimming.
14. I wonder if José failed the test.
15. We will probably arrive late (miss the first act).
16. Mel must have a lot of debts. Mel probably does not budget his money.
17. . . . must have arrived . . .
18. He must be a good employer. He probably received a promotion.
19. . . . must be 20 (any number) years . . .
20. Jake must be nervous. He must be rehearsing right now.

## EXERCISE 126

Answers will vary.
1. He was probably the new director (a professor, an artist, . . .)
2. It was probably (must have been) eight o'clock (any time).
3. They must have been very happy.
4. He must have trained very hard.
5. He must not have studied. He must be very unhappy.
6. He must have been tired. He must have enjoyed his trip.
7. They must have been sailing on the high seas. They must have a lot of money.
8. She probably didn't feel good. She must have had an early class. She probably had to get up early today.
9. They must have been sick. They must have had to work today.
10. He must have enjoyed the movie.
11. It must have rained earlier.
12. He probably got good grades in all of them.
13. She must have been very tired.
14. Your check has probably cleared by now.
15. It must have arrived about 10 o'clock (any time).
16. There were probably 50 (any number) people there.
17. They probably went (must have gone) to Gatlinburg.
18. He must have seen it 10 times. (any number)
19. I was probably eight years old. (any age)
20. They must have announced the winners on Saturday. (any day)

## EXERCISE 127

| | | | |
|---|---|---|---|
| 1. pass | 6. peck | 11. gives | 16. speaks |
| 2. talks | 7. throws | 12. sees | 17. rides |
| 3. sits | 8. come | 13. decides | 18. says |
| 4. feeds | 9. know | 14. is | 19. is |
| 5. fly | 10. approaches | 15. has | 20. takes |

## EXERCISE 128

| | | |
|---|---|---|
| 1. clashes | 8. have | 15. Was |
| 2. is | 9. distribute | 16. looks |
| 3. has | 10. is | 17. offers |
| 4. walk | 11. come | 18. say |
| 5. are | 12. contain | 19. breaks |
| 6. are | 13. is | 20. photograph |
| 7. grow | 14. was | |

## EXERCISE 129

| | | | |
|---|---|---|---|
| 1. has | 6. are | 11. requires | 16. represents |
| 2. are | 7. wants | 12. hurt | 17. goes |
| 3. likes | 8. frightens | 13. seems | 18. solve |
| 4. is | 9. trains | 14. spend | 19. drive |
| 5. need | 10. excels | 15. costs | 20. occur |

## EXERCISE 130

1. *Death of a Salesman* was written in 1949.
2. The fort was captured by the attacking troops.
3. Monticello was designed by Thomas Jefferson.
4. The Declaration of Independence was signed in Philadelphia.
5. Rain is being predicted for tomorrow.
6. Most of the prairie was destroyed by a forest fire.
7. Many trees will be cut down by the lumberjacks to build twelve new homes. (Twelve new homes will be built after the trees have been cut down.)
8. Before the ceremony had begun, the candles were lit by the altar boys.
9. Houdini had been locked in a box for one of his tricks.
10. The final episode of the program was watched by thousands of viewers.
11. The author's name is not known.
12. *Passion* was directed by Mel Gibson.
13. The treaty was signed in 1863.
14. Five hundred speeding tickets were issued yesterday.
15. The stock market will be closed on July 4.
16. A program on Spain will be featured on Channel 5 on Wednesday.
17. Plans for a celebration have been made by the committee.
18. The old church had been torn down before 1875.

## EXERCISE 131

1. The salesman ordered a new car.
2. The technician analyzed the water to see whether it was polluted.
3. I (any name) am sending your package air freight.
4. We (someone) will sing the national anthem before the soccer match.
5. The painters are painting Frank's house this week.
6. The fishermen are catching fish in large numbers
7. Mel Fisher has discovered much treasure from the sunken ship *The Atocha*.
8. The orchestra played my favorite song.
9. At one time the French occupied St. Augustine.
10. Nancy bought her dress in Atlanta two weeks before the wedding.

## EXERCISE 132: BEAUTIFUL HAWAII

The pilot flew a planeload of tourists out of Los Angeles toward Hawaii. The flight crew served a wonderful meal on board. The passengers enjoyed the beautiful scenery en route to the island paradise. Upon arrival, native women wearing grass skirts greeted the tourists. They were swaying to Hawaiian melodies of traditional music that the local musicians were playing on their ukuleles. Many consider these instruments to be native to the islands. One of the lovely natives gave each of the tourists a colorful lei of tiny orchids. The citizens of this Pacific island received the tourists warmly.

## EXERCISE 133: STONEHENGE

In 2750 B.C. an agricultural tribe of sun worshipers built Stonehenge, a megalithic structure located in England. Scientists have proposed a number of theories about the purpose of such a structure and the mystery of Stonehenge. In 1963 a British astronomer, Gerald S. Hawkins, proposed the most accepted theory regarding its significance. He believed that Stonehenge was a giant stone calendar and observatory. "Heel stones" in the center of the complex marked the point at which the sun rose during the midsummer solstice. A religious sect called Druids performed rites there that anthropologists say date back to the time of Atlantis. Scientists discovered that historically and chronologically, however, the Druids and Stonehenge are from different eras.

## EXERCISE 134

| | | | |
|---|---|---|---|
| 1. to tease | 6. drive | 11. to be | 16. to study |
| 2. see | 7. to eat | 12. to accept | 17. to pay |
| 3. apologize | 8. to visit | 13. move | 18. to get |
| 4. take | 9. live | 14. to give | 19. dance |
| 5. to write | 10. to appear | 15. to arrive | 20. swim |

## EXERCISE 135

(verbs only)

| | |
|---|---|
| 1. had gone | 6. could have gotten |
| 2. had had | 7. had not been snowing |
| 3. could have cooked | 8. had not had to make |
| 4. had been | 9. could have typed |
| 5. hadn't had to take | 10. would have bought |

## EXERCISE 136

Answers will vary.

## EXERCISE 137

| | | |
|---|---|---|
| 1. had bought | 5. had | 9. had not been |
| 2. had not driven | 6. knew | 10. read/could read |
| 3. had gotten | 7. had not drunk | |
| 4. had taken | 8. would dry | |

## EXERCISE 138

We wish Solange hadn't had to work late. I wish I hadn't had to wait for her to shower and dress. We wish we hadn't arrived late at the party and missed so much of the fun. We wish we would have been able to hear Johnny Durango. We wish we could have eaten more than just the leftovers. I wish I could have danced with Pete Sinclair. (I wish Pete Sinclair had danced with me.) Solange wishes she hadn't drunk so much and gotten sick at the party. She wishes she hadn't lost her keys. We all wish Tom hadn't offered to drive us home. I wish he weren't such a bore! I wish Solange hadn't gone to bed at 11:00. I wish I hadn't watched (hadn't had to watch) television. I wish I had stayed home that night!

## EXERCISE 139

| | | | | |
|---|---|---|---|---|
| 1. told | 3. says | 5. tell | 7. said | 9. telling |
| 2. said | 4. tell | 6. told | 8. tell | 10. told |

## EXERCISE 140

| | | | | |
|---|---|---|---|---|
| 1. to tell | 3. said | 5. said | 7. tells | 9. says |
| 2. says | 4. told | 6. tell | 8. tell | 10. say |

## EXERCISE 141

1. Helen asked where he was going . . .
2. The project director said we would raise . . .
3. Dr. Janske said that my (your, our) case was unusual.
4. No one moved when the president said that he was resigning his office.
5. Yolanda asked what kind of job it was.
6. Columbo said that he wondered where the murder weapon was.
7. In tomorrow's speech, the ambassador will say that we (they) would negotiate this treaty.
8. Danny asked his teacher when the exam would be.
9. Mark Antony said that he had come to bury Caesar, not to praise him.
10. Saundra asked whether Harlan knew how to fill out these (those) forms.
11. The mayor asked what we (they) could do to improve the park.
12. The strikers said that they would not return until working conditions improved.
13. The old lady said that Debra looked silly in that dress.

14. The unhappy flood victims said that there was nothing left for them to do.
15. Flora insisted (by saying) that she would discuss . . .
16. Milo always says that nobody understands him.
17. The policeman said that he was afraid that he would have to give me a ticket . . .

## EXERCISE 142

1. Jane asked me if (whether) I planned . . .
2. A famous American patriot told his soldiers not to fire until they saw . . .
3. The Customs inspector told us to open . . .
4. The boss told Thomas that if he worked very hard, he would be . . .
5. The witness told the judge that he (she) had nothing . . .
6. Trudy is telling the contestants that the judges' decision will be final.
7. The restaurant manager told his customer that he was sorry that he/she did not enjoy his/her veal cutlet.
8. Kerry told a group of physicists that the company had to concentrate on. . . .

## EXERCISE 143

Yesterday Carlos and I went to visit some friends of ours. While we were there, our host said that he wanted to make an addition to his house and that he was looking for someone to help him with the project. Carlos said that he was interested in his project and would gladly help him with it.

After hearing that, our host told Carlos the he would show him exactly what he had planned to do and asked him to give him some suggestions on how to do it.

While the men were looking at the house, our hostess took me into their green-house and showed me her lovely collection of plants. She told me that this was the first year that all of her plants had bloomed. I asked her whether the cold bothered them. She told me that she had a small gas heater installed to use on cold nights.

We all went inside to discuss plans for the new project.

## EXERCISE 144

| | | | |
|---|---|---|---|
| 1. told | 6. said | 11. told | 16. said |
| 2. said | 7. tell | 12. told | 17. said |
| 3. told | 8. told | 13. says | 18. said |
| 4. told | 9. tell | 14. tells | 19. said |
| 5. told | 10. said | 15. told | 20. told |

## EXERCISE 145

1. The professor said, "The class will meet at 11."
2. My friend said, "They (We) are going to Europe for the spring."
3. John said, "I always feel better in the morning."

4. Mary said, "I am going to the dance tonight."
5. The secretary said, "I remember mailing the letter."
6. Frank's daughter said, "My friend has graduated with honors."
7. The doctor said, "I need your help."
8. John asked, "Where did you go on your vacation last month?"
9. The lawyer asked, "Where is the courthouse?"
10. The students asked, "When will the class begin?"

## EXERCISE 146

1. Our neighbors said that they were going to buy a new car.
2. The politician said that poverty would be abolished.
3. The professor said that the students were all present.
4. The lawyer told Mr. Green that he thought he could help him.
5. The senator will tell his constituents that he is interested in conservation.
6. The guest told the hostess that her dinner was delicious.
7. The coach told the players that they had to practice more.
8. Mary asked John if (whether) he enjoyed classical music.
9. The waitress asked me if (whether) I was ready to order.
10. The diplomat asked whether (if) the meeting had already begun.

## EXERCISE 147

| | | | | | |
|---|---|---|---|---|---|
| 1. A | 4. A | 7. B | 10. B | 13. A | 16. B |
| 2. B | 5. A | 8. A | 11. B | 14. C | 17. A |
| 3. A | 6. B | 9. B | 12. C | 15. B | |

## TEST ON VERBS

| | | | | |
|---|---|---|---|---|
| 1. A | 6. A | 11. B | 16. B | 21. C |
| 2. B | 7. B | 12. B | 17. A | 22. C |
| 3. A | 8. C | 13. B | 18. B | 23. A |
| 4. C | 9. C | 14. B | 19. B | |
| 5. B | 10. A | 15. B | 20. A | |

# NOTES